P9-DMH-641

Praise for *What Stands in a Storm*

"The writerly brilliance—the terse dark poetry—of this debut book explodes from every page. Yet Kim Cross is too much of a writer to let mere masterful writing suffice. She has enlisted her sentences in the service of her tremendous reportorial mission: to recover and make sense of the thousands of fragmentary incidents, images, voices, and glimpses of human character ennobled by loss and imminent death—the sum and substance of the most catastrophic mass-tornado attack in recorded American history. This young writer has done the impossible: she has out-written apocalypse. A new star has appeared in our literary sky."

—Ron Powers, Pulitzer Prize–winning journalist and coauthor of *Flags of Our Fathers*

"Amid so much terror and pain and death, there is an overflowing of life here in *What Stands in a Storm*, gathered together in a blessing of uncommon decency and indelible beauty. If you want to know what shape your heart's in, read this book and learn, through Kim Cross's extraordinary reportage and artistry, that stories are as much a gift as life itself. Stories, in fact, are our afterlife."

—Bob Shacochis, author of *The Woman Who Lost Her Soul*

"Whether you live in tornado country or not, everyone should read this book. Heartbreaking and heroic."

—Fannie Flagg, author of *Fried Green Tomatoes at the Whistlestop Cafe*

"Turn off your cell phone. Call in sick. Tell your family whatever you need to tell them, because you're going to have to have eight hours of uninterrupted time once you begin Kim Cross's book. Her verbs pulsate, her narrative web sucks you in. Mostly, Cross makes you care about the people in *What Stands in a Storm*, their quirks and aspirations. You won't look at a coiling sky the same way after reading this powerhouse debut."

—Beth Macy, *New York Times* bestselling author of *Factory Man*

"*What Stands in a Storm* is a dramatic and carefully reconstructed account of nature's unexpected and explosive power and the strength of humans to bond together in its destructive wake."

—Peter Stark, author of *Astoria* and *The Last Empty Places*

"With exhaustive, on-the-ground reporting, spellbinding prose and voices of the living and the dead recounting every haunting moment of the storm's three-day reign of terror, Kim Cross has produced a spine-chilling narrative. *What Stands in a Storm* will tear apart, forever, our complacent sense of security when we look at a dark sky overhead."

—George Getschow, writer-in-residence,
The Mayborn Literary Nonfiction Conference

"A powerful book, unforgettable in its recreation of a horror that swallowed entire communities. Kim Cross brings to life the soul-searing experience of people standing prostrate as a monstrous storm tears their lives to shreds. But there is joy in this horror. She shows us how ordinary people in the worst-hit areas discovered what they and their communities were made of as the sky fell around them."

—Winston Groom, author of *Forrest Gump*

WHAT STANDS IN A STORM

Three Days In the Worst Superstorm to Hit the South's Tornado Alley

KIM CROSS

FOREWORD BY RICK BRAGG

ATRIA BOOKS

New York London Toronto Sydney New Delhi

ATRIA BOOKS
An Imprint of Simon & Schuster, Inc.
1230 Avenue of the Americas
New York, NY 10020

First Atria Books hardcover edition March 2015

ATRIA BOOKS and colophon are trademarks of Simon & Schuster, Inc.

Interior design by Paul Dippolito
Maps on pages xvi and 230–231 are by Fredrick Fluker of énFocus Media Group

Manufactured in the United States of America

10 9 8 7 6 5 4 3 2 1

Library of Congress Cataloging-in-Publication Data is available.

ISBN 978-1-4767-6306-4
ISBN 978-1-4767-6308-8 (ebook)

For those who lost their lives to this,
and for everyone who loved them

CONTENTS

AUTHOR'S NOTE

April 27, 2011, became the deadliest day of the biggest tornado outbreak in the history of recorded weather. It was the climax of a superstorm that unleashed terror upon twenty-one states—from Texas to New York—in three days, seven hours, and eighteen minutes. Entire communities were flattened, whole neighborhoods erased, in seconds, by the wind.

This was an epic storm in an epic month: April 2011 saw three separate outbreaks and a record 757 tornadoes—nearly half of which (349) occurred during the April 24–27 outbreak that inspired this book. This anomalously stormy month blew away the previous April record of 267 tornadoes in April 1974 (and the record for any month, topping the May 2004 count of 542).

The storm left in its wake long scars across the landscape, $11 billion in damage, and at least 324 people dead. Most of them died in Alabama, which now leads the nation in tornado deaths. On April 27, a total of 62 tornadoes raked the state; in some moments, there were six or more on the ground at once.

This book tells the story of this storm through the characters who lived it. All the characters and events in this book are real, based on more than a year of research and one-hundred-plus hours of interviews with responders, meteorologists, survivors, and the families of those who died.

Any dialogue in quotation marks was taken directly from an audio or video recording, or from transcribed interviews in which those conversations were recounted directly to me. Time-stamped posts were recorded directly from Facebook, Twitter, and chat rooms.

Text conversations were retrieved from victims' salvaged phones and shared with me by their families. These conversations have been left raw and intact, with no editing for grammar, spelling, or punctuation. Emergency radio transmissions were transcribed from time-stamped recordings. A person's thoughts set in italics were based on social media posts by that person, or were remembered by primary sources present when the character said what they were thinking.

I have attempted to check and double-check my scientific facts with the help of many experts, including respected research and forecast meteorologists and a fact-checker trained in science writing. That said, any errors are mine.

FOREWORD

Almost nothing stood.

Where the awful winds bore down, massive oaks, one hundred years old, were shoved over like stems of grass, and great pines, as big around as fifty-five-gallon drums, snapped like sticks. Church sanctuaries, built on the rock of ages, tumbled into random piles of brick. Houses, echoing with the footfalls of generations, came apart, and blew away like paper. Whole communities, carefully planned, splintered into chaos. Restaurants and supermarkets, gas stations and corner stores, all disintegrated; glass storefronts scattered like diamonds on black asphalt. It was as if the very curve of the earth was altered, horizons erased altogether, the landscape so ruined and unfamiliar that those who ran from this thing, some of them, could not find their way home.

We are accustomed to storms, here where the cool air drifts south to collide with the warm, rising damp from the Gulf, where black clouds roil and spin and unleash hell on earth. But this was different. A gothic monster off the scale of our experience and even our imagination, a thing of freakish size and power that tore through state after state and heart after Southern heart, killing hundreds, hurting thousands, even affecting, perhaps forever, how we look at the sky.

But that same geography that left us in the path of this destruction also created, across generations, a way of life that would not come to pieces inside that storm, nailed together from old-fashioned things like human kindness, courage, utter selflessness, and, yes, defiance, even standing inside a roofless house.

As Southerners, we know a man with a chain saw is worth ten with a clipboard, that there is no hurt in this world, even in the storm of the century, that cannot be comforted with a casserole, and that faith, in the hereafter or in neighbors who help you through the here and now, cannot be knocked down.

—Southern Living, *August 2011*

I wrote, after the winds had died, that we would never look at the sky the same way again. But it changed us in more ways than that.

Before April 27, 2011, the wail of the warning sirens might have caused some concern, some pause. After, after the winds bore down and into this place, the sirens struck us with dread, and sent us moving for basements and strong buildings not in panic, maybe, but aware—certain—of the destructive power that swirled somewhere nearby.

Before, we looked at the weatherman with the remote control in our hands and heard his warnings, certainly, but it seemed distant, that danger, something we could just flip away from at any time if we wanted, and hide inside an old movie, or the cooking channel, or ESPN. After, we searched for him, quickly, because he had been the only warning a lot of people had.

Before, we looked at things like concrete blocks and red bricks, like lumber and nails and poured cement, as solid things, substantial things, something stronger than the elements. After, we saw steel twisted into ribbons and bricks scattered like bread crumbs, saw cars crumpled like wadded-up newspaper and trees snapped like Popsicle sticks and whole streets swept raggedly free of houses; in some cases of whole neighborhoods.

Before, we took the darkening skies as a kind of inconvenience, thought to ourselves how inconvenient it might be when the lights winked out. After, the funerals lasted for days.

Most of us could only imagine the horror of April 27, 2011. Some of us were very lucky, and only came home to the great sadness of the destruction of splintered houses and lives. We drove back into our neighborhoods to see only material things smashed and hurled about, and knew nothing of the deeper misery, in places like Rosedale, the Downs, Forest Lake, Holt, Alberta City, and other places.

I had been about three hundred miles away and watched the storm—disconnected, somehow—terrify people I knew and leave many of them homeless, and when I came back into the city in the awful calm I was not even sure where I was, because the lovely trees and the landmarks had been erased.

I felt lost, in this splintered place, but I didn't know what lost was.

Now, because of the work Kim Cross has done in re-creating the drumbeat of horrors of that terrible day, I realize more than ever how lucky I was, how lucky we all were, to only lose wood and bricks and trivial things such as cars and trees.

Because of her meticulous re-creation, we know more about what it was like to live through that time, and, tragically, what went through the minds of some who did not.

Much has been written and said about the goodness of the people who responded in various ways after the winds died down. Those people can never be repaid, never be thanked sufficiently. People whose names I did not know sweated and even bled in my neighborhood, for strangers.

We have, many of us, counted our blessings and moved on, until the next siren, the next darkening sky. The dead are buried, and prayers have been said, and love overflowing has washed through the pain.

What Kim has done here is perhaps the oldest service a writer can supply. She has helped put a human face on the people inside those winds, and, maybe, etched their faces a little deeper into memory. At least, that is what we writers would like to believe.

Rick Bragg

In times of trouble,
the things that tear our world apart
reveal what holds us together.

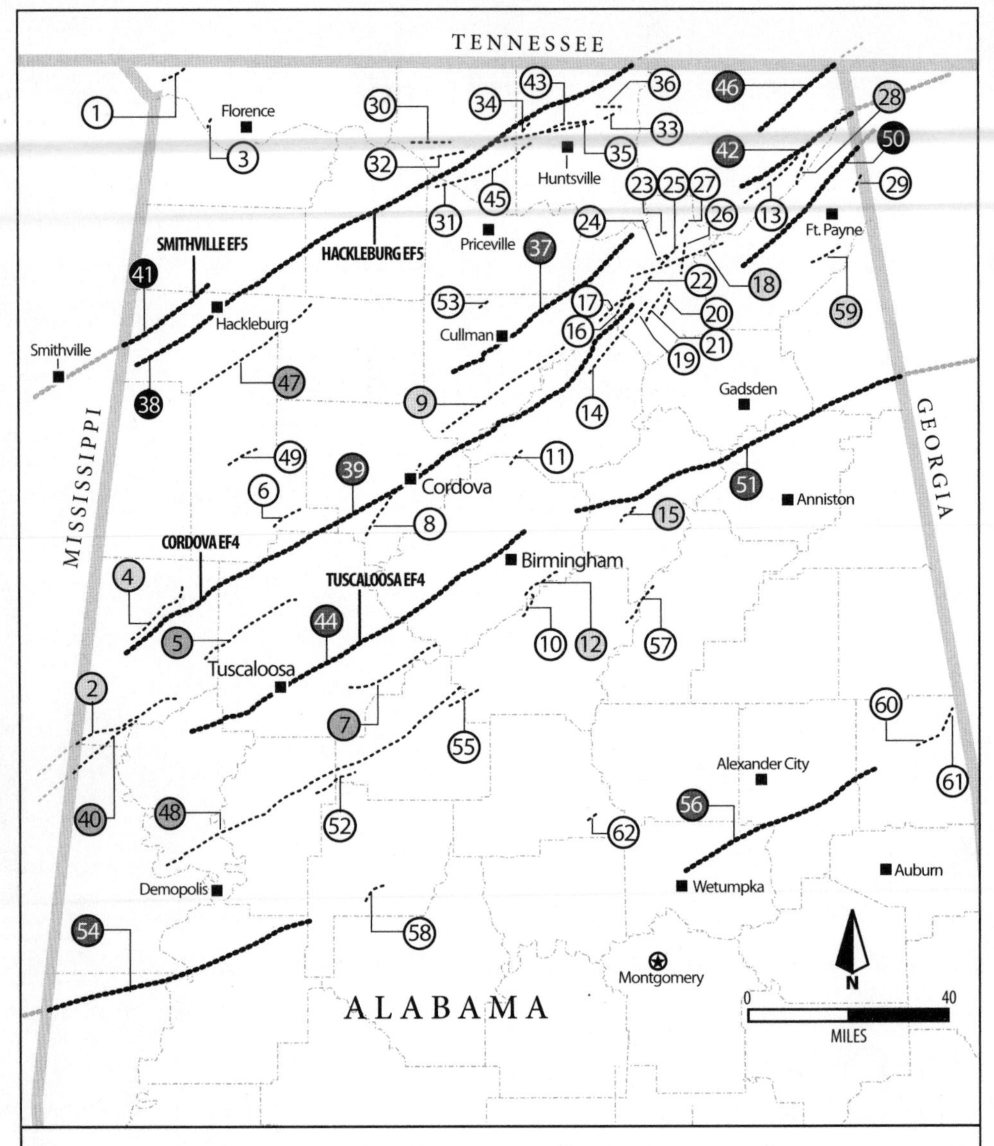

APRIL 27, 2011

HISTORIC TORNADO OUTBREAK

Tornadoes are numbered chronologically based on the time of touchdown in Alabama on April 27.

The tornadoes occurred in three rounds that began at 4:16 a.m. and ended at 9:50 p.m.
For an interactive timeline, see Whatstandsinastorm.com.

Sources: National Weather Service, Birmingham, Alabama, and TornadoHistoryProject.com

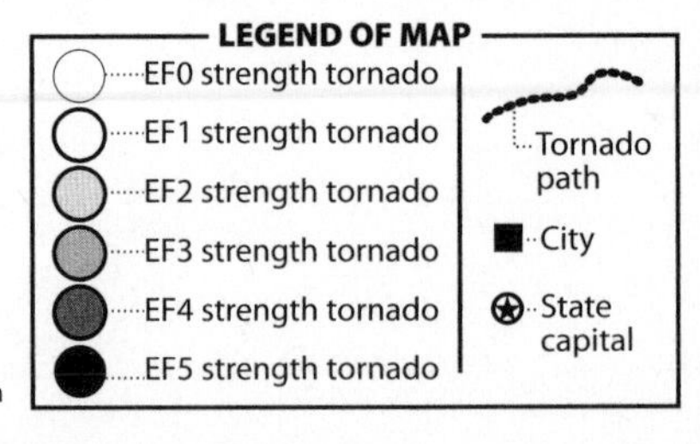

PART I

THE STORM

CHAPTER 1

RACING THE STORM

3:44 P.M., WEDNESDAY, APRIL 27, 2011—SMITHVILLE, MISSISSIPPI

Patti Parker watched the dark funnel grow until it filled the whole windshield, blackening the sky. Its two-hundred-mile-per-hour winds were furious enough to blast the bark off trees, suck the nails out of a two-by-four, and peel a road right off the earth, and it was charging at sixty miles per hour toward everything she loved most in the world—her children, her husband, their home. She was racing behind the massive storm, down the seven-mile stretch of rural highway between her and the life she knew.

Smithville, Mississippi, was much smaller than Oxford, the postage-stamp of native soil that William Faulkner called home. Too tiny to appear on some maps, it was a 1.5-square-mile speck of a town about ten miles west of Alabama and twenty miles southeast of Tupelo, where Elvis was born. Set on the banks of a dammed river some locals believed tornadoes would not cross, Smithville was a place where women put on makeup before going to the Piggly Wiggly, planned dinner around choir practice, and took their families to Mel's Diner for fried catfish and the town's late-breaking news. It had one stoplight and five churches.

Smithville's earsplitting tornado siren, just fifty feet from Patti's house, had been screaming so often this spring that she found herself sleeping through the warnings. A high-pitched, lugubrious wail, it sounded just like the air-raid sirens of World War II. When people heard it, they would run into their closets and bathrooms, although many would pause first and go outside to stare up at the sky.

The sirens had interrupted Patti's work again today in the neighboring small town of Amory, Mississippi. The executive director of the local United Way, she had been at her desk answering e-mails and reviewing disaster plans. When the sirens screamed she sighed and joined her colleagues in the stairwell, pausing by the coffeepot along the way to pour another cup.

Tornado season hovered like an unspoken question over every spring in the South. It was just part of living here. But this time, when someone opened the metal doors beneath the stairs to peek outside, Patti noticed a sinister shift in the wind. She had told her husband she would wait it out and come home when the warnings expired, but she felt the urgent need to be with her kids. If she left now, she thought, maybe she could beat this thing to Smithville. Driving on the road was quite possibly the worst place to be in a storm, aside from a mobile home. But the pull of family overcame logic.

And now here she was, caught behind a mile-wide tornado that was rushing immutably toward the center of her universe.

▪ ▪ ▪

At home in Smithville, Patti's son, Johnny Parker, one day shy of his seventeenth birthday, was leaning into his computer, peering at the radar maps. What he saw made him prickle with fear. Severe thunderstorms were popping up across the state, dotting the screen with red and yellow tie-dyed splotches marching steadily northeast. He knew some of these storms were pregnant with tornadoes. A student of the weather since the age of four, when a storm nearly crushed his house with a toppled tree, he studied the maps, searching for patterns and clues that might foretell what the sky would do. His fingers flew over the keyboard, dashing off an e-mail warning to the hundred friends who followed his weather dispatch, which he always typed, because cerebral palsy hijacked his words somewhere along the path between his mind and his mouth. Johnny could type a blue streak and you would never know, reading his forecasts, that he struggled to speak.

Johnny's concentration was broken by the sound of his father yelling, calling him and his fourteen-year-old sister, Chloe, to come out and look at the sky. Together, they stared up at the terrible beauty: steel-colored clouds that whorled around like dishwater circling a drain. Johnny turned his head, and all he could hear was the terrible roar. He knew without looking what it was, and that it filled the Mississippi sky.

"Get inside!" yelled his father, Randy.

Johnny and Chloe raced to the innermost hallway, where a parade of tiny handprints on the wall, growing bigger through the years, marked the passing of their childhoods. They knelt and tucked themselves into balls, covering their heads with interlaced fingers, just as their teachers had taught them during tornado drills. The roar turned deafening, so large and loud they could feel it rumbling inside their chests. Their ears popped with the sudden drop in pressure as the walls of their home began to shudder. And then, in a moment most meteorologists will never experience, Johnny's house came apart around him.

▪ ▪ ▪

Four miles away on the two-lane highway, Patti pounded the steering wheel, stuck behind a slow-moving pickup truck. Rain and hail were sheeting down, and wind gusts were shaking her car, but this pickup was creeping down the two-lane road as if the world was not about to end. She wanted to pass, but through the curtains of rain she could see the silhouettes of falling trees, huge and ancient pecan trunks crashing across the road. The truck went around them, and she followed its blurry taillights through the sluicing rain. And then the truck stopped dead in the road, blocked by live power lines and mountains of debris.

Patti stopped the car, flung open the door, and ran to the driver's window. An old man looked at her mutely. Her auburn hair snapped like a flag and her green eyes squinted into the wind as she heard her own voice, as if in a movie, rising in pitch with panic.

"I've got to get through this! I've got to get home!"

The old man watched her as she started running, guided by some primal compass through a splintered landscape that, stripped of all landmarks, didn't look anything like home. She ran through the mud, hurdling limbs, dodging live wires, and finding her way through the shredded remains of homes she had passed that morning. Her heels scraped on the asphalt, her stride abbreviated by her pencil skirt, her jacket flapping like frantic wings. The storm had roared on into Alabama, leaving in its wake an eerie quiet that amplified the muffled cries emanating from broken heaps. It registered that these were the voices of friends, of neighbors, of people who desperately needed help—of people who might be dying. But her legs would not stop moving under the directive that looped through her mind:

Get home—Get home—Get home!

The house on the corner was mostly gone, but the piles of yellow brick signaled she was close to home. A neighbor crawled out of a gutted house and called out to her, and Patti yelled back, but could not stop her legs from running. As she approached the spot where her home once stood, she screamed for her husband.

"*Randy!*"

In her hand, her mobile phone lit up with a message from Johnny, the last thing his friends and family would read before the long silence.

Get to a safe place NOW!!

CHAPTER 2

TROUBLE ON THE HORIZON

Four Days Earlier . . .

SATURDAY, APRIL 23, 2011—ACROSS THE COUNTRY

Somewhere west of the Mississippi River, the ingredients of violent weather began drifting into place. A blanket of warm, humid air slid north from the Gulf of Mexico to hover languidly over the South. Storms were hammering the Rockies, wringing moisture from the air, dumping snow upon the mountains, and lurching east as a cold front. A large trough of low pressure stretched from Arkansas to the Great Lakes, rippling slowly eastward over the Central Plains like a giant ocean swell. Behind it, the mass of cold, dense air from the Rockies was grinding east like a plow, shoving up the warm, moist air in its path. Along the invisible boundary between these clashing bodies of air—the dryline—blue skies began blooming with thunderstorms.

The thunderstorms began as the innocuous white cauliflower of cumulus clouds that formed in the beautiful dance of convection that resembles a boiling pot in time-lapse movies. The sun beat down and warmed the earth, heating the blanket of air from the Gulf, as hot and wet as a fever sweat. From it, great blobs of muggy air broke off and rose like invisible hot-air balloons, penetrating the cold, dry air above. The rising air left behind a wake of low pressure that the surrounding air rushed to fill, creating a fountain surging upward as fast as one hundred miles per hour. As the moisture rose and cooled, it condensed into microscopic droplets, a veil of white on blue. Those droplets merged into bigger and bigger drops and, when they became too heavy for the updraft to keep aloft, fell to the earth in a shimmering gauze of rain.

As vapor became liquid, the state change released latent heat—the fuel of thunderstorms—feeding the air fountain with a new surge of power. The top of the fountain cooled rapidly, crested over, and sank to the ground, only to be warmed again by the surface and sucked back into the storm. These rushing currents created a self-perpetuating loop, a monster that fed itself. The storms mushroomed upward into towers that loomed thirty thousand feet and higher, grazed by screaming upper-level winds that sculpted their classic anvil tops, and caused the storms to tilt and rotate. The thunderstorms throbbed with power, releasing more energy than the atomic bomb dropped on Hiroshima. And these self-feeding monsters stalked steadily east.

Meteorologists frowned into their screens at NOAA's Storm Prediction Center on the plains of Norman, Oklahoma. Their weather models were painting apocalyptic futures, projecting what the weather community had been worrying about for days: a widespread, multiround outbreak of violent long-track tornadoes.

The conditions intimated an outbreak of epic proportions, an event of a scale that many scientists had never witnessed in their lifetimes. But it was impossible to forecast exactly when and where the storms would form. Tornadogenesis is still a mystery not yet decoded by science. Meteorologists have deciphered the conditions that give rise to tornadoes—moisture, instability, wind shear, troughs of low pressure and ridges of high pressure that ripple through the upper air like ocean waves—but not the proportions. Much as bread dough with too much water or too little yeast will fail to rise, the ingredients for tornadoes must be present in very precise amounts. "We know the ingredients," some meteorologists liked to say, "but not the specific recipe."

This week these ingredients were present in generous quantities, making the atmosphere ripe for the kind of tornadoes that could stay on the ground for hours. But the best that science could do was map out the probability in any given area. That picture grew clearer with each passing day, as the weekend ended and the workweek began. The map looked like a target, with concentric circles of decreasing risk radiating from the bull's-eye.

That bull's-eye was beginning a slow drift toward Alabama.

This April had already seen two outbreaks, and one was the worst in years. Just days ago, on April 14–16, 178 tornadoes had raked across sixteen states from Oregon to Virginia, killing thirty-eight people. Towns in Alabama, Mississippi, and Kentucky were still picking up the pieces.

Three days later, on April 19, the second outbreak barged through the Midwest and southern Great Plains, unleashing hail-spitting thunderstorms and seventy tornadoes in Oklahoma, Missouri, Ohio, Illinois, Kentucky, and Indiana. One of the biggest struck the St. Louis area a little before eight in the evening on Good Friday, carving a twenty-two-mile path through the suburbs, barely missing downtown. Nearly half a mile wide, it damaged 2,700 buildings and pounded the airport, blowing out terminal windows and buffeting three commercial airplanes full of passengers waiting on the tarmac. Damage to the airport, which would close for four days, was nearly $30 million.

Astonishingly, no one died. Broadcast meteorologists had warned St. Louis with thirty-four minutes of lead time.

April was usually the peak of spring tornado season, but this April was exceptionally fierce. Around two hundred tornadoes had struck North America so far this month. The tally would rise to 757, making April 2011 the most active tornado month in recorded history. But most people would not remember these first two outbreaks, because a third was brewing with such malevolence that it would come to eclipse them both.

▪ ▪ ▪

James Spann, the lead meteorologist for Birmingham's channel ABC 33/40, had been monitoring conditions intently. In nearly three decades of forecasting Alabama weather, he had watched the atmosphere turn deadly many times. As a teenager he had witnessed the worst outbreak ever previously recorded, the Super Outbreak of April 3, 1974. That was the first time he had ever seen death up close, and now, as a broadcast meteorologist, he felt a personal responsibility for every fatality on his watch. He could recite the victims' names and life stories; he attended their funerals and grieved with their families, some of whom became his friends.

Karen Spann had been with her husband for his entire career. Married for nearly thirty years—they joked that she was a "weather widow"—she could read the forecast in the shadows of his face and in the fog of preoccupation that clouded his eyes whenever a storm approached. She was accustomed to the silent withdrawal that occurred whenever he was in the zone. But something about this storm struck her as particularly ominous.

"This has a huge potential for disaster," Spann told his wife quietly at the kitchen table one morning as they sipped their coffee. Breakfast was the one slow moment of his day, after calling in forecasts to twenty-seven radio shows, filming his daily online Weather Xtreme video, and getting their thirteen-year-old son off to school. Today as they talked, he was troubled, his forehead etched with concern. "Somebody could die in a setup like this."

The computer models were not always right. But atmospheric conditions looked alarmingly similar to those of past outbreaks, and models were all pointing to a day when the sky would convulse with long-lived supercells bearing families of tornadoes. He expected to see funnels of unfathomable size and power that could stay on the ground for a hundred miles—maybe more. Spann felt certain this was going to be a red-letter day. He had come to this conclusion more than a week before the storm.

"Wednesday the twenty-seventh—that could be a pretty active period for strong or severe storms," he had warned viewers the past Tuesday, eight days out, on his Weather Xtreme podcast. "Hey, this is April in Alabama, when things like that can happen—and often will."

CHAPTER 3

THE CALM

SUNDAY, APRIL 24, 2011—TUSCALOOSA, ALABAMA

Danielle Downs awoke on Easter Sunday to the unusual quiet of an empty house. Both her roommates were with their families, and in their absence the house lacked the comfortable chaos of three students with colliding schedules. Danielle wished she could be home today, too, with her parents and younger sister. But she had the weekend shift again at the Wingate, an interstate hotel where she worked the front desk. In the slanting light of spring, this rare and velvety silence tempted her to sleep in. But she decided to get up for Easter Mass, even if she had to go alone.

A mile north of campus, her house stood in the lowest point of Beverly Heights, a sleepy street of middle-class homes and college rentals shaded by trees in new leaf. The neighborhood lacked the couches-on-porches ambience of the Strip, that thumping stretch of University Boulevard where Lynyrd Skynyrd blasted at any hour from the belly of a sticky-floored bar. At twenty-four, Danielle was over that. She liked this house, with its wraparound deck seasoned with late-night laughter and spilled drinks, where the white wooden railing was still wrapped in Christmas lights. It was quiet, but not too quiet. Through her second-floor window she could hear invisible trains rumble by, hidden by curtains of tall pines.

A senior in social work, Danielle was one of thirty-four thousand students attending the University of Alabama, the biggest school in the state and an academic juggernaut that dwarfed the historically black Stillman College (one thousand students) and two-year Shelton State (around five thousand) in their semesterly occupation of Tuscaloosa. Graduation was less than two weeks away, and all three schools were pulsating with the fugue of procrastination and panic that whirled through finals week.

One last paper stood between Danielle and her diploma. Working seventy-hour weeks between her full-time hotel job and her field placement for the School of Social Work, she had been rushing to finish papers and tie up loose ends in the scraps of time between double shifts. When she learned that she had qualified to graduate, the swell of relief yielded a smile so big that her almond eyes disappeared. Her family called this look her "Chinese eyes." It meant she was really happy.

She loved walking to class across the grassy Quad, the focal point of campus, beneath cherry trees that rained pink blossoms in the spring and rust-colored leaves in the fall. On one side of the Quad sat the musty-smelling fortress of Gorgas Library; on the other towered Denny Chimes, the redbrick obelisk that announced the hour with a melody. Ancient oaks knit their branches into a canopy above University Boulevard, shading the white double staircase of the President's Mansion, one of seven antebellum buildings that survived the burning of campus five days before the end of the Civil War, when this was a military college. Beside the mansion was Danielle's School of Social Work, headquartered in Little Hall, a former gymnasium named after an 1892 transfer student who introduced a game he had learned up north: football. The university now claimed a football dynasty that could easily double the population of Tuscaloosa on game days, when students must move their cars off campus to make room for convoys of motor homes filled with fans of the Crimson Tide.

Soon there would be no more tailgating on the Quad, admiring the chocolate fountains and flat-screen TVs clustered under vast alumni tents. No more all-nighters over textbooks or beer pong. No more struggling for a passing grade in classes that tested theories but not those unteachable realities that underlay her calling to social work—compassion, integrity, tenacity, patience. Well, maybe not patience. She was itching to move on.

Her little sister's wedding was a week from Friday, and Danielle was the maid of honor. Michelle was marrying her high school sweetheart, a meteorology student, just a few days after their graduation from Mississippi State. The day after the wedding, Danielle would walk across her own stage in Tuscaloosa. After pulling on one more bridesmaid's dress for a good friend's wedding in May, she could get on with her own postcollege plans to move to the snow-white beaches of Florida's Gulf Coast. She hoped to find a job at Eglin Air Force Base, counseling families through deployments.

Danielle had not been to church in a while, and as she entered the sanctuary of Holy Spirit, a large marble fountain of holy water bubbled as if to welcome her back. An Irish priest delivered a touching Mass, the altar behind him lit by the late-morning sun streaming through the stained-glass window, which depicted a white dove in flight among golden rays. Around Danielle's neck swung a medal depicting her patron saint, Joan of Arc, an inexpensive piece of jewelry that she almost never took off.

After church, she treated herself to the jazz brunch at Five Bar, a gastropub in old downtown known for its Bloody Mary bar, beignets, and fried chicken 'n' waffles. Customers filled the bistro tables on the sidewalk patio as temperatures rose comfortably into the mid-eighties—a good bit warmer than normal for April. A gentle breeze drifted in from the south while a local jazz trio played in the background. It was not a bad way to spend Easter, even if she could not be with her family. She paused to muse on Facebook:

1:16 p.m. Mass was pretty amazing . . . but I wish I could have spent it with family and friends . . . Happy Easter and just be thankful to be with the ones you love today!

At 3:01 p.m. she clocked in and took her place behind the wood-and-marble front desk at the Wingate. As comfortably familiar as any chain, the five-story stucco-and-stone hotel joined a Cracker Barrel and a Howard Johnson among the gas stations off Interstate 20/59 on the outskirts of Tuscaloosa. It offered clean, predictable rooms and a free continental breakfast to visiting UA parents, interstate travelers, and a few French and German employees attending meetings at the nearby Mercedes-Benz plant.

Danielle was still upset with her boss, who had cut her hours as punishment for her recent confrontation with a customer, a man who had been complaining aggressively. She took pride in her ability to smile and let customers vent. But she was no pushover, and this man had been condescending. She had tried to offer a calm reply, but he had cut her off and talked down to her. She had raised her voice, not to the point of yelling, but enough to ensure she was heard.

Her boss was furious. Coworkers and nearby customers had defended Danielle, calling the customer out on his behavior. But it had not made any difference. She was dropped from the schedule Mondays and Wednesdays. And with two weddings coming up, and her own move in May, she desperately needed the money.

Her Sunday shift passed uneventfully, and after clocking out at 11:12 p.m. she went home to a house that was no longer quiet. Her roommates, Kelli Rumanek and Loryn Brown, were back and getting ready for Dead Week, the window of all-night voracious cramming that preceded final exams. It was good to have them back.

The girls were aware that a dangerous storm was expected midweek. The TV meteorologists were working themselves into a lather. Danielle was not afraid of storms, but she constantly reminded everyone she knew to stay prepared and take shelter. Loryn, on the other hand, was terrified of storms and had just bought a weather radio, which would wake them up with a loud alarm if a tornado warning was issued in the middle of the night.

As Dead Week commenced, the bars on the Strip got at least as busy as the library, and students sauntered in small groups across campus dressed in the unofficial coed uniform of T-shirts, shorts, and flip-flops. It was starting to feel like early summer.

CHAPTER 4

THE PRELUDE

MONDAY, APRIL 25, 2011—ACROSS THE SOUTH

As Monday slid into afternoon, the sky to the west began stirring. Tornado-producing thunderstorms were forming on the leading edge of a cold front nosing its way across Arkansas, chasing a surface low. Hail drummed the ground, growing as big as hen eggs, golf balls, baseballs, and softballs, pocking cars and cracking windshields. Ending months of abnormally dry weather, the skies spilled themselves upon Arkansas in what would become, in many parts of the state, the wettest April in years. Rivers swelled and escaped their banks, engulfing roads and sweeping cars away in the swiftly moving water. Six people died in those cars. A house was flushed from its foundation. In Missouri, the Black River seeped over the crest of its levee in more than three dozen spots, oozing toward the thousands of people who lived in its floodplain.

And then came the wind. A rash of tornadoes broke out across Texas, Oklahoma, and Arkansas. Around 7:25 p.m., a large tornado struck Vilonia, a one-block town in Arkansas, thirty miles north of Little Rock. A husband and wife who tried to ride it out in a big rig were killed when the truck was tossed into a pond. Two others died in their mobile homes. The phalanx of storms marched east in a nearly vertical line that crossed the Mississippi River around 10:00 p.m., beating Mississippi with straight-line winds and leaving in its wake a lingering rain.

Before Monday was over, ten people were dead in Arkansas. The governor declared a state of emergency.

"And you know," he said, "it may not be over."

CHAPTER 5

THE OPENING ACT

11:00 P.M., TUESDAY, APRIL 26, 2011—BIRMINGHAM, ALABAMA

Jason Simpson never slept well before a storm. He was half-awake when his alarm clock buzzed, and he rolled over in the dark beside his sleeping wife and glanced at the laptop glowing on the bedside table. The radar showed a red streak moving east across the Mississippi River. It was a squall line, a wall of thunderstorms marching in an angled line across northern Mississippi. This triggered a twinge of surprise. Things were expected to get ugly the coming afternoon, but this squall line was sneaking toward Alabama in the middle of the night. Moving steadily east, it would cross the state line well before daybreak.

I've got three hours, Jason thought, now wide awake. *Time to get to work.*

He rolled out of bed and dressed quickly in the dark, careful not to wake his wife. Seven years into his job as a weatherman at ABC 33/40, Jason still worked the morning shift, which began at 4:00 a.m. He was accustomed to starting his day in the dark and functioning on five hours of sleep, but Lacey, four months pregnant with their first child, needed all the rest she could get. Her belly was beginning to swell, and today was the ultrasound appointment that would send her shopping for pink or blue. He hated to miss that tender moment, but the weather does not wait.

Jason went into the kitchen, brewed six cups of coffee, enough for one big mug and a thermos to take into the TV studio. Three pieces of bacon and three sausage links crackled on the George Foreman Grill, the breakfast he ate every day while trolling the weather maps on his laptop at the breakfast counter. It was part of his pregame ritual, the daily routine that made him feel ready for anything, and he didn't like to miss any part of it, especially before a big storm. He had gone to bed earlier than normal so he could have plenty of time to prepare for what he expected to be a harrowing day. He deviated from his ritual only slightly, nuking a few chicken fingers and throwing them in a plastic container for later. If the weather got dicey, at least he would have protein.

Jason had been on edge for the past week, along with every other meteorologist in the South, as he had watched, with mounting concern, the atmosphere beginning to simmer. Around twenty-two hours earlier, at 1:00 a.m., the Storm Prediction Center had released a two-day outlook with a warning that had made the weathermen shiver:

> ***POTENTIAL FOR A SIGNIFICANT/WIDESPREAD SEVERE WEATHER EVENT—INCLUDING THE POSSIBILITY OF A TORNADO OUTBREAK—REMAINS EVIDENT THIS FORECAST . . . CENTERED ON THE MID SOUTH/TN VALLEY AREA.***

Tension had swept through the weather community. The professionals hunkered down over weather maps and computer models at the National Weather Service (NWS) and at the National Oceanic and Atmospheric Administration (NOAA) offices. Amateur weather buffs flocked to the chat rooms to fill them with speculation. Conditions were very similar to those of past outbreaks, and the models painted probabilities that looked downright apocalyptic. Yesterday the Storm Prediction Center in Norman, Oklahoma, issued a two-day forecast warning that conditions were ripe for long-track tornadoes in parts of Alabama, Mississippi, Kentucky, and Tennessee.

Again? Jason thought. *So soon?*

The last outbreak—the worst in years—was less than two weeks ago. Now the potential for another outbreak was clear and present, but it was hard for Jason not to feel a little skeptical. What were the odds of another one, so soon after the last? Would it strike the same place twice?

In his kitchen just before midnight, Jason puzzled over his weather maps. *These look like fake numbers. This can't be real.* The wind shear was off the charts, approaching a level he had never seen.

He followed the squall line across his screen. There would probably be damaging straight-line winds, maybe a small tornado or two. But large and violent twisters are rare when thunderstorms march in a line. The individual storm cells in a squall line often compete and interfere with one another, throwing off the recipe for supercell tornadoes. But by midnight, the thunderstorms had begun dropping tornadoes on Mississippi. Around 1:00 a.m., going against type, Jason called a director and told him to meet him at the station. By 3:00 a.m., he was standing in front of the green screen and talking into the camera.

Going on air during a severe weather event is a two-meteorologist job. One monitors the radar behind the scenes while the other performs between the camera and the green screen, connecting with the audience. There is a lot of information to take in, and one look at a weatherman's laptop screen, jammed with maps and chat rooms and camera feeds, is enough to make an average head explode. The screen displays two radars: one showing radial wind velocity; the other, precipitation. Five private chat sessions with National Weather Service offices scroll with internal messages and public warnings. Another chat room buzzes with Sky Watchers, amateurs trained to spot the harbingers of storms. A window shows live feeds from the SkyCams, which must be driven by remote control so that they point in the right direction. And now on Twitter and Facebook, viewers on the scene supply photos that can be useful—as well as ground observations that a seasoned pro knows better than to trust. To the untrained eye, a funnel-shaped cloud can resemble the vortex of a tornado. And some tornadoes look like a thunderstorm sitting on the ground.

Jason usually drove the radar, in the studio. But right now, he was flying solo on the weather desk, doing his best to cover both jobs, translating the gist of what he saw into the black eye of the camera. He asked two early morning anchors on the early shift to help him.

"Look for power flashes, low-hanging clouds," he told the anchors, "anything that looks weird."

At 4:16 a.m., while most Alabamians slept soundly and unaware, the first tornado reached into the dark of rural Alabama and filled the air with a lonely roar and the snapping of tall pines.

■ ■ ■

Across town, lead meteorologist James Spann was startled awake by the loud bleating of his smartphone. It was just a few minutes before his regular alarm went off, as it did every weekday at 4:52 a.m., but the sound startled him, and he surfaced through a fog of surprise and alarm. His weather app was doing its job, waking him up with the day's first warning. He pawed around on the nightstand for his phone, which lay next to the weather radio, glanced at the radar, and shot out of bed.

Oh, Lord!

Thunderstorms were developing up and down the state, and the National Weather Service was already pumping out warnings in six counties. It took a minute for him to confirm he was not dreaming. In three decades of reading the patterns of the atmosphere, James had seen the weather unleash a Pandora's box of maelstroms, but not like this one.

"When it comes to thunderstorms," his colleague Al Moller always said, "expect the unexpected."

These predawn storms had surprised him with both their timing and severity. Every single conventional forecasting method had failed him. In yesterday's broadcast, he had warned emphatically about the potential for dangerous storms to rumble through the afternoon. But he had said nothing of a morning outbreak.

James fought the queasy feeling that he had botched the forecast. He showered quickly and threw on the uniform he wears every day in front of the green screen: dress shirt, tie in any color but green, and dark trousers held up by suspenders. He stuffed his MacBook Pro in a bag, grabbed his jacket, and jumped into his silver Ford Explorer. The sky was black and the clouds hung hot and low. Stealing glances at the weather radar glowing on an iPad mounted to his console, he raced—his wife would kill him if she knew how fast—to the TV station on the other side of town. Thank goodness the roads were empty at this hour. The commute takes twenty minutes on a regular day. Today he got there in ten.

This was rare form for Alabama's favorite weatherman. In a state where only the Gospel is gospel, James Spann's word is considered the next best thing. A common refrain is: "My mama says, if James Spann says it, it must be true." Wives have learned not to talk to their husbands during the Iron Bowl or anytime James Spann is on the air.

Spann, fifty-three, bald on top, gray on the sides, delivered the weather in a deep, crisp baritone. Many of his viewers were outright fans. They called him "my hero," and "the Man." They knew if they e-mailed or tweeted him a question, they would get a personal answer. They read his blog and watched his weekly online video talk show, WeatherBrains, on which he and other self-professed "weather weenies" talked shop about meteorology. Spann had more Twitter followers than some national celebrities and had reached Facebook's max on friends. He may be the only weatherman in history to have his own bobblehead doll.

Spann fans swore that they could glance at a muted TV and tell you how bad the weather was based on what they could see of Spann's uniform. *Uh-oh, I see suspenders—where's the tornado?* Those visible suspenders meant he had removed his coat, a signal that weather conditions were getting serious, and you had better pay attention. If his sleeves were rolled up, it was time to hide in the closet. "The day the tie comes off," said one fan, "will be a very, very bad day."

When Spann burst into the studio, jacket under his arm, Jason could still hear the sleep in his voice. James looked at Jason and read his face: conditions were bad. They had been a team for seven years and could communicate whole paragraphs with a glance and a gesture. Without a word, they swapped places. Spann stepped in front of the green screen, opened his laptop on a mobile podium, and addressed the black eye of the camera. If he turned his head to the right, he could see himself in front of the weather map on a small monitor just off camera. Beyond that, he could see Jason on the weather desk, behind a row of six monitors that showed the disaster unfolding in many dimensions. Jason gave him a hand signal and the show went on.

Above them, above the wires and the studio lights and the acoustic dampeners, above the rooftop of the ABC 33/40 station on the hill in south Birmingham, the sky was already churning.

■ ■ ■

Jason would never forget the first time he met James Spann. It was April 1998, his senior year at Holly Pond High School. The guidance counselor had pulled him aside and said, "Jason, there's somebody here I think you need to talk to." The Storm Link minivan had pulled into the parking lot, and out climbed James Spann, there to give his meteorology talk to the students, to dazzle them with his science. Jason helped carry in a projector and a twenty-pound laptop. On their walk down the hall, the high school senior gushed. When he was bored in class, he drew pictures of megastorms, radars dotted with hook echoes, the supine commas that signaled spiraling winds around a ball of debris. James looked at the kid, and saw promise.

"How would you like to intern with me this summer?" James said.

"Really?" Jason said. "That would be great!"

It was seventy miles from his house in rural Holly Pond to the TV station in Birmingham. But that was back when gas cost seventy cents a gallon. He could make the round trip in two hours and on four dollars. Like a young Jedi, Jason studied James. He watched the way he moved, the way he talked, the clues he noticed, the words he chose. But the kid was one of about thirty interns that year. How could he ever hope to make a lasting impression on the master? One night he got his chance: his first taped weathercast.

He had thought it would be easy, because James made it look effortless. But in front of the green screen, it was not so easy. Jason found himself with his back to the camera—a broadcast sin—floundering around as he tried to figure out where the heck on the blank wall to point. You could almost hear the air whooshing out of his ego like a balloon as he trudged off the set, chin to chest. James had been in the control room, watching the boy unravel. He met him at the door.

"Don't worry about it," he said. "It gets easier."

That was classic Spann. Little words. Big message. Unforgettable truth. Jason had a seventy-mile drive home to let that marinate. By the time he pulled into his driveway in Holly Pond, he had talked himself out of quitting. *It gets easier.* Those three words prevented him from giving up on this career.

After that, Jason worked with James whenever he got the chance. James taught him everything. Most important, he taught him to be himself. Authentic. Viewers could smell a fake across two counties. "Don't be a blow-dried boob," James would say, nodding at the stiff-haired guys on the national news. "You be you. You're from Holly Pond. You remember that. Don't ever forget where you came from." Jason watched, listened, and learned. He got a job in a smaller TV market and practiced. In August of 2004, shortly after the ten o'clock news, his phone rang. It was James.

"What do you think about coming to work for me?"

"I think it'd be pretty good."

Jason could not wait to work a severe weather event with James, to be his right-hand man. But it did not happen right away. In the first bad storm, he found himself third on the totem pole. Jason stormed out of the studio that day, hurt that he was not trusted to do the job that James had hired him to do. But James knew he was not ready. Eight or nine months later, Jason had learned how to anticipate what James needed.

It got easier.

In the studio, Jason drove the equipment while James went on camera. Jason had studied James for so long that he knew what he wanted, sometimes even before James did. The hand signals would come in handy today.

■ ■ ■

Seven hundred miles away, at the Storm Prediction Center in Norman, Oklahoma, the warning coordination meteorologist Greg Carbin was watching the Birmingham radar closely. He spotted a bow echo forming—a line of storms pushed out into an arc, like a hunter's bow. The storms' position at exactly 5:52 a.m. looked to him like a giant question mark, punctuated by a storm cell at the bottom. It was poised over central Alabama, spreading over roughly eleven counties. Carbin shook his head and thought: *Even the atmosphere doesn't know what it's doing.*

Like a canoe paddle moving through the surface of a lake, curling the water into whirls within swirls, the squall line moved through the atmosphere, stirring up small to midsize tornadoes. Some dissipated minutes after they formed. Others grew to a size that could shred a double-wide trailer into ribbons. One stayed on the ground for twenty-three miles. They coursed insidiously through the rural lands of west-central Alabama, across counties where timber farms outnumbered stoplights.

At 5:18 a.m., the fifth tornado of the day to strike Alabama had come straight down the main street of downtown Cordova, a small town an hour's drive northwest of Birmingham, shattering storefront windows along Commerce Street and leaving a trail of bricks and broken glass.

As that storm raged on for another nineteen miles, another tornado, a sneaky one, was born on the outskirts of Tuscaloosa. In a blink of the radar's eye, what looked like a straight-line gust of wind mutated into a tornado. By the time it appeared on Jason's radar, the funnel was already on the ground, tearing up Coaling, crossing the interstate, and heading toward the Mercedes-Benz plant.

While he was on the air, Jason felt his mobile phone buzz. He stole a quick glance at the screen. It was his cousin Bob from Holly Pond.

Why are you calling me? he thought, annoyed. *You know I'm on the air. You know I can't answer the phone.*

He hit ignore and returned to the radar. That's when he saw it, the angry red comma passing over Holly Pond. Over his parents, aunts, uncles, and cousins. The family farm.

Yeah, he knows I'm on the air. That's why he's calling. They must have been hit. A surge of emotion made him blink and swallow. The storm was suddenly personal. Things just got real. James read his face, gave a nod.

"Go take a minute. Get some air."

Jason stepped out of the studio and into the white cinder-block hallway with a beat-up striped couch, and tried calling his family. No answer. He choked up and called his wife, who had been trying to reach them, too, with no success. Jason pulled himself together and went back into the studio. The midstate storms began to dissipate, and the morning event wound to a close. The northern third of Alabama was still being pummeled by weak tornadoes, but the sky above Birmingham was clearing up—for now. When the ON AIR light went dark and the studio dimmed, Jason looked at James, and James looked at Jason.

They said nothing.

That said everything.

■ ■ ■

Around 7:00 a.m., Central Alabama woke up to blue skies and sunshine. Several storms were still spinning upstate, but Birmingham and Tuscaloosa looked deceptively clear. Thirty-one tornadoes had struck Alabama, but many of the people outside their path had no idea anything had happened until they turned on the morning news or picked up the phone. Some of them wondered, *Was that it? Is it over?*

James rushed straight from the weather desk to his office, a windowless room the size of a closet located in the middle of the building. This morning's outbreak was just the opening act. Today's atmosphere was a powder keg, and the source of energy that would set it off—the sun—was beginning its rise. If the morning had been this bad already, the afternoon would likely be off the charts. People would die. How many? That answer was something he considered a direct reflection of how well he did his job.

Between his radio interviews and hundreds of e-mails, the damage reports poured in. A quarter of a million people in the state had no power. Five people were dead. Mobile phone towers had been knocked down, and the network was overloaded. Landlines were not working. Cable was gone. The Internet was out. It was a hot mess.

The damage crippled the weather community. The storm had taken out equipment they needed to forecast and broadcast warnings. Meteorologists lost their radar feeds. Weather radio transmitters were disabled. SkyCams were busted. Communications systems were groaning under the weight of everyone calling at once to check on family and friends.

"Okay, let's start over," James told his technicians. "Instead of telling me what is *not* working, tell me what *is*."

While workers raced to fix downed cameras and broken lines, Jason joined a morning news show called *Talk of Alabama*. He had to get the word out—at least to people who could still turn on a TV—that the day was far from over. This blue sky was a lie.

"Please, pay attention this afternoon," he said. "This is not what you think it is. Get ready. This might be the last time some of us talk."

After the show ended, Jason walked over to the newsroom to brief the reporters. Usually when there is a weather situation brewing, he steps into the news director's office and closes the door. But today it was time to make sure that everyone heard the alarm. He stood on a platform behind the news desk and swore the apocalyptic warnings were not hyperbolic.

"Gary," he said, turning to the news director. "Have I ever told you that we were going to have a horrible tornado outbreak?"

"No."

"Well, today is that day. Get ready for mass casualties if these things hit cities."

"When does it start?"

"An hour or two."

"Where do you think the first one will be?"

"It could be anywhere."

CHAPTER 6

GROUND TRUTH

It could be anywhere.

In an age when we can map the human genome, gather dust from a comet hurtling through space, and engineer synthetic DNA, science cannot predict exactly when and where a tornado will form. A radar cannot "see" tornadoes. It can only detect conditions known to be present when they form, such as signs of strong rotation. And the presence of those radar features does not prove a tornado exists. The only way to confirm a tornado is for a human to lay eyes on it. This, in meteorology, is called ground truth. It is one of the most valuable tools meteorologists have today.

Ground truth is the difference between probability and reality. It is a key factor in the false alarm rate—the percentage of warnings issued by the National Weather Service based on conditions seen on radar when in fact no funnel has materialized on the ground. The problem is, supercells that bear tornadoes look almost exactly like supercells that do not. So when a radar signature glows with the inflamed comma of a hook echo—a sign of strong rotation—but no ground truth ensues, a warning coordination meteorologist at the NWS must decide whether to issue a tornado warning based on circumstantial evidence alone.

A tornado warning triggers a ripple effect of communication and action, beginning with countywide sirens. Broadcast meteorologists such as Spann have no authority to issue a warning, but they shoulder a great responsibility to disseminate it quickly and broadly to the public. They are the town criers, informing the legions who still do not get their warnings directly from the NWS via weather radios, websites, or smartphone apps.

Herein lies the great dilemma: Warnings issued without ground truth are often false warnings. The sirens sound. People run to their basements. Then nothing happens. After a few such occasions, people stop running. They grow complacent. They stop trusting meteorologists or, worse, accuse them of crying wolf. Then, when they hear the next alarm, they go outside to scan the sky for confirmation. Or they simply ignore it.

To warn or not to warn? That is a loaded question. In weighing the consequences of being wrong in either case, it would seem logical to err on the side of warning. But overwarning has dire ramifications, too. At the time of the outbreak, the false alarm rate at the NWS office in Birmingham—and nationwide—was hovering around 80 percent.

Ground truth is one of the reasons James Spann spends a great deal of off-the-air time teaching children and adults about storms. The best storm chasers may be able to put themselves in the right place at the right time to catch a twister—sometimes. But storm spotters, who stay put, are everywhere. The 290,000 volunteer spotters across the country scan the skies above trailer parks, small towns, rural farms, and other places the SkyCams cannot reach. Most of them have attended two-hour classes that teach them how to tell a violently rotating column of air from a harmless funnel-shaped cloud. Spann's classes are eight hours and often draw four hundred people of all ages and walks of life. When something wicked comes their way, they photograph it, film it, e-mail it, tweet it, and post the valuable real-time information in private chat rooms where Spann and others can harvest info from trustworthy sources. They are one of the most valuable tools meteorologists have today.

Education is, as Spann sees it, a critical part of his duty, not only to enlarge his network of ground truth but to teach people how to save themselves. Teaching the public to be weather-wise is just as important as devising and broadcasting accurate forecasts. An old friend and colleague, the tornado researcher Chuck Doswell, summed it up:

If our forecasts are perfect but the users don't receive the message, don't understand the message, don't know what to do with the message, and don't act upon the contents of the message, then our time and effort have been wasted.

Spann spends hundreds of unpaid hours every year teaching storm-spotter classes, giving presentations at public libraries, and preaching the gospel of weather safety to just about anyone who will listen. His favorite audience, without question, is children.

Every morning during the school year, Spann drives to an elementary school somewhere in Alabama. For more than two decades, he has been giving this weather talk—the same one he gave the day he met Jason Simpson in the high school parking lot—and it has evolved into a presentation with stunning photographs and cool videos that make students gasp and laugh and wonder. Teachers book him a year in advance.

The students are anywhere from first to sixth graders, and they cannot wait to meet a celebrity they watch every night on TV. To welcome him, they color posters of tornadoes and sleet and hurricanes and hang them all over the halls, or the school library, or the auditorium where they gather for a celebrity assembly.

"He's a superstar!" teachers say. "When he comes here we get as excited as the students, 'cause we always learn something, too."

Spann's talk lays an approachable foundation for understanding the atmosphere and, ultimately, tornadoes. He does this to get kids excited about science, because whatever the kids learn, they go home and teach their parents. And when the weather turns, they will herd their parents into the hall closet and shame them into wearing a football or bike helmet.

On a recent talk, James addressed several fifth-grade classes gathered in an elementary school library.

"Everybody breathe in!" James said to the assembly. "Breathe out!"

The library audibly exhaled.

"That was a science experiment!" James said. "You proved that there's *air* in here!"

The fifth graders giggled. Air has weight, he explained—not enough to feel—but a little weight that can be measured by a . . .

Barometer! the fifth graders yelled in unison. They always knew more than the first graders, and he could count on their participation. He was most comfortable around people this age, more so than around adults, and certainly more so than around the seventh graders, who were approaching the evil age of thirteen, when it is no longer cool to yell out in an assembly.

"Yes! That's where these numbers come from," James said, the screen behind him flashing to a picture of today's weather map. "These are units of pressure called millibars, and when the barometer's like, really really high, what letter shows up?"

H!

"When you see an *H* on a weather map, that means the air there is kinda heavier than the surrounding air. And when something's heavy, it doesn't go up. It goes where?"

Down!

"When air sinks, it crushes the clouds away. It's like, sunny. So typically, when you see an *H* it's kinda sunny. And in the winter it's also kinda what?"

Cold!

"Cold air is heavy. But around these lows, air tends to be light. The winds converge. Air goes where?"

Up!

"When air goes up, you get clouds and rain. So half my job is figuring out if air is going up or if air is going . . ."

Down!

"Wait a minute. If air is going up, and air is going down, that means air has what?"

Silence.

"Waves—like the ocean. You just can't see them," James said, showing them a pressure map that looked like a topographical map, with blobs of concentric circles and contour lines that depicted barometric pressure instead of altitude.

He showed them a video of the National Weather Service releasing a weather balloon, explaining that this happens every day, twice a day, all around the world at exactly the same time. In the video, the man holding the balloon, twice his height and filled with hydrogen, was nearly dragged off his feet by the wind. The students cackled with laughter. Once he let go, the balloon rose into the atmosphere, carrying a radiosonde, a toaster-size box of instruments that measure wind, temperature, pressure, and moisture. A radio transmitted the measurements, which were compiled into the weather maps he studies every day, like a soothsayer reading tea leaves. Eventually the balloon would pop, and the radiosonde would float back to earth on a parachute. Radiosondes that don't land in lakes or oceans or trees are discovered in fields and backyards and mailed back to the National Weather Service. Less than 20 percent are ever returned.

James also showed them a photo of a satellite 22,500 miles over the equator, moving in an orbit that matches the planet's rotation, hovering above the same spot on the earth. If you gazed up at it at night with the naked eye, you might mistake it for a star. Weather satellites take a picture of the planet every few minutes; shown in succession, they look like a movie of break-dancing clouds.

"I can't imagine doing my job without these, and they didn't have these before about 1960. We also have a tool that lets us see where the rain is falling. It is called a . . ."

Radar!

The radar device looked like a giant volleyball perched on top of a tower. Inside the white sphere (a protective cover that keeps out the elements) is a machine that looks like a giant gun.

"This thing is on a motor and it spins around all day long and shoots out little pulses of electromagnetic energy," James said. "What's cool about these little pulses, when they run into a target, like a raindrop, part of the energy will bounce off the raindrop and bounce back to the antenna. Happens faster than you can blink your eye. We make maps of where the bounces are, and the maps look just like this."

The screen looked like a tie-dyed shirt from the 1960s. Blues and greens mean light rain, he explained. The angry splotches of yellow and red mean heavy rain or hail, and those splotches sometimes come in the shape of a comma that had fallen over on its face. Most kids would first notice the fiery colors of the arc, but the dot of the comma is where the danger lies.

"That's the debris ball," James said. That invariably excited them.

At least once a semester, the kids in his audience practiced a tornado drill, which meant curling into the "tornado turtle" in the halls, or putting books over their heads. Every student in the state had done it.

The most valuable thing Spann teaches the kids is this: When a meteorologist says to get to a safe place, he means the smallest room on the lowest floor, in the center of the house, away from windows. And: *Do not wait to hear a siren.*

"A lot of people think they need to hear a siren. Please, guys—*no!*" he said, over and over, to countless parents and to school and library groups. "I hate sirens. *I hate 'em!* There are days I want to take 'em down and burn 'em."

Spann and other experts believe that sirens are a deadly problem. People wait to act until they hear a siren, but sirens cannot always be heard indoors. Intended to warn people working outdoors and far from better sources of weather information, sirens are an anachronistic WWII relic unworthy of the authority people place in them. Lives are lost because people wait to hear a siren before taking shelter.

Spann called this misplaced faith in sirens the "siren mentality." The National Weather Service is required to issue a warning for tornadoes of any size—even the smallest, which may dissipate in seconds and rarely cause much harm. A warning triggers sirens across the whole county, even though the actual path of danger is considerably smaller. And so when people hear an alarm, they notice it is often closely followed by . . . nothing. Spann believes that meteorologists are overwarning, in part because improved technology is better at detecting smaller, weaker tornadoes that would have been missed in the past.

Spann hoped to be part of the solution, though he could actually change little about the warning system. But he had changed the ways Alabamians received and understood his forecasts, using Twitter, Facebook, blogs, and podcasts—any tool he had—to warn of approaching storms. Unlike TV weather, which provided him exactly two minutes three times a day, new media allowed him enough air time to fully qualify his forecasts with an explicit degree of uncertainty. He could respond to viewer questions and send updates as often as needed. He tried to answer every question viewers sent by e-mail, which numbered into the hundreds on any given day.

James wrapped up his elementary school weather talks by handing his video camera to a student and filming the children waving and cheering. He told kids he would put them on the news that night, but only if they promised to do an urgent homework assignment:

"If you don't have a weather radio, go home and pester your parents till they buy one. That sounds the alarm in your home. You'll know the tornado is coming and you'll turn on the TV and I promise we'll be there, and you can see how close you are and you can do something if you need to. But everyone needs a weather radio. That's a baseline."

Spann always ended his talks—to audiences of kids and colleagues alike—with a reminder that this was a science of probability, not certainty, and that it was easy to get overconfident.

"The greatest thing our science needs is humility," he said. "We still have a lot to learn."

CHAPTER 7

SCANNING THE SKIES

9:30 A.M., WEDNESDAY, APRIL 27, 2011—SMITHVILLE, MISSISSIPPI

At Smithville High School, the hallways were humming with talk of tornadoes. As the screams of the sirens penetrated the cinder-block walls of the school, students and teachers stopped Johnny Parker between classes.

"Is it over?" they asked.

Johnny shook his head and responded, word by halting word.

"More . . . are . . . on . . . the . . . way."

Johnny had been monitoring discussions by the National Weather Service and Storm Prediction Center since last week. This morning at six o'clock he had bent his six-foot frame over the desktop computer in the study, examining the swirling radar and scanning the severe weather updates. Dr. Greg Forbes of the Weather Channel was predicting a 90 percent chance of seeing a tornado within a fifty-mile radius of any given point in Johnny's stretch of Mississippi. That was the highest probability that Johnny had ever seen.

At 6:17 a.m., Johnny dispatched an e-mail forecast that warned of the possibility of strong tornadoes, baseball-size hail, damaging winds up to eighty miles per hour, and flash flooding. His warning left no room for misinterpretation:

> A major and very dangerous tornado outbreak will occur across the South today. The greatest threat for Tornadoes will

be from Northeast MS, most of Alabama, Southern parts of Tennessee, and parts of Georgia.

Most weathermen can remember a childhood storm, a meteorological awakening that inspired their lifelong passion for weather. Johnny's defining storm had toppled a magnificent apple tree that stood guard over his front yard, a lovely canopy in whose shade he had spent long childhood afternoons swinging and playing. That this benign and giving tree could turn murderous seemed inconceivable until he saw how closely it had come to crushing his house. He was only four, with bright blue eyes and dirty-blond curls, but the details of the storm were tattooed into his memory—the streaks of lightning, the house shuddering in gusts of wind, the crack and grumble of thunder all through the angry night. When the sun came out, the young boy stood before that ancient, mangled tree, grasping for the very first time the awesome, staggering power of the sky. But instead of fear, Johnny felt a hunger to know, to study these storms, to understand what made them go and how something invisible could be so powerful. If he came to understand these storms, could he warn his family? Could he keep them safe?

As Johnny grew, so did his fascination. In elementary school, he preferred the weather over cartoons. In middle school, he would stand in the living room and gesture in front of the TV, mimicking the motions of the local weatherman. He made a hobby out of tracking hurricanes and longed to live on a coast so he could one day see the middle of one. He read meteorology books for fun, and he parked himself in front of the Weather Channel during every big event: Andrew. Wilma. Katrina. Ivan. He collected hurricanes as if they were baseball cards. When he was fourteen, he spent a year cataloging every hurricane that had spiraled around the world. His list dated back to 1492.

That same year he attended a National Weather Service seminar to become a trained storm spotter. For every Christmas and birthday, instead of wishing for video games, he begged for radar software. He taught himself how to read weather maps and how to write a forecast. In eleventh grade, Johnny went to Tupelo to visit his idol, the WTVA meteorologist Dick Rice, whom he had previously interviewed for a high school project, and helped compose the day's forecast, which Rice delivered on the ten o'clock news.

Johnny also idolized Jim Cantore, the Weather Channel celebrity whose presence in any coastal town assured residents of a coming hurricane. Johnny believed he would one day become, like Cantore, an operational meteorologist, focusing on forecasts, even though his speech impediment precluded a broadcast career. As he typed his daily forecasts, he dreamed of ways to become a new kind of weatherman, and by seventeen, he had started his own private meteorology company, Parker Weather Service, to practice his craft.

The idea came as Johnny was sitting at his computer, thinking of new ways to dispatch his forecasts. He glanced down at his phone and had an idea: a weather text. He started out with thirty-two "customers"—mostly friends and family who supported his passion—and he texted abbreviated forecasts to batches of ten, the maximum his phone carrier would allow. When the word got out, he got so many new requests that he couldn't keep up with the texts, so he added daily e-mails. He had a pretty good forecast batting average. Every once in a while he hit a home run, like he did on the Christmas of his junior year, when he predicted the rare and beautiful event of a Mississippi white Christmas.

■ ■ ■

The technology now readily available to meteorology students and enthusiasts—from modeling software to online satellite and radar feeds—is remarkably similar to what the pros use. Johnny's hero, Jim Cantore, who taught a college meteorology course, marveled that his students were mastering many of the tools he used every day at the Weather Channel. In the span of his lifetime, how the tools had changed.

In the era before satellites, Doppler radar, and powerful computers, meteorology was a relatively crude science. Before the end of World War II, researchers had little at their disposal besides intermittent observations and a few limited mathematical models based on idealized versions of real conditions. The idea of forecasting was still a pipe dream and the early prophets of weather prediction sometimes found themselves singing in the wind.

The first scientific inquiry into tornado forecasting met curious resistance. In the 1870s, John Park Finley, a farmer's son from Michigan, began what he called "a systematic study of the storms of the United States, especially those of a violent character, namely, tornadoes." In his twenties, he was working at the US Army Signal Service (later renamed the Signal Corps) in Philadelphia, where he devoted his spare time to studying tornadoes. He compiled his findings in an elaborate report that was submitted and approved for publication, but then, mysteriously, lost.

The six-foot-three, two-hundred-pound young man with the handlebar mustache was not easily deterred. He got a break in 1879 when the Signal Corps sent him out to survey a disaster zone in the wake of a tornado outbreak in the Central Plains. Afterward, he suggested that a warning unit should be established in Kansas City, Missouri, to obtain weather reports and spread the word locally when conditions in the area were ripe for twisters. Subsequently, he gathered every known tornado report in the last century to look for patterns. Finley's 1882 report, "The Character of 600 Tornadoes," was the most comprehensive treatise ever written on the matter and became the basis for his later forecasting efforts. He traveled throughout the Central Plains, enlisting more than 957 "tornado reporters"—the precursor to today's storm spotters. And he continued to analyze hundreds of storms, including a famous outbreak of sixty funnels that killed an estimated eight hundred people on February 19, 1884.

Once or twice a day throughout the stormy months of March and April, he specified when conditions were both favorable and unfavorable for tornadoes. "It requires as much, and often more, study to say that no tornadoes will occur as to make the prediction that conditions are favorable for their development," he wrote. (He could say that today and still be right.) When conditions were unfavorable, he was 99 percent accurate, but when he specified conditions favorable, tornadoes occurred only 28 percent of the time. Still, not bad for a relatively nascent science. And Finley's efforts to compare his forecasts to what actually happened were the beginning of what is now called forecast verification.

Unfortunately, at the peak of Finley's career, forecasting got political and a hot debate raged about whether the weather service should be under military or civilian control. Ultimately his superiors terminated his tornado studies in the late 1800s and ordered him to halt all predictions, discouraging use of the word "tornado" on the grounds that it would incite public panic—a harm they judged greater than injuries and damage inflicted by the storm itself. The word remained verboten for decades, and tornado research and forecasting fell into a dark ages of sorts until the late 1940s.

In 1945, the Thunderstorm Project began—a collaboration between the Weather Bureau, the Army Air Forces, the Navy, and the National Advisory Committee for Aeronautics (NASA's predecessor). World War II was coming to a close. Radar had been invented recently and, almost by accident, discovered to be useful for meteorology. As radar detected the presence of enemy aircraft and ships, military operators noticed signals irritatingly "cluttered" with weather echoes, but meteorologists saw the silver lining: radar made a mostly invisible phenomenon visible, providing something akin to a sonogram of a thunderstorm being born.

The Thunderstorm Project aimed to dissect a thunderstorm, inside and out. Trained military pilots flew directly into thunderstorms in twin-propeller fighter planes rugged enough to withstand the strong winds. Stacked five high every five thousand feet, the pilots penetrated a thunderhead over and over, and relinquished their controls to the mercy of the winds inside.

This science was not for sissies. No storm was to be avoided, no matter how large or violent it appeared. During the summers of 1946 and 1947, pilots participating in the study logged seventy flight-hours inside seventy-six thunderstorms. Planes were struck by lightning twenty-one times. But the pilots pulled off 1,362 storm penetrations without a single accident.

As the planes sliced through each storm, their instruments measured turbulence, updrafts, and downdrafts. Equipped with radars, the P-61C Black Widows also had transponders so they could be tracked from the ground as they passed through the storm. The cockpit instrument panels were continuously photographed, and evidence of pilots "flying" their planes in ways that might compromise the data meant that data would be thrown out.

While the pilots were getting buffeted around in the thunderheads, a two-mile grid of surface observation stations scanned the skies; weather balloons measured temperature, dew point, and wind speeds at different altitudes; ground radars tracked and monitored the thunderheads and guided the pilots through them; and radar-wind stations measured wind speeds. The result was a sort of meteorological MRI, a constellation of data that painted a vivid picture of the bowels of the thunderstorm.

Scientists at the University of Chicago analyzed the data by hand over the next three years—their findings on the life cycle of a thunderstorm underpin our understanding of severe-weather phenomena today.

A few years after the Thunderstorm Project, the first tornado forecast in the history of meteorology was made. It was also the first accurate one and was issued on Tinker Air Force Base near Oklahoma City on March 25, 1948. Until that day, tornadoes were considered to be an "act of God" (a phrase that still haunts today's homeowners insurance policies) and forecasting them was not regularly done.

Five days earlier, a large tornado—we don't know the rating because the scales used today did not yet exist—had struck the base only eight minutes after it was spotted by a nearby airport. The funnel was lit up from within by lightning and stormed through the air force base, flinging aircraft, shattering the control tower windows, and causing $10 million in damage (nearly $100 million in today's dollars).

The day after that storm, the base commander, General F. S. Borum, ordered two officers at the base weather post, Major Ernest J. Fawbush and Captain Robert C. Miller, to investigate thunderstorms to try to predict which are likely to produce tornadoes—and to give people enough advance warning to prepare or escape. The officers spent the next few days feverishly poring over weather maps, looking for patterns in the conditions that precede storms.

On the morning of March 25, Miller and Fawbush noticed conditions disturbingly similar to those leading up to that week's earlier tornado. The same surface lows hovered over the west-central plains. The dryline again lurked west of Tinker, inviting a warm, humid air to flow north from the Gulf and smother the base with a mass of muggy air, the jet fuel of thunderstorms. The atmosphere was unstable, with blobs of warm air rising rapidly through cool air above, like great invisible hot-air balloons. High up, the "balloons" encountered strong winds blowing in different directions, which caused them to spin like tops. The jet stream screaming through the upper atmosphere further enhanced the wind shear. Recognizing this pattern, the officers briefed the general that they thought the likelihood of tornadoes was high enough to justify a warning. The word "tornado" in a public broadcast was still avoided, but the general announced the beginning of a new era with his terse order:

"Do it!"

At 3:00 p.m. that day, Miller and Fawbush issued their warning to the base, sending military personnel into severe-weather mode as they braced for the storm's arrival, predicted between 4:00 and 6:00 p.m. Aircraft were moved to hangars, loose objects were tied down, and people prepared to retreat to safe places. At 6:00 p.m., as if following marching orders, the week's second large tornado struck the base, causing another $6 million in damage—but less than it would have without preparation.

This warning paved the way for a civilian program in the 1950s and beyond. Miller and Fawbush became pioneers in the field, creating the Air Force Military Warning System, a team that eventually forced the United States Weather Bureau to change its policy of forbidding tornado warnings and to create the Severe Local Storms (SELS) unit in 1953. It was the beginning of modern tornado forecasting.

The research meteorologist who would establish the field, Tetsuya "Ted" Fujita, a diminutive Japanese, came to the United States in 1953 specifically to study tornadoes. A professor at the University of Chicago, Fujita had meticulously surveyed the damage of the atomic bombs detonated over Hiroshima and Nagasaki. The starburst pattern in which trees fell in bomb-struck areas showed remarkable similarities to the trees downed by certain thunderstorms, inspiring his theory of microbursts, the sudden powerful downdrafts that could knock airplanes out of the sky.

Nicknamed "Mr. Tornado" among colleagues and friends, Fujita spent years walking the damage paths left by tornadoes, looking for patterns that might yield insight into their power and formation. He studied tens of thousands of photographs of tornadoes forming, frame by frame, a technique called photogrammetric analysis. His approach was unique, fresh, and often outside the established norms of meteorological research, and some members of the scientific community frowned on his unorthodox methods. Yet even his critics had to admit that he arrived at groundbreaking conclusions that evaded other researchers.

In 1971 Fujita developed the Fujita Scale, or F-Scale, which enabled scientists to categorize the magnitude of tornadoes through assessment of the damage they left behind. Using indicators of damage to vegetation and man-made structures, the F-Scale ranked tornadoes on a scale of F0 (little damage) to F5 (foundations of well-built houses swept clean of debris). In 1974 he spent hours flying over Alabama and other states to study the tornado tracks of the Super Outbreak. This was "the pinnacle of his analysis of a tornado outbreak," wrote one colleague. "For many of the 148 tornadoes, he was able to map the entire path in Fujita Scale-Intensity contours." He also mentored a fresh crop of meteorology students who are among today's leaders, including Dr. Greg Forbes, the tornado expert at The Weather Channel, and Dr. Roger Wakimoto, who became the director of the National Center for Atmospheric Research.

Years after Fujita's death, the F-Scale was revised to better account for new variables such as the quality of construction of the buildings damaged by the storms. The Enhanced Fujita Scale, or EF-Scale, was adopted in 2007 by the United States (in 2013 by Canada) with the same basic six categories, EF0 to EF5. It is still in use today.

And April 27, 2011, the biggest of all—an EF5—was forming near Smithville, Mississippi—the second of four to strike the South that day.

■ ■ ■

As Johnny and Chloe sat in class at Smithville High, the atmosphere began recharging. The morning storms had wrung moisture from the air, depleting the storms of their fuel. The rain had cooled the air as it fell. These slight and subtle changes threw off the recipe for supercells, and the atmosphere relaxed, cleared, and brightened into a deceptive, menacing calm.

Now, as the midday sun heated the Mississippi River Valley, the ingredients were once again shifting into dangerously perfect proportions. The morning storms had left behind a wake of rain-cooled air, but that air began to warm in the afternoon sun. A slight high along the Gulf Coast had cleared the skies, sending sunshine in buckets and heating the land, which radiated heat into the low-lying air, which was thickening with moisture rising from the Gulf in hot vapors.

The winds were shifting favorably. The seventy-mile-per-hour winds at three thousand feet began to mix with surface winds. A gust front, the windy leading edge of a thunderstorm, rippled east through northern Mississippi and Alabama. A low-level jet stream swooshed up from the south, nudging the blanket of muggy coastal air north, directly in the path of the gust front. As that warm air undercut the cold, dry air aloft, the atmosphere once again began to simmer with instability. Vast bubbles of warm air began to form, break free, and ascend. The pot began to boil.

West of Mississippi, the upper winds screamed northeast, sliding over slower-moving surface winds coursing northwest. This wind shear encountered a rising bubble of air, causing it to rotate. At the surface, surrounding air rushed to fill the areas of low pressure left by the rising blob, converging like water around a drain, but spiraling up, not down. The effect was like a spinning ice skater pulling in her arms until she became a blur. This rotating column of air—a mesocyclone—transformed into the most dangerous and powerful kind of thunderstorm on earth, spitting lightning within itself and onto the ground.

A supercell was born.

CHAPTER 8

TORNADO DOWN

11:30 A.M., APRIL 27, 2011—TUSCALOOSA, ALABAMA

On Fifteenth Street, inside a small brick building that contained a thrift store, a few offices, and a tiny lobby with a sliding glass window, Danielle Downs took the last decorations off the gray walls of her cubicle, one of two squeezed into the office she shared with a graduate student from Huntsville. Without the Mardi Gras beads and the banner of purple, green, and gold fleurs-de-lis, the cube felt empty and soulless. Today was her last day of work at Temporary Emergency Services (TES), the field placement requirement to graduate.

The last semester of her college years had ticked away here, from eight to five, four days a week. TES was a small nonprofit that served the poor, providing bread, clothes, diapers, and occasional help with the power bill. Of all the jobs Danielle had held in unbroken succession since high school, this was by far her favorite. An unpaid internship required by her program, this was the last stop before graduation. She had fallen behind the rest of her class, which had completed field placement last semester, but her professors had granted Danielle a special extension to help her graduate with the others.

In these four months Danielle had found her element at last and flourished exactly as her professors had hoped. Her confidence bloomed as she proved to them—and more important, to herself—that she had every bit of what it took to be a great social worker, even if that didn't translate to her GPA. At last, a test she could pass with honors. Danielle felt relieved and a little sad.

When the morning storms rattled through, they came loud and hard, and the skies above 31 Beverly Heights had shuddered with awful thunder. Danielle had bolted awake at 5:13 a.m., emerging from the fog of sleep with the distinct thought that someone had put a strobe light in her room. She blinked into the flashes until her eyes adjusted.

Nah, just a ton of lightning, she thought. *I am soo tired of these stupid storms!* The thunder even woke up Loryn, who on top of being a very sound sleeper was worn out from a four-to-midnight shift waiting tables at Baumhower's Restaurant. The sky was still flashing at 5:20 a.m. when Loryn realized she was hungry. Danielle, within hollering distance down the hall, happened to be trolling Facebook, too.

5:20	Loryn Brown	can you still use a microwave during a storm . . . 'cause I reallyyy want some oatmeal
5:22	Danielle Downs	I think it'll be okay . . . just stand away from it in case of a power surge lol

Even though Loryn had a good weather app, she usually forgot to plug in her phone at night, and now the battery was so low that the app didn't work. She felt scared enough to call her mother and wake her up around 5:30 a.m. Her mother was always the first one she called, and they spoke at least once a day.

"Mama, pull up your weather app and see what the weather's like."

Ashley Mims woke up in Wetumpka, Alabama, looked at the radar on her phone, and saw a small polygon—the area of possible danger for this tornado warning—passing over Tuscaloosa.

"Baby, it's just a little triangle," she said. "It should be over in just a few minutes."

Danielle had always enjoyed the symphony of a thunderstorm. When she was younger, she would sit on the front porch and watch the light show dance across the sky while her sister, Michelle, ran inside and cried. Something about today was different, though. When she went to work at 8:00 a.m. as usual, she obsessively watched the weather.

She had also checked on others all day. She called her mother, who was working at a part-time job with the Army Corps of Engineers in Huntsville. Terri Downs was an air force wife—independent, capable, and not easily scared. Her voice was low and raspy, with a hint of a Cajun accent and a matter-of-factness that some people mistook for gruffness.

"Are you safe?" Danielle said.

"Yeah, we're in the Federal Building," her mother said. "They built it pretty good."

In truth, the building felt downright flimsy and Terri swore she could feel the walls shake every time a colleague walked down the hall. But Terri didn't want her daughter to worry. That was her job.

"I want you to be safe, too," Terri said. "Go to the library—you said you always felt safe there."

But the sky outside looked innocuous, and Danielle's boss did not seem worried. Clients were streaming into TES at the regular pace. So Danielle just kept an eye on the TV in the lobby, where James Spann was making noises about more storms coming.

▪ ▪ ▪

Early in her internship, Danielle had been browsing in the TES thrift store when she had found a poster of Rosie the Riveter that she couldn't pass up. It assured her: "We can do it!" She kept the framed eight-by-ten on her desk, with its good message to remember on the hard days. And there were many hard days.

Life had taught Danielle that no situation is ever as simple as others think, and she was cut out for this job better than most. Understanding other people's problems was her special talent. Some days she felt like a therapist, nodding into the phone as a single mother unloaded her burdens on the other end. With others who were more reserved, Danielle could tease out pertinent details by asking the right questions. Helping others made her happy, which everyone noticed.

Danielle had an innate talent for bridging the gaps of race and education to connect with her clients. And she knew what it felt like to struggle, especially with money and the limits of minimum wage. She had watched her parents stretch their military salaries to care for their aging parents, and she understood that even when you work hard, life throws curveballs that can set you back.

As noon approached, a coworker suggested going out for a farewell lunch to celebrate Danielle's last day. So they drove the twenty minutes to Southland Restaurant, a Cottondale meat-and-three not far from the Wingate hotel. On the drive, the sky was leaden and brooding, with sudden gusts that whipped the trees.

■ ■ ■

At the house, Loryn Brown was cramming for the Spanish final she was taking at 6:00 p.m. It would be her last exam at Shelton State, capping off her associate's degree in time to transfer to the University of Alabama in the fall. Her father, Shannon Brown, was an Alabama football hero, and with her looks, bubbly personality, and Crimson Tide pedigree, she had a potent package for a career in sports broadcasting. Her dream job was to work for ESPN. A little more than a week ago, she had launched her own personal sports blog, the Lo Down. The blog's icon was a hot-pink sequined football, which matched the color of her room.

The youngest of the three girls who shared the house, Loryn had just turned twenty-one a few weeks ago in March. For her birthday, she and a group of friends had taken the train to New Orleans to spend St. Patrick's Day in the French Quarter. They had paraded her down Bourbon Street in a rhinestone tiara and a pink pageant sash that announced BIRTHDAY GIRL.

The weathermen were talking about afternoon storms in a way

that made Loryn nervous, so she called her mom again. It was lunchtime, and the weather wasn't due to get bad for another couple of hours. Ashley Mims had begun to pack a bag and told Loryn she'd gather her younger sisters and brother and they'd all come to Tuscaloosa. But Loryn, watching TV, was afraid of all those storms forming across the state line.

"It's already getting bad in Mississippi," she said. "I don't want you driving."

"Baby, it's not that bad," Ashley said. "I'll get to Tuscaloosa before it gets bad."

"No, I don't want you on the road."

"Okay, we'll wait here. But I'll come later if you want me to."

"No, Mama!"

This went on for twenty minutes. Loryn won.

"Just call me if you hear anything else," Loryn said before they hung up.

"I'm gonna run to town," her mother replied. "I'll call you back."

Ashley stepped outside the house and felt sunshine on her face as she walked to the car. In Wetumpka, the weather was beautiful, but about a hundred miles northwest, in Tuscaloosa, the muggy air seemed ominous. The wind felt shifty, as if it couldn't decide which way to blow. Loryn hoped her Spanish exam would get canceled, because she did not want to leave the house in this weather.

On the bright side, Will Stevens would be coming over soon.

Danielle's good friend from high school, Will was tall and athletic, with a strong jaw and dark brown hair that hung just above his hazel eyes. A small-town boy raised on a farm next door to his grandparents, he was quiet at first meeting, but when he finally opened his mouth, he usually made people laugh. At twenty-two years old, a senior in college, he was not embarrassed to admit that he called his mama every day at 1:15 p.m., right after she got off work.

Will had been a three-sport athlete at Priceville High: quarterback, forward, and pitcher. Six-foot-two and 170 pounds, he didn't have enough meat on him to play college football, and he looked custom-built for basketball, but it was his pitching arm that won him a full-ride baseball scholarship to Stillman College in Tuscaloosa. At the historically black college, he found himself a minority for the first time in his life, a new but not unpleasant experience that only enlarged his ample circle of friends. Some of the guys there referred to him fondly as Mr. Quiet Optimism.

Will would graduate in ten days with a history degree and move back to Priceville to coach high school baseball. He would move back in, temporarily, with his parents, who managed around five dozen beef cattle on the family farm. On a recent visit home he had told his high school coach, only half joking, "I'm coming home to take your job." This was not a surprise to anyone, least of all the coach. When Will was a high school freshman, that same coach had asked his team to write on a sheet of paper where they saw themselves in ten years. Will wrote:

Probably teaching and coaching a sport. Or being a broadcaster on TV, or hopefully on ESPN.

Will was the same age as Danielle's sister, Michelle, who had been his homecoming date the year before she met Clay, her fiancé. In the formal photo Will wore black trousers, a Hawaiian shirt with black and tan palm fronds, and an oddly serious expression. He had been trying to hide the jawbreaker in his mouth.

Danielle had poor luck with boys herself, but she loved matchmaking and considered Will perfect for Loryn, given their farm upbringings and ESPN dreams. They would make a good-looking couple as well, with their dark hair, tanned skin, and hazel eyes. One rode a tractor; the other a horse. Will had helped deliver his first calf when he was two years old. Loryn loved barrel racing.

Will regularly came over to fix Danielle's car and always turned down their offers to pay him for the work. Instead, they fed him and let him do laundry. They would play Xbox games and eat pizza while the drier rumbled. Not long ago, Danielle had called him to help a guest at the Wingate, a young lady whose car would not go. After fixing her car, he pumped her gas, and the three of them went out to dinner. When the young woman asked how she could pay him back, he said, "Let me take you out." She said yes.

But that was before Loryn. There was something special about this girl. Even his family remarked that she was just the kind of girl who would have caught his eye.

"They just looked like they went together," Will's mother would tell her friends.

They had been out on a date but were taking things slow. As pretty as she was, Loryn had not had a serious boyfriend yet. She was waiting for the right one to come along rather than suffer dates with fools. Will had felt the sting of heartbreak and was in no rush. But Will had mentioned Loryn to his younger sister. And Loryn had told her mom about Will.

Will joined the girls often for movie night—he loved popcorn and Harry Potter—and he had been spending more time lately over at the house. After her last-day-at-work lunch, Danielle glanced at her phone and saw his text.

1:49	Will	so when we gonna make up movie night
2:32	Danielle	well I'm off tonight :-p
2:33	Will	well then tonight it is what time you'll be home
2:33	Danielle	should get there by 5 now my room is a mess so we can watch a movie downstairs LOL plus my place might be safer than ur place
2:34	Will	sounds good to me
2:44	Danielle	ok I'll text you when I'm heading there

On the TV in the lobby of TES, the voices of the weathermen rung with urgency. James Spann was showing live video from a SkyCam above Cullman. A textbook supercell thunderstorm was hovering on the horizon, with a bright rain-free base on the right and a dark curtain of rain on the left.

Danielle and a coworker stood in the small lobby and watched the scene unfold on a small TV. On the screen, a dark finger reached down from the cloud and began to claw the earth. The camera zoomed in. Fragments of debris were visible, whirling. It was 2:46 p.m.

"We've got a tornado down," James Spann said on the air. "This is a tornado emergency for the City of Cullman."

The charcoal mass writhed malevolently against the milky sky. To a storm spotter, the funnel looked like a textbook specimen from Kansas or Oklahoma. It was rare to see one so clearly defined in the South, where funnels often come in disguise, cloaked by a curtain of rain.

Danielle watched the monster grow on the TV screen, thickening, darkening, and churning mercilessly toward the heart of Cullman.

The church!

Sacred Heart church, where Michelle would be married next week, was a landmark of downtown Cullman, a city of fifteen thousand about an hour's drive north of Birmingham. Built in 1916, the Romanesque church was one of the prettiest Catholic sanctuaries in the state, with a roseate window framed by steeples topped with twin golden crosses. Its stained-glass windows, crafted in Germany, were so exquisite that they had been buried during World War I to protect them from the bombings, and later shipped to America. Inside, one of the largest pipe organs in northern Alabama echoed off the vaulted ceilings. Michelle had always dreamed of getting married there.

Danielle worried about her sister. A student at Mississippi State University, Michelle lived in Starkville, a college town eighty miles west of the University of Alabama. Storms forming in Mississippi would hit her at least an hour earlier. The state had more than half a dozen warnings in effect, and an EF5 was pounding Philadelphia, a tiny town about sixty miles south of where Michelle sat studying in her apartment. Danielle's phone was broken—the caller could only be heard on the speakerphone setting—so she texted her sister to check in.

2:52	Danielle	have u seen the storm in cullman?
2:52	Michelle	no.
2:53	Danielle	theres a huge tornado in downtown cullman we're watching it right now on abc 33 40 go online

Michelle and Danielle had a relationship straight out of a Hallmark card. Michelle, two years younger and two inches taller, looked up to Danielle, figuratively at least, and called her "my little-big sister." As military brats, the girls had seen each other through the hardships of deployment and relocation. Their father, an air force ground crew chief, had been sent to Iraq during the first Gulf War, and their hardworking air force mother held the family together when he was away. By high school the girls had lived in three states, and during the many moves they had learned to make friends easily but also let go and move on. The one constant was each other. When Michelle was a baby, her parents could not understand her first garbled words. Three-year-old Danielle would translate, and Michelle would nod as if to say, "Yep—that's what I said!" When they were older, they'd test this unique ability in the bathroom mirror while brushing their teeth. Michelle would mumble through a thick lather of toothpaste; Danielle always knew what she said.

Danielle had become like a second mother to Michelle, whom she had potty-trained, taught to ride a bike, and guarded fiercely. They were two sides of the same coin. Michelle was the sweet one, tall and willowy with sky-blue eyes, a guileless smile, and more book smarts than common sense. Danielle, shorter and built like a swimmer, had knowing eyes the color of almonds, a disarming smile, and the ability to smell bullshit a mile away. Danielle stood up to bullies and broke up fights, and got in the face of anyone who dared to tease her sister.

Michelle hid behind her, followed her, and admired her for the traits they did not share. Danielle was a coxswain on the rowing team. Michelle played clarinet in the marching band. Danielle picked the biggest school in Alabama. Michelle preferred smaller Mississippi State. They had briefly considered sharing an apartment halfway between the two but couldn't afford the commute.

The sisters texted almost daily, but the last time they had spent time together in person was during Christmas at their parents' house in Priceville, a small town on the outskirts of Huntsville. A rare Alabama snow had closed the roads, so Danielle couldn't go back to work. The sisters pulled on parkas and ran out to catch snowflakes in the front yard. Feeling like kids again, they built a real-size snowman—not the dirt-colored midgets made with spatulas, which is usually all that can be made from a Dixie snowfall. They posed for a photo on either side of their "rock-star snowman," made with pinecone eyes, a carrot nose, and a pine-needle mohawk.

■ ■ ■

Danielle watched the funnel grow on the screen. Suddenly it appeared to divide into three, with two small tendrils swirling diagonally around a large central column. The weatherman called it a multiple-vortex tornado. It looked like a dancing strand of DNA, with a strangely hypnotic, haunting beauty that made it hard to look away.

"This is the time to go to a safe place!" Spann said. "A small room, hall closet, bathroom . . . lowest floor, near the center, away from windows."

With live footage, there was no need to put the radar screen on TV, but all across the country weather buffs were admiring the textbook signature: a bright red dot at the center of a tie-dyed spiral. That dot was the debris ball, the vortex of the tornado, where the beam of the antenna was bouncing off shredded bits of trees and earth and buildings. The shape grew on the screen, thickening as it headed at fifty miles per hour straight toward downtown Cullman.

"This could be a half mile wide," Spann said. "This thing is probably going to stay on the ground for a long time."

On the screen, specks of debris were lofted into the air. From a distance, it appeared to rotate in slow motion. But inside that funnel, winds were ripping and shoving and tearing around at 175 miles per hour.

"That's pieces of buildings in downtown Cullman flying apart," Jason Simpson said as he watched the EF4 tornado penetrate the heart of a town filled with people he knew.

The funnel plowed straight through the business district, ripping the roof off the courthouse and lofting it thousands of feet into the sky. It knocked down the Busy Bee and flattened Christ Lutheran Church, just a few blocks from Sacred Heart, where the priest who would marry Michelle and Clay ran outside the church and gaped. It peeled the redbrick facade off A Little Bit of Everything, a curio shop, revealing the wall underneath where a painted ad for Fuller Bros. Ford Motor Cars had been covered up for so long that most locals never knew it existed. It bent the NOAA Weather Radio Transmitter Tower like a twist tie.

On the SkyCam, the antenna tower from Channel 52 was a faint line that quivered and vanished, snuffed out by the dark finger. Just as it grew into a wedge about a mile wide, the image froze on the screen.

"We just lost power," the weatherman said.

▪ ▪ ▪

About that time, Ashley Mims called her daughter from Walgreens to tell her about the bronze cowboy boots she had bought her at the mall.

"Mama, did you see what happened in Cullman?" Loryn interrupted. "I'm getting scared."

"Yeah, baby, I saw it," Ashley said. "Me and the little kids are coming there."

"No, Mama, you can't!" Loryn said. She was crying now. "You can't get on the road now. It's too late!"

"Well, you get in that basement," Ashley said, her voice calm and reassuring. "You get those pillows and blankets, and you start studying down there."

The house didn't have a basement, but Loryn knew what her mother meant. She started gathering books and blankets to move to the windowless hallway beneath the stairs. The safest place in the house. It was nearing 3:00 p.m. and her mind was not on her Spanish exam.

"Have they canceled classes yet?" Ashley said.

"Not yet."

At 2:54 p.m., above a rural stretch of Newton County, Mississippi, a new supercell was born.

CHAPTER 9

BIRTH OF A WEATHERMAN

1962—GREENVILLE, ALABAMA

Little James Spann stared out the window of his classroom, watching the clouds go by. He was six years old, and the white billowing shapes parading across the skies of Greenville, Alabama, were considerably more interesting than whatever was being taught in first grade.

At the head of the class was his first-grade teacher, the fearsome Mrs. Porterfield, who looked to be least a hundred years old and had the disposition of a water moccasin. Edna Porterfield was feared and reviled by misbehaving schoolboys. She was known to yank them out of the classroom and into the hall, where she would wear the cotton out of their britches with a wooden paddle. Mrs. Porterfield was strong for an old lady, and she could make hallways ring with the yelps that followed each echoing *whap!*

If she caught you with a piece of chewing gum, you had to trade it for a stale one from the gum jar, and the notion of tasting someone else's spittle on a calcified wad instilled in James a fierce and lifelong aversion to gum. Mrs. Porterfield addressed students by their last name, and McClendon, who would grow up to become Mayor McClendon, spent all of first grade believing that his best friend's name was Spann. Which in Greenville was pronounced with two syllables: Spa-yunn.

"Spann!" Mrs. Porterfield yelled in the middle of a lecture.

Six-year-old James pulled his wide eyes away from the window, certain his life was about to end. "Spann! Get out here *now*!"

He trudged across the snickering classroom and into the hallway with lead feet and mounting dread. He had never felt the sting of a paddle.

It's all over, he thought. *I'm dead.*

In Mrs. Porterfield's hand was not a paddle but a book.

A library book. About clouds.

Mrs. Porterfield, who was indeed old but not blind, had noticed James staring out the window day after day and figured out his interest. From that book in her hands, James learned the shape and name of every cloud in the sky. From Mrs. Porterfield, he also learned that people are often not what you think. Both lessons would guide him like a lighthouse through the rocky shoals of life.

Greenville, Alabama, in the 1960s was a hard place and time to grow up without a father. The small lumber mill town in south Alabama was populated by boys who came to school flush with stories of hunting and fishing with their daddies. Young James Spann had no such stories to share, and he listened with silent longing. More than a rod or a hunting rifle, he yearned for a baseball, a wooden bat, and a well-worn glove. And as much as he wanted those simple things, which his mother could not afford, he longed for one thing more: a father to play catch with.

His father had walked out when James was six. For a while, he would come back from time to time to visit his only son. On one occasion, his mother dressed him up in his nicest clothes and sat him in a chair by the door. Little James sat in that chair for hours, waiting for a father who never came.

Mrs. Spann worked hard, loved her son, and supported him in her job as the high school secretary—the best job she could get in Greenville without a college degree. She would never remarry and she remained a single working mother in an era when that was not common.

In fifth grade, James and his mother cut loose from Greenville, hoping to find better luck and employment in the bigger city of Tuscaloosa. Only the fifth-largest city in Alabama, Tuscaloosa still felt vast and bewildering to a twelve-year-old small-town boy. Spann and his mother would live in an apartment the size of a bathroom until Mrs. Spann was able to finish her degree and get a job teaching high school English. But in this new town they met people who encouraged and helped them in ways he would never forget. With the blind fortune he would later relate to in the movie character Forrest Gump, James stumbled under the wing of several father figures who taught him many useful things and treated him like a son.

A physician who lived in a fancy neighborhood taught James how to operate an amateur radio and gave him his first equipment. James would later study electrical engineering in college. He was fascinated by structures and buildings, and he took things apart and put them back together to understand how they worked. It made him giddy to think that a wire antenna could enable you to talk to someone on the other side of the world. He took up ham radio with a passion eclipsed only later by his love of weather.

When he was fourteen, James paid a dime to Radio Shack for a little book that taught him how to go about getting an FCC radio license. He had to learn Morse code and take a written exam that was only offered twice a year in Birmingham. He climbed on a Greyhound bus for the hour-long ride to the biggest city in Alabama, walked a few blocks to the courthouse, and took the test in front of an FCC commissioner who came from Atlanta to proctor.

That license became his ticket into a world of new friends and confidence. Before he could drive, James helped cover severe weather as the network controller for the Office of Civil Defense, where he served as an operator for a nationwide network of storm spotters who radioed in ground truth. Once he was old enough to drive, he joined them in the field, chasing storms. He spent long, delicious hours driving the back roads of the Alabama Black Belt, climbing towers to hang repeater antennas, talking to the locals who congregated at gas stations, always turning his tires down the roads less traveled. Along the way he developed a mental map of Alabama geography that would make him one of the best broadcast meteorologists of his time.

At sixteen, James was offered his first paying job, at a local commercial radio station. It was 1972, when stations still used giant reel tapes, which James fed into an automated machine that played them on the air. This was an FM station, but back then AM was the big thing, and James dreamed of one day speaking into a mic that would project his voice over the AM waves. Six months into his reel-loading job, he got that chance. His boss invited him to do an AM shift.

It was a cold November Sunday night, and in his mind, every single person in the range of that 250-watt station was listening when he played his first song, "Jessica," by the Allman Brothers Band. He picked a longer song because he needed all the time he could get to curb the adrenaline coursing through his veins like a current. When the song ended, his heart was still pounding as he leaned into an open mic and spoke his first words on the air:

"The Big 1230, WTBC-AM!"

His skin broke out in goose bumps. The moment was—and remains to this day—the most thrilling of his career.

The summer before his senior year, James got together with some fellow radioheads and started a school radio station at Tuscaloosa High. Located in the attic of the school, it had two turntables and a microphone, and the signal reached no farther than the parking lot. James was beanpole-thin with a mop of brown hair, which was long enough to cover both ears and parted on the left. He wore collared shirts with stripes and sleeves that reached to his elbows, and headphones bigger than earmuffs. He still spoke with a Forrest Gump accent that would gradually vanish, along with his hair.

■ ■ ■

Two months before James's eighteenth birthday, the ingredients for a massive tornado outbreak came together in just the right recipe, and the atmosphere above thirteen central states convulsed with violent thunderstorms. Warm, moist air—the fuel of a storm—drifted north from the Gulf of Mexico. A mass of air chilled and wrung dry by the Rockies slouched east. The cold front wedged itself under the warm air, further encouraging that less-dense air to rise. An area of low pressure hovered over southern Wisconsin, and air from surrounding areas rushed to fill it, as milk converges toward the spot in a glass being emptied by a straw. High above the earth, where airplanes fly, the river of air known as the upper-level jet stream shot northeast. A lower jet, closer to land, flowed north. Together, they spun the massive blob of rising air like a giant, invisible top. The rotation set into motion whorls within swirls, like curls of smoke.

On April 3, 1974, the sky unleashed 148 tornadoes upon a geographic alley that stretched from Alabama to Ontario. Many of them came in "families," multiple tornadoes spawned by the same supercell thunderstorm. A staggering proportion of these funnels were large and violent: Seven F5 tornadoes and twenty-four F4s were confirmed in a twenty-four-hour period. At the crescendo of the outbreak, sixteen tornadoes raked the earth at once. When the winds died down, 319 people were dead. Alabama saw three F5 tornadoes that day and lost seventy-seven lives, more than any other state. It was the largest tornado outbreak ever recorded, an event that would be unparalleled for decades.

Tuscaloosa was not hit that night, but several other towns in Alabama were. In southern Limestone County, the small rural town of Tanner was destroyed by a one-two punch of tornadoes that hit thirty minutes apart. Each scoured the state for at least twenty miles. The first one sucked a water pump out of a well house and ripped power-line truss towers from their anchors and threw them; one was never found. The sun had already set and rescuers were rushing to help bleeding victims when the second killer emerged from the cloak of night. The two tornadoes killed more than fifty people, most of them in Tanner, and injured at least four hundred. One victim who had been critically injured by the first tornado was rushed to safety in a nearby church, but when the second tornado struck the church, he died in its collapse. Ninety-seven miles south, the town of Guin was left in ruins by the longest-lived tornado of the day, an F5 that is considered one of the most violent ever recorded. It stayed on the ground for eighty miles.

As the storm raged into the night, James broadcast tornado warnings from the radio station. When he got off work at midnight, he rushed to the Civil Defense office and asked how he could help. He was dispatched with a police escort to Jasper, a small town about an hour north that had been obliterated by an F4. The Red Cross needed someone there with a radio, because the hospital was overwhelmed and had lost all lines of communication with other towns. Spann set up his ham radio in the emergency room of People's Hospital in Jasper.

Until that night, James, like many storm chasers, had wished for storms the way most boys wish for their team to win the World Series. Lightning and thunder were exciting, and the prospect of tornadoes—and the chase they inspired—was downright exhilarating to a teenage boy. He was happiest when the sky churned.

One night in the ER changed all that. What he saw in that hospital would give him night terrors for months. He could not erase the indelible sounds, smells, and images from his memory. He had seen death before, but not like this. Broken bodies. Torn flesh. Missing parts. Faces that mothers could not recognize. People killed and disfigured by airborne pieces of their homes. Only then did he understand what horrors the wind could inflict upon the human body. When it blew hard enough, household objects became missiles. Windows shattered and turned into shrapnel. If the wind could drive a pencil three inches into the trunk of a tree, if it could hurl a dump truck farther than a football field, if it could scour an entire town from the earth—what could it do to flesh and bone?

The smell the tornado left in its wake combined pine, sulfur, and natural gas with the sickly sweet smell of death. It was a nauseating, desperate smell that clung to his nostrils and turned his stomach in every disaster zone he would ever visit. After one tornado, a man looked at him with ancient eyes and described the smell in words he would never forget: *It comes from the pit of hell.*

But it was the people's eyes that would haunt him most. They were filled with terror, anguish, pain. In his nightmares they followed him pleadingly, looking out from bodies that were bleeding, impaled, and grossly disfigured. He wanted so badly to help these people, but he felt powerless to do so. Those eyes stabbed and wounded him in a place deep inside that would never fully heal. Spann would never speak in detail to anyone of what he saw.

"I saw things that no child should ever see," he would later say. "That was the night I lost my innocence."

■ ■ ■

3:00 P.M., APRIL 27, 2011—BIRMINGHAM, ALABAMA

James Spann had not had time to roll up his sleeves today. His jacket never made it on. The atmosphere was about to explode. The Cullman EF4 was still the only tornado on the ground in Alabama. But as it moved northwest toward Huntsville, other supercells were brewing in its wake.

The news desk had received encouraging reports from Cullman. The downtown had indeed taken a direct hit, but its buildings had been mostly vacant. The people who worked there had heard the warning sixteen minutes before the storm hit—enough time to flee to safety. The hospital had been spared by a narrow margin, and so far was reporting no fatalities.

Okay, maybe we're fine, Spann thought. *Maybe we're gonna get through this.*

In the Birmingham office of the National Weather Service, Meteorologist-in-Charge Jim Stefkovich leaned into his monitor, fighting the queasiness welling up in his stomach. He was not looking at the Cullman tornado. His eyes were trained on Mississippi, watching the next round beginning to form.

It's about to happen, he thought. *It's about to become the nightmare we said it would be.*

Spann slid on his reading glasses and squinted at his laptop, where data streamed in from many different sources. Eight chat rooms were scrolling with warnings from eight NWS offices around the state. Twitter was exploding with ground truth. Spann's Facebook page was abuzz with live photos posted by viewers. The storm-spotter chat room was churning with observations, questions, and speculation.

Spann scanned and processed the data, quickly translating what he saw into something a third grader could understand and act upon. He thought of something a wise friend once told him:

The first storm of the event will talk to you. It will tell you a story. It's up to you to read the story.

The friend, Chuck Doswell, was one of the most respected research meteorologists in the study of severe weather, though he would scoff when people called him "the nation's foremost tornado expert." At the National Severe Storms Laboratory in Norman, Oklahoma, Doswell had a reputation not only for his pioneering scientific study of storms but also for his blustery charisma. A six-foot-two native of the Chicago suburbs, he wore a battered straw cowboy hat, often paired with a Hawaiian shirt, and a Fu Manchu mustache that underscored a withering glare, which he aimed at anyone who professed "facts" about tornadoes that science had not proven.

Spann read everything he wrote but dreaded the prospect of giving a presentation with him in the audience. No one was immune from Doswell's concern for accuracy in presenting the science.

The two meteorologists had become good friends despite their many differences. A war veteran who spent eleven months in Vietnam, Doswell was a staunch and vocal atheist who described religion as a "narcissistic comfort in a myth . . . virtually certain to be a false comfort." Spann was a devout Christian and a children's minister who spent his weekends teaching Sunday school. Doswell was liberal, Spann conservative. They approached meteorology like two mountaineers climbing the same summit on different routes.

A forecaster, Spann focused on predicting future conditions using models based on past weather patterns. Doswell, a researcher, focused on studying, recording, and measuring severe weather, to understand the mechanics of storms (though early in his career he had been a part-time forecaster). Ultimately complementary and equally vital to the progress of the science, one looked to the future, while the other analyzed the past.

Doswell joined his fellow research tribesmen in a landmark study—VORTEX1 (the Verification of the Origins of Rotation in Tornadoes Experiment)—that aimed to record and measure the entire evolution of a tornado, up close and in great detail.

Live tornadoes are infrequent, irregular, fleeting, and erratic—the most resistant subjects. You can't study them in a lab. You can't control the environment. You could engineer an outdoor lab with the finest instrumentation, but even if you built it, they might not come.

To reckon with all these variables, VORTEX1 created a mobile lab that could follow supercells as they formed. A fleet of planes flew into the supercell and recorded measurements. A Doppler on Wheels (literally a big radar mounted on the back of a truck) provided three-dimensional maps of the winds swirling inside the tornado.

During the 1994 and 1995 storm seasons, VORTEX1 succeeded in documenting the entire life cycle of a tornado. (It also inspired the movie *Twister*.) But one of the study's key questions—*What is the difference between supercells that produce tornadoes and supercells that do not?*—still could not be answered.

Thus, the scientific sequel: VORTEX2. Actually, it was a mega-sequel, at least from a production standpoint. At a cost of more than $10 million, this project was as logistically mind-bending as the invasion of a small country. Pulling it off required orchestrating one hundred-plus researchers from labs and universities, more than forty vehicles, mobile weather balloon launchers, aerial drones, and deployable pods that would measure the inner workings of a tornado. To maximize the number of potential intercepts, the study area spanned 750,000 square miles—a sizable chunk of the Great Plains that stretched from the Dakotas to southwest Texas, from Wyoming to Iowa.

VORTEX2 deployed its scientific battalion in the quieter-than-average tornado seasons of 2009 and 2010 and intercepted around thirty supercells and twenty weak or short-lived tornadoes. In June 2009, Wyoming gave the scientists a long-lived tornado that remains the best-sampled tornadic supercell to date. But, like a fishing trip that yielded a cooler of keepers but no whopper, VORTEX2 closely studied a season that failed to cooperate by delivering the necessary action. The watched pot refused to boil. Nonetheless, VORTEX2 yielded important insights about triggering mechanisms for tornadogenesis, the inner structure of a tornado, and wind damage. Scientists are still analyzing the data, but their findings should improve tornado warning lead time.

"The average warning time nationally is thirteen minutes," said Joshua Wurman, president of the Center for Severe Weather Research in Boulder, Colorado, and one of the principals of VORTEX2. "If we can increase that lead time from thirteen minutes to half an hour, then the average person at home could do something different. Maybe they can seek a community shelter instead of just going into their bathtub. Maybe they can get their family to better safety if we can give them a longer warning and a more precise warning."

CHAPTER 10

RED-LETTER DAY

3:07 P.M., APRIL 27, 2011—TUSCALOOSA, ALABAMA

Danielle stood in the TES lobby, watching James Spann and wondering what to do. Everyone in the office was starting to murmur anxiously about the storm. But through the glass door, the sky did not look menacing. Just gray and cloudy. The temperature was a balmy eighty-two degrees, the dew point sixty-nine and rising. A gusty wind blew in from the south, tugging on flags up and down the street. Beyond the TES parking lot, the traffic roared by at its regular pace on the four lanes of lower Fifteenth Street.

Danielle recalled the rash of tornadoes that had come through less than two weeks ago. Her power had gone out that night, and her alarm clock had failed. What were the chances of getting hit again? She planned to weather the storm at home with friends, playing board games and watching movies until it passed. She invited her grad-student colleague to join them. He could hang with Will, talk baseball.

The Cullman tornado had been on the ground for more than half an hour now, and it was headed toward Huntsville, the big city northeast of her parents' house in Priceville.

James Spann was waving at a new scary-looking splotch on the radar aimed north of Tuscaloosa. An angry spiral with an evil red eye, it was headed northeast at a steady clip, and at least three small towns lay directly in its path—Hamilton, Hackleburg, and Phil Campbell. It was scary enough by itself, but west of the storm, in Mississippi, the brigade of storms stacked up behind it was chilling to behold.

"This is going to be one of those red-letter days," Spann said, looking over the tops of his spectacles. "We're just gonna sit back, take a big deep breath, and we're gonna get through this thing together."

Now there was a new tornado warning for a cell coming out of Mississippi and entering Pickens County, just west of Tuscaloosa.

"This thing is wrapped up like a top," Spann said, "and that's crossing the state line."

The producers cut to live video streaming from the dashboard of two tornado chasers trolling the lonely back roads of Alabama, trying to intercept the tornado. Their camera showed nothing but window wipers and black asphalt scrolling between shadowy pines and a sliver of white sky.

Danielle was annoyed. She could not see the whereabouts of the storm headed her way, and it was making her grumpy. Why wouldn't they zoom out? Just then, her phone pinged with a text from her sister.

3:18 Michelle storm headed your way. Be careful!

Within four minutes, the atmosphere was boiling with no fewer than ten supercells raging northwest across Alabama, Mississippi, and Tennessee, bearing litters of tornadoes. The thirty-eighth tornado of the day was on the ground in Alabama, and dozens more were forming behind it.

Danielle's boss, Karen Thompson, made an announcement to the staff.

"You know what? Let's just go home," she said. "Everybody go home."

No point in staying. Schools were letting out and the city was shutting down. Thompson, who had lived in Tuscaloosa all her life and was accustomed to storms, was not all that worried. It was just a part of living here, and according to her memory, tornadoes had more or less followed Highway 69, a hair west of Tuscaloosa. She heard the weathermen saying it was going to be bad. But they always said that.

Danielle packed up her last few things. Her desk was clean. She said her last round of good-byes and texted Will.

3:34 Danielle I'm leaving now

3:35 Will Let me know when you get there

Normally at this hour on a Wednesday she would be driving to work at the Wingate. But not today, since her boss had cut her hours. As she walked across the parking lot to her car, the sirens began to wail and a stiff wind tossed her hair. Steel-wool clouds curled across the sky, hanging so low they looked like they might snag on the treetops. The muggy air lay upon her like a soggy towel. Under the curdling clouds the world took on a heavy cast, and the streets were still wet from the morning storms, giving them a slick, metallic sheen. It looked like it might rain again.

Her grad-student friend said it sounded like a fun way to weather a storm, but he was tired and decided to just go home. She wasn't sure whether she would see him again between graduation, the wedding, and her move to Florida. Over the past four months of working closely together, they had become friends. Danielle delivered a big hug, just in case this was good-bye.

The nine-minute drive from TES to 31 Beverly Heights began east on Fifteenth Street, a corridor of college haunts that have fed, entertained, and distracted generations of college students. Inside Fifteenth Street Diner, a meat-and-three tucked in a strip mall, waitresses in Crimson Tide T-shirts crisscrossed the black-and-white checkered floor, delivering plastic plates of fried catfish, okra, and hush puppies to diners squeezed into the red vinyl booths. Central High had let out early, and the parking lot was empty. Danielle followed the string of taillights past Bama Bowl to the intersection of Fifteenth Street and McFarland Boulevard, where the scent of fried donuts at Krispy Kreme sometimes mingled with the meaty smoke curling from the pits of Full Moon Bar-B-Que.

As Danielle drove home, Loryn was already in the hallway, burrowed in a nest of blankets and pillows. She had not bothered to put on makeup or straighten her hair—no way was she leaving the house in this weather. If she inched toward the living room, she could peek around the wall at the meanness outside the bay window. She had dragged the large flat-screen TV from its stand in the living room, stretching the cord to a place where she could watch James Spann from the safety of the hallway.

The blotch on the radar behind Spann was growing bigger and bigger. It looked to be pretty far north of her, but still it scared her into hiding. She sought comfort from friends on Facebook.

3:42	Loryn	i doonnntt like this tornado . . . i was fine until i saw that tornado hit Cullman. sooo now im in the hallway and i have so many pillows around me a tornado will not even know i am hiding.

Danielle walked in and laughed at Loryn's hallway blanket-fort but decided to join her. This weather was getting serious.

Across town, Will shoved his laptop in a blue-and-black backpack that he carried everywhere. It was warm out, and he was wearing a black Priceville High Baseball T-shirt with black-and-white athletic shorts that gaped around his skinny knees. He climbed behind the wheel of his sand-colored Ford F-150 pickup, setting on the console the Alabama wallet his uncle gave him on Christmas.

It wasn't an easy thing for a southern boy to admit, but tornadoes scared him, too. He was easily spooked, by strangers at the front door of his parents' house or unfamiliar noises in the night. Anytime he was home alone in Priceville, his family would come home to find the blinds closed and every light in the house blazing. He had joked during the April 15 outbreak that "this is my kind of weather," but today he had been keeping a nervous eye on the news. He called his mother to check in.

"They say it's gonna get bad down here," he told his mom, Jean Stevens. "Danielle wants me to come over to her house to just hang and watch movies."

First he needed to turn in a history paper—his very last college assignment—and meet with his professor. But it was getting late. His phone buzzed with Danielle's text, letting him know, as promised, that she had gotten home.

3:43	Danielle	here
3:44	Will	OK I'll be over as soon as I meet my teach

Danielle did not approve of this plan, and she was not afraid to let him know it. James Spann kept telling people to go to a safe place, and the radar screen behind him was painted with so many angry spirals it was hard to count them all. Seven? Ten? Two big ones were leaving Mississippi and entering Alabama, headed northeast at fifty miles per hour. One of them was aimed at Tuscaloosa.

3:47	Danielle	umm u know we're under a tornado warning now I think u can meet ur teach later
3:48	Will	yeah it's going north of us and I'm trying to get a job LOL
3:48	Danielle	OKK
3:49	Will	haha yeah
3:54	Will	coming now
3:57	Danielle	OK!!

4:00	Will	Turn it to CNN
4:00	Danielle	There's nothing on

On ABC 33/40, James Spann was zooming in on an evil-looking spiral far north of them. The significant tornado index read 17.5. Until today, he had thought it was a scale from 1 to 10.

"That's a debris ball," he said. "That's the radar beam bouncing off the stuff in the tornado. Cars could be in there. Boards, bricks, glass, nails, shrapnel, pieces of homes."

Danielle and Loryn hunkered down in the hall, listening. Danielle's phone buzzed again with another text, this time from her father. Ed Downs had been nervously eyeing two storms tracking directly toward his daughters. He fired off a quick text to them.

4:07	Dad	Hey, there is cells heading toward both of you. Be careful. Love you.

One hundred miles north of Beverly Heights, a road was being shucked from the earth. A small bulldozer cartwheeled through the whipping dirt, and a dump truck careened fifty yards through the air, crumpled like a soda can. A two-ton utility trailer launched into a mile-long arc and cratered the earth with its impact. A Corvette flew 641 feet. At the Wrangler plant, a flock of blue jeans launched into flight, flapping like denim birds. A memory quilt that told the story of a life was carried over two counties.

Somewhere, a mother watched the blackness swallow the town where her children waited.

CHAPTER 11

UNBROKEN

3:44 P.M., APRIL 27, 2011—SMITHVILLE, MISSISSIPPI

The pastor of Smithville Baptist Church was sitting on the red brick steps that had led to 520 Sunday sermons, watching the funnel part the horizon. It was off in the distance, maybe a mile or two—he could see where it was, but not where it was going—and two heartbeats later he could feel it breathing down upon him. He turned to his youth minister and said, "It's here," and the two of them began running. They sprinted across the parking lot to the two-story Sunday school wing, the oldest and strongest part of the church, and ducked into a low-ceilinged room where eleven others—children, parents, a small dog—were huddled together, terrified.

For fifteen long seconds, the world hung suspended. The winds punched through the windows and pelted the people with pieces of trees and homes and dreams. It peeled tiles off the ceiling and tugged at them like a great, invisible hand trying to turn the church inside out. They held fast to the walls, to a bookshelf, to anything still there. With a thunderous clap, two large sheets of metal from the fellowship hall slammed down over the two nearest windows, shielding Pastor Wes and his people from the blender of debris. One room over, the storm speared a two-by-four through the wall. So loud was the roar that they did not hear the church fall.

Two blocks away, Johnny Parker cowered in his hallway with his sister and father. He had always dreamed of seeing a tornado but never imagined he would find himself caught in the teeth of an EF5. His ears popped, muffling the roar that sounded like a 747 jet screaming inches from their heads. Even through the deafening noise, Johnny's father heard a voice. It was a man's voice, deep and loud.

MOVE!

Randy reacted reflexively, not pausing to question.

"Get in the bathroom!"

Chloe clawed her way through the dark on her hands and knees, dizzy and disoriented. It felt like the room was spinning. She felt Johnny in the tub and clambered on top of him, holding his head as he screamed. In the sliver of light through the bathroom door, she saw the south end of the house implode, sending a doorframe and a crystalline shower of glass hurtling down the hall where they had just been.

But where was her father? She could not see him, and she knew, in the deepest part of her gut, that if he was not in the bathroom, he was dead. In those eternal seconds of thrashing, pounding horror, she felt certain that her mother was dead, that she and her brother were orphans. The thought made her preternaturally calm, because she knew she would have to be the one to find their parents' bodies, to take care of Johnny. They could move in with their grandparents, if they both survived.

The windowless bathroom became a Tilt-A-Whirl, and she felt the floor dropping out from under her. But the floor was not dropping. Chloe was levitating, sucked from the grips of gravity and into the terrible mouth of the storm.

The supercell towered three miles above the earth as its funnel-child tore mercilessly through the heart of Smithville in a tantrum of annihilation. It plucked a red Ford Explorer up like a Matchbox car and hurled it into the town water tower half a mile away. The SUV flew another quarter mile and cratered a field. The storm lifted the cab of a tractor-trailer, flung it more than a quarter mile into a field, where it landed and crumpled like foil. It blew the town hall apart, wrapped cars around trees, and smashed apart buildings, flinging cinder blocks like Legos. It plucked trees from the ground and scoured the bark off the few that stood. The tornado sucked homes right off their foundations, leaving nothing behind but lonely slabs with the anchor bolts that once held down the walls. It sucked people into a hateful sky and pelted them to death with shards of the places they trusted to protect them.

■ ■ ■

Patti Parker ran up, breathless, to find the front of her house shorn off, the scraps of her walls heaped on the porch. She began screaming for her husband.

"Randy!"

The past and the future dangled in the moment, her universe suspended in the purgatory of uncertainty. Somewhere under the house lay three pieces of her heart. They were alive. Or they were dead.

A movement on the side of the house caught her eye, and within seconds the world had shifted again. It was Johnny, walking around from the back. She could hear Randy's voice, and it sounded strong. Then Chloe emerged through a gap in the wall and sobbed when she saw her mother. They all ran to one another and embraced, sinking gratefully to the ground in a knot of elbows and tears.

Blocks away at Smithville Baptist, Pastor Wes and his people picked their way out of the fallen church. No one in the church was killed, but their sanctuary was buried under a mountain of bricks and glass. And yet: A single window somehow survived with only one small crack. It was the stained-glass window of Jesus, with outstretched arms, which Johnny's grandparents had donated.

CHAPTER 12

CHASERS

4:00 P.M., APRIL 27, 2011—NEAR CORDOVA, ALABAMA

The storm chaser squinted at the rectangle of sky framed by his windshield, glanced at the radar, and stepped on the gas. Duct taped to the dashboard of his Chevy Avalanche, a video camera was trained on the road and plugged into a laptop strapped to the center console with a threadbare bungee cord. It wasn't fancy, but the rig was ready to stream live footage to ABC 33/40. On the laptop, the radar showed a spray of moving targets—storm cells that were stuttering out of Mississippi and gathering intensity as they stalked northeast. The biggest one was headed toward Hackleburg, and he was trying to catch it.

A retired meteorologist, Brian Peters was not out for a glory chase. Though he could not deny the exhilaration of chasing, his mission was to intercept a tornado in time to save the people in its path. He worked closely with James Spann, who affectionately introduced him to storm-spotter classes as "the man who looks like Santa Claus." Other colleagues called him Colonel Sanders. With a bemused smile and a quick laugh, he talked about the weather with the unbridled glee that other men reserve for football. He had spent years working for the National Weather Service as a Warning Coordination Meteorologist, in charge of tornado warnings. After each storm, he would walk the damage path, looking for the telltale signs of wind speed—an empty foundation, debarked trees—that were used to determine the

EF rating. Yet in his forty-five years as a meteorologist, he had not seen a single tornado.

In the passenger seat—he never chased alone—his partner, the meteorologist Dr. Tim Coleman, was watching the radar and navigating. Coleman had been just sixteen years old when he started working for Peters as an unpaid volunteer for the National Weather Service. Like Peters, he discovered a passion for the weather at the age of three or four. In high school he volunteered after school and on weekends at the NWS, where he read the warnings on the NOAA weather radio—a job that was later replaced by a computer-generated monotone. As soon as he could drive, he began chasing storms. After years of schooling, jobs at the NWS and at TV stations as a broadcast weatherman, Coleman completed a PhD and worked in research meteorology at the University of Alabama, Huntsville. He studied everything from tornadoes to atmospheric waves, and he loved, by his own admission, to "geek out about the weather."

The two men had started a meteorological consulting business together and became steady chase partners during outbreaks. One would drive; the other would navigate. They trusted each other implicitly.

"Everything is north of us," Peters said, stealing a glance at the radar.

"But where is that giant hook going?" said Coleman, pointing at a cell coming out of northeast Mississippi.

"Let's do a loop and see what happens."

They played the radar scans, taken every few minutes, in a continuous loop, studying the cells' evolution. That was all the confirmation they needed: the cell ahead of them was rotating.

"So there's probably a tornado ahead of us."

"I wouldn't be surprised."

Coleman tracked the storm across the radar screen and searched the maps for a road that would place them in a safe position to capture it on film. They needed to be within camera range—a few miles away—but somewhere well in the safety zone: south of the tornado's march northeast.

In Alabama, this was not easy. The country roads spaghettied all over the hills, and the trees blocked their view of the sky. It was much different from chasing tornadoes in Kansas and Oklahoma, where the roads are straight and gridded, and the cornfields so flat and bare you could stand on a tuna can and see all the way to forever. For this reason, most glory chasers favored the heartland and avoided Dixie Alley.

Today every road seemed like a tunnel of trees that curved in the wrong direction. The sliver of sky between the pines was white, in stark contrast to the wet asphalt, which mirrored occasional headlights. The big one was on the ground and tantalizingly close, but there wasn't a road that would put them in a place where they could safely stay out of its way. These roads provided no sure escape route, and Coleman didn't feel safe. They let the big fish go.

Just then, two new supercells caught their eyes, running northeast on parallel tracks, one trailing the other slightly. The northern one, which led the pair, was headed their way, on track to hit Cordova. Coleman bent over his laptop, tracing the tornado's vector on the screen with his finger, stopping at their target location. He compared this to their dot on the GPS. The tornado was still a county away. It looked like they had time to get into position to catch it roaring by.

But just barely.

Cutting a diagonal path across the state, the tornado would pass just south of their current position. This was the most perilous place for a chaser to be. If this tornado came wrapped in rain, they would not see the funnel. It would look like a wall of water, veiling the monster lurking behind it. And if it wandered off course, if it veered slightly north, they would be caught directly in its path.

In an act of faith and mental triangulation, Coleman calculated the window of time they had to get themselves south of the storm. It was closing rapidly. Like a car racing to cross the railroad tracks ahead of a speeding train, they would have to dash south, crossing its path, a few minutes before it arrived in Jasper. On the radar, that path took them straight across the giant red eyebrow that preceded the debris ball.

"We are thirty-eight miles from Jasper," Coleman said. "It says we'll get to Jasper at four forty-six. What time is the tornado gonna get there?"

"Four fifty-five," Peters said.

Nine minutes. That was their window.

The time was 4:08.

The Chevy Avalanche roared down I-22, its speedometer needle leaning precipitously . . . eighty . . . ninety . . . ninety-five miles per hour. Through the sheeting rain, only a few blurry taillights were visible. That was good—they could not risk an accident. It was fortunate, too, that Brian had put new tires on his car. Every advantage would matter today. With every minute that changed on the digital clock, their blood surged with another wave of adrenaline. It was dizzying to think that they were on their way to seeing their first tornado.

And then they lost radar.

Data lines, ripped by the morning storms, had limited their radar feeds to patchy or nonexistent. They had different phone carriers, which helped a little, but way out in the sticks coverage was not known to be good even in fair weather. They needed eyes on a live radar, or else they would have to abort. They knew better than to risk driving blind through the rain to meet an oncoming storm.

"I don't want to die, you know," Coleman said.

"I don't want to die either."

Through the rain they saw blue lights flashing ahead. Peters braked instinctively, but the state trooper was parked beneath a highway overpass, taking shelter. They stopped here, too, out of the clamor of rain, so Coleman could hear his wife on the phone.

"Listen, we're under the bridge near Jasper," he said. "We have no Internet. We have nothing."

Jennifer Coleman had been a weather wife long enough to confidently read the radar. At home in Birmingham, glued to the TV set and attached to her computer, she became the chasers' lifeline. She relayed what she saw and heard to her husband, who repeated it to make sure he had it all right.

"It's southwest of Oakman? That's live? You're watching Spann?"

Coleman turned to Peters.

"Okay. It's moving east-northeast."

In the shelter of the overpass they had no time for discussion. Every second they spent deciding put them a second closer to danger. Peters's gut made the call.

"We can do it."

They sped off into the rain.

■ ■ ■

Storm chasers have been chasing storms for centuries. Unaided by technology, the act began as simple observation of a phenomenon that inspired great speculation and a considerable amount of pre-urban myth.

Benjamin Franklin was one of the first to document a chase on American soil in April 1755, twenty-one years before the birth of our country and 115 years before the creation of the US Weather Bureau. Franklin, then forty-nine years old, was on a gentleman's ride in Maryland when he spotted "a whirlwind." It appeared in the form of a sugarloaf (a cone-shaped block of refined sugar) "spinning on its point, moving up the hill towards us, and enlarging as it came forward," he wrote. As his companions stood gaping, Franklin urged his horse alongside it, watching the dust swirl up into a funnel the size of a barrel. Testing the commonly held belief that shooting a bullet through a waterspout would cause it to dissipate, Franklin tried cracking his whip at it repeatedly, with no effect. He chased it into the woods, where it stirred up leaves and bent tall trees with "a circular motion [that] was amazingly rapid." After it dissipated over a tobacco field, Franklin turned to the colonel he was riding with and asked whether such whirlwinds were common in Maryland.

"No, not at all common," the colonel replied pleasantly, "but we got this on purpose to treat Mr. Franklin."

Centuries of amateur storm chasing followed.

Scientific storm chasing became a regular practice in the 1970s, when Doppler radar and numerical cloud models brought about a revolution in the understanding of storms. When Doppler signals bounce off an object and return, the device can "hear" subtle shifts in the echoes that indicate whether that object is moving closer or farther from the radar source. Using data from multiple Doppler radars, scientists could now calculate the speed and direction of winds swirling within storms.

Numerical cloud models produce three-dimensional simulations of developing storms, and these realistic simulations enable researchers to quantify the forces of storms. Unlike earlier models, which simply strived to *understand* these processes, new models could help *predict* them.

Today's scientific storm chasers span a pretty wide spectrum. In popular chasing territories in parts of Oklahoma and Kansas, scientists may find themselves sharing the roads with chase teams driven by very different motives. For some, it is research. For others, glory. Others are there because weather tourists have paid them for the wild ride. Since the inception of YouTube and reality shows like the Discovery Channel's *Storm Chasers*, a growing number of nonscientific glory chasers take to the road in storm season with more nerve than knowledge.

The tour groups do not often chase in Dixie Alley.

■ ■ ■

As Peters and Coleman were driving straight into the heart of their storm, another chase team seventy miles south was gunning to intercept a large storm on a parallel track. Their radar showed the hook echo heading northeast at a steady clip, approaching the Tuscaloosa county line. Avoiding other teams on nearby storms, they chose this unclaimed supercell and sped southwest to meet it.

Behind the wheel of his Toyota Highlander, meteorologist John Oldshue stared intently through the wipers. On the radar, the echo was a perfect red hook. There was no way of knowing for sure until they saw it, but instinct told him this was real, and it was somewhere on the ground.

Throughout his years of chasing, Oldshue had caught four tornadoes—one of which had nearly caught him—and he knew their mercurial nature. Now retired, he had spent most of his decade at ABC 33/40 in front of the green screen, but during outbreaks he drove the StormChaser van. Today he was chasing as an unpaid volunteer, supporting his former colleagues.

Oldshue was another case of a weatherman who had found his calling as a child. He was three years old when the 1974 outbreak captured his fascination forever. In elementary school, James Spann became his hero. Oldshue remembered the date Spann got his first color radar—July 27, 1977—because it was Oldshue's seventh birthday, and the advent of color radar was just as much cause for celebration.

When Oldshue was a freshman in college, there were no meteorology programs in the area. So he enrolled in his next choice, the veterinary program at Mississippi State. During an internship with a large-animal vet, he met the cow that changed his career. The cow was suffering from constipation, and the vet had Oldshue don a rubber glove that stretched all the way to his shoulder. In the middle of the procedure, a thunderstorm broke out, and Oldshue realized that he was more into the weather than he was the cow. Which was, at the moment, saying a lot. Mississippi State had recently introduced its broadcast meteorology program, and Oldshue promptly changed his major.

Oldshue thrived in the program. When it came time for his college internship, he knew just whom he wanted to work for. He looked up the phone number of his childhood hero and left a gushing message on Spann's answering machine.

"You don't know me," he said, "but I have watched you since I was in diapers and I want to be a TV weatherman. I want to be your intern."

Spann called him back and left him a message Oldshue would save and replay for the next three weeks, perplexing his future wife with the magnitude of his man-crush.

"John, this is James Spann. I've never had an intern, but I'd love for you to become my first."

Oldshue interned with Spann for the next two summers, an apprentice to the master. When he graduated, Spann helped him land his first job at a TV station in Tuscaloosa. After a succession of jobs in and outside of meteorology, Oldshue returned to 33/40 as the weekend weatherman. During tornado season, he drove the back roads looking for ground truth. He was one of the best chasers at the station.

His most famous catch was the F4 tornado that had struck Tuscaloosa on December 16, 2000, a monster spawned by a winter outbreak that scarred the land from Mississippi to North Carolina. Oldshue had been chasing that twister through Tuscaloosa, trying to capture live footage for Spann to broadcast. It was his fourth tornado, and prior experience informed his calculated risks. He had a wife and kids to think about, as well as the reporter riding along in the StormChaser van. He did not take this responsibility lightly. For safety, he wanted to give this huge storm a wide berth, and his conservative calculations should have kept them in the safe zone. But tornadoes can never be trusted to behave as expected. This one had veered suddenly. It was one of the small percentage of funnels that moved due east instead of northeast. Oldshue and his colleague were standing in the parking lot of a Hampton Inn, looking at what he thought was a wall of rain.

Those birds wouldn't be flying out here if this was a tornado.

Then he looked closer.

Those aren't birds. Those are car bumpers.

As it barreled toward them, Oldshue and his colleague ditched the van and ran inside the Hampton Inn, joining the manager and a group of guests taking shelter in the hallway.

They took a direct hit. No one at the hotel was hurt, but that storm killed eleven Tuscaloosans, nine of them in a trailer park. Oldshue walked outside to find the StormChaser van nearly totaled, an incident that his colleagues would never let him live down. It was no small consolation, however, that he and Spann would win an Emmy for their coverage.

Oldshue did not get his livestream that time, but other live footage, captured by a remote-controlled SkyCam, had saved countless lives and ushered the station into a new era of warnings. It had proven that live footage was more motivating to viewers than the most detailed, cutting-edge radar.

Now, years later, Oldshue was gunning for another shot at getting a tornado live on TV. But with wireless signals patchy from the morning damage, that was going to be a matter of luck and timing.

Riding shotgun, Ben Greer was a close friend who found Oldshue's chasing stories captivating. Greer worked in the film industry, setting and lighting scenes, and had hoped one day to film a live tornado. He had brought along a high-definition camera to use alongside Oldshue's streaming weather-cam, which he was now rushing to assemble with nervous hands. In his lap was a bird's nest of unfamiliar wires, cameras, and gadgets that Oldshue had dumped in the passenger seat and was trying to talk him through.

Today's decision to chase had been last-minute. The friends had talked about chasing together for years, but the right opportunity had not yet presented itself. Earlier that week, when Greer had seen an outbreak on the forecast, he picked up the phone. Oldshue, who had long since left his job as a broadcast weatherman, demurred.

"Let's go," Greer said. "Let's do it."

"No," Oldshue said. "I'm retired. I'm done."

They hung up, but the prospect nagged at Oldshue. Once you're bitten by the storm-chasing bug, it was hard to cure the fever. He called Greer back.

"Can you be here in thirty minutes?"

They planned to head west of Tuscaloosa until they learned that another chase team—a third pair working with 33/40—was already on that storm. So they set off to find an unclaimed supercell. This one, farther south, looked promising. When supercells come in pairs, the second often grows stronger, fed by the storm before it.

"Nobody's on it," Oldshue said. "Let's go catch it."

They shot down the interstate, dodging traffic as they headed toward a rural area about twenty miles southwest of Tuscaloosa. Greer downed a Snickers and a Coke, plugged cords into cameras, and tried to stay calm. Oldshue looked for an exit with a high point. In this part of the state, the foothills of the Appalachians give way to the coastal plain. There are not many hills. But the trees that blanket the undulations turn some roads into tunnels. They hoped they could find a hill high enough to let them see the horizon.

As he drove, Oldshue told Greer to open his computer and send a message to 33/40. He knew his old colleague Jason Simpson would be running the radar and scanning the chats for ground truth. Those guys would be slammed and he would not bother them unless he felt there was a high likelihood that he would have a storm to show. Today, he had that feeling.

4:09 Oldshue yo

4:12 Simpson hey man just got your email

4:17 Oldshue we are going south to tuscaloosa county line

4:17 Simpson ok

They pulled off the interstate at an exit where they thought they might find the highest point and turned into the parking lot of Frontier Bingo. Greer stayed at the car while Oldshue ran into the establishment, searching among the bleeping gaming machines for an authority he could ask for permission to film on the property. An old man in overalls and a younger man in a suit both gave their blessing. He ran back out to meet Greer.

From here they still could not see the horizon, but they watched the sky to the south, above a roadless hill, for the shape of a funnel. The mercury was dipping.

■ ■ ■

Pursuing the northern storm, Peters and Coleman raced through the rain. The wind was bearing down upon them, licking the truck with sudden gusts. On either shoulder of the interstate, trees had been cleared, providing a rare wide swath of sky. But they could not see much through the downpour. Raindrops spattered on the windshield faster than the wipers could sweep them away, and through the sheets of water they could see little more than the blurry taillights of the trucks they passed. They were pushing ninety miles per hour.

The air filled with the scent of pine. Small needles and twigs flecked the windshield, catching in the wipers before getting brushed away. Falling leaves were a telltale sign that they were somewhere inside the supercell. Their options here were slim. They could try to punch through to the other side, risking a slight miscalculation that could get them hurt or killed. Or they could quickly find a place to hunker down and pray as the storm crashed over them. Either way, it was an all-in bet.

The clatter on the roof grew louder. Hail. It sounded so big that Peters worried that his windshield might shatter. Hail occurs near the core of a supercell, which meant the funnel could be near. They wondered whether it would emerge at any moment from the grayness that enveloped them.

"Do we want to get under the overpass?" Peters said, spotting shelter.

"We're directly in the path of the tornado now. I see the rain-free base. I see a lowering. We've just got too many trees and hills in the way."

They pressed on through rain and fear. They had passed the point of turning back. Coleman looked up from the radar and out the window with mounting anxiety.

"You haven't turned southeast yet," Coleman said, voice rising several octaves in panic. "It's coming at us!"

"I know it. I know it."

"You gotta keep goin'."

"We don't want to get off here?"

"No!"

Coleman knew this landscape well. He had a cabin on nearby Bankhead Lake, where he loved to fish for bass and bream. He had driven these back roads many times. He knew where they went, and where they did not. With a lack of escape routes, he knew they were in danger. Coleman believed they were punching the core of the storm. Peters disagreed that they were core punching but sensed the danger, too.

"We're gonna have a view right up here," Peters said. "Let's see what we can see."

"Okay. But keep your engine running."

As they climbed the slight hill, Coleman looked behind them.

"There it is, Brian!"

In the sky behind them was a gathering gray, rotating slowly on the ground, like a giant top. Coleman rolled down the passenger window and pointed his video camera toward the back of the truck as Peters pulled onto the grassy shoulder. Semi trucks roared by, seemingly oblivious, kicking up spray from the asphalt. The trees and fields lost their hopeful spring green as the land darkened under a yellowing sky. The tornado was four or five miles away, and it was either growing bigger or getting closer. Maybe both. The air smelled of cut grass and wet asphalt.

"I'm stopping on the interstate to give James a play-by-play of what we can see from our vantage point," Peters said.

Their video camera captured Peters's voice, excited and unafraid. Coleman's carried the edge of primal fear.

"We can't stay here long," Coleman said.

"Tim, that's it!"

"There's the tornado!"

It swayed like an elephant's trunk. Around it, the entire sky was rotating slowly, looming ominously and winking with lightning. Peters stared at it in awe and said a silent prayer of gratitude.

Thank you, God. It's in the woods. I get to see one where nobody's going to get hurt.

They guessed it was four or five miles away as it crossed the interstate. From this distance, it almost looked like it was moving in slow motion. But it was actually charging at sixty miles per hour, snapping hardwoods, tossing cars, splintering chicken houses. Ropelike at first, the funnel leaned like a plow tilling the ground, the supercell dragging it across the land. It fattened and darkened with bits of trees and dirt and asphalt. Then a second vortex formed beside the first. Were they looking at twins? Peters was standing on the side of the highway juggling his digital still camera and his phone as he dialed the number of the ABC 33/40 studio. The managers patched him through to Spann on the air.

"We're looking at what appears to be two tornadoes. One has lifted, and the second one is definitely on the ground. We're not going to be able to stay here very long. This thing is actually coming at us."

"Brian, you get out of there," Spann said. "Don't worry about me. If you've got to hang up, you go. But do you notice any debris falling out of the sky?"

"No sir, but it is definitely on the ground. We can see the visible funnel."

In the background, a woman on the side of the interstate screamed, "*It's right there!*"

■ ■ ■

Outside Tuscaloosa, waiting for the southern storm, Oldshue and Greer stood outside the bingo parlor, cameras rolling on a pregnant sky. A handful of cars remained in the parking lot like sleeping dogs awaiting their owners. The meteorologist and the cameraman stood on either side of the dark blue Highlander, which had both doors splayed open, giving the vehicle a birdlike quality, as if it stood poised to take flight.

Oldshue set up his camera to stream live footage to the studio. His laptop sat on the hood of the car, attached with a cord to his video camera, which he had detached from the dashboard so he could hold it. Using a private chat, Oldshue pinged Jason Simpson to make sure his live video stream was working. He had muted the volume for the test run; one less source of noise for Simpson.

4:18	Oldshue	can u see video
4:20	Simpson	what is your stream?
4:22	Oldshue	in the email
4:22	Simpson	yes i see u
4:22	Oldshue	in knoxville exit 52
4:35	Oldshue	got video?
4:35	Simpson	yes
4:35	Oldshue	knoxville bingo hall
4:37	Simpson	let me know if you see somthing

Oldshue tore his eyes from the laptop and turned them toward the sky. Above the ridgeline, the wet cotton was beginning to flicker with static electricity. The cloud-to-ground lightning was another sign that a tornado was forming inside the gray mass. A bolt crackled to the earth. Then another. And another. Strangely, the wind was not gusting. The air around them felt restless and humid. Oldshue felt it, the storm breathing down his neck, like a predator ready to pounce.

4:41	Oldshue	lots of cg lightning
4:45	Oldshue	may have tor behind ridge
4:47	Simpson	ok. we have col sanders on with live torn right now

Oldshue knew Colonel Sanders meant Brian Peters. What he didn't know was that Peters was on the air, describing a tornado about to deal Cordova the second blow of its day. Oldshue's mind was racing too fast to comprehend this because of what he saw in front of him.

The charcoal monolith emerged over the southeast ridgeline, hulking and formidable. Set against the stark white sky, its edges were clearly defined, though its ropelike bottom was truncated by the ridgeline. Now there was no question.

4:48	Oldshue	think we have a tor
4:49	Oldshue	tor!
4:49	Simpson	I see it

Click.

The tornado was live on the air.

As he steadied his hand on the camera, Oldshue blocked out the cacophony that surrounded him. The car door was dinging, the Emergency Broadcast System was squawking, and a phone was going unanswered. Spann's voice was booming from the dashboard.

On the other end of the line streamed a silent picture. Oldshue had muted it for testing, and now knew better than to change his setup and risk breaking the tenuous connection between eyewitness scene and viewer: camera, computer, cell tower, Internet, computer, broadcast microwave. The silence made it feel as if time had warped into slow motion.

In the studio, Spann faced an unprecedented situation: Two tornadoes. Two towns. One moment in time. Cordova's storm was slightly more imminent. Tuscaloosa's endangered more people. He had video from one, audio from the other.

Which one should be put on the air?

Both. Peters's voice overlapped Oldshue's video in a surreal moment that captured a thumbnail of the chaos breaking loose above Alabama. The sky was exploding with supercells, with no fewer than five violent, long-track tornadoes raging through the state at this moment. Still more were lined up behind them in Mississippi.

The atmosphere was boiling. As in a pot of water on a heated stove, great bubbles of air continued rising into the colder upper air. The wind shear was extreme: blowing twenty miles per hour on the surface and seventy miles per hour at three thousand feet up, which spun those rising air-blobs like tops. Higher still, at thirty-four thousand feet, the wind speeds screamed at a hundred miles per hour, feeding the momentum of the mesocyclone, the rotating mother storm. Wind shear was a key ingredient missing in summer storms, when towering anvil-shaped thunderstorms grow straight and tall. Hot blobs of air still rise, but the rain falls straight down into the updraft, cooling and curbing its ascent. In effect, they rain themselves out.

But now, spring winds were careening through the upper air, shoving the tops of those towering thunderstorms until they leaned like the Tower of Pisa. Curtains of rain and cool air descended on the leeward side, too far over to cancel the updrafts. With nothing to stop their ascent, the updrafts coursed unchecked like great fountains of air, sucking in the fuel of humidity and growing even more powerful.

These rotating supercells had evolved into something like living organisms, with inputs and outputs that flowed in a vicious circuit unbroken for many hours and miles. They consumed the warm and humid air, sucking it up like food. They discharged cold air in fierce downdrafts. Without anything to break the circuit, the biggest of these monsters stalked the earth that day for more than eight hours and one hundred miles, some bearing multiple tornadoes.

Upstate, two EF5 tornadoes were coming out of Mississippi, and an EF4 was crossing over into Georgia. But those were now the concern of the Huntsville TV station. Spann was focused on the two EF4 killers in his market, aimed point-blank at Cordova and Tuscaloosa, approaching simultaneously.

"We've got a large tornado crossing into Cordova," Spann said. "I've got John's video of a separate tornado. We are calling a tornado emergency for Tuscaloosa and Northport . . . based on that live stream, be in a safe place. This includes the campus of the University of Alabama."

CHAPTER 13

SAFE PLACE

4:38 P.M., APRIL 27, 2011—TUSCALOOSA, ALABAMA

The girls were getting scared.

Camped out in the hallway, a mile from campus, they could hear the sirens howling. On TV, two terrifying spirals crossed the radar behind James Spann. The bottom one was headed toward Tuscaloosa.

"Get a bicycle helmet on your kids," Spann said. "In many cases the treating physicians in the ER have told us that if the kids had had a bicycle helmet on, they would have survived."

The girls had no helmets. They had no basement. All they had was this hallway at the bottom of the stairs, filled with soft things to protect them. It was everything Spann said a safe place should be: a small room, in the center of the house, on the lowest floor, away from windows. Still, Danielle did not like it, and she said so on Facebook:

4:39	Danielle	once again the sirens are going off . . . have I mentioned that I'm so tired of these storms? But I hope everyone stays safe!!

Beside her, Loryn was on the verge of tears, and Will was trying to comfort her. The hallway dimmed and the TV flickered shades of blue across three solemn, frightened faces.

In Wetumpka, 130 miles southeast, Loryn's mother opened her front door and stepped out onto the porch. The sun was shining down on her farmhouse, its warmth breaking through the gently rolling clouds. Intermittent shadows chased the little kids running in the yard. Back inside, Ashley flipped through the channels, trying to find news about the weather in Tuscaloosa. In this TV market, she was struggling to find out what was happening on the other side of the state.

From the hallway, Loryn chatted with friends on Facebook. Some of them teased her about her fear.

Next to her, Danielle was texting friends and family. Many people out there still had no power and might not be able to see what she was seeing on the news. She was particularly worried about her little sister in Mississippi, where so many tornadoes were forming.

4:43	Michelle	FWD: MAROON ALERT 4:38 p.m.—Tornado warning for Starkville campus
4:52	Danielle	Yeah we're under a warning too. :-/ very lame
4:52	Danielle	U guys okay? U should pull up abc 33 40 online and see the tornado heading to Tuscaloosa.
4:55	Michelle	the power is out for the whole town
4:56	Danielle	Not good guys have the radio on? U safe?

Spann's voice cut through the hallway with a chilling report.

"We are calling a tornado emergency for Tuscaloosa and Northport. At the same time, we are calling a tornado emergency for Walker County, specifically around Cordova."

The tornado had passed out of sight of the chase team. Spann cut to the SkyCam bolted to the roof of the Tuscaloosa County Courthouse, on the other side of town from 31 Beverly Heights. Above the dark seam of the horizon, the sky was a light box, flat and white.

Like a shadow, it slunk into view. At first it just looked like a thunderstorm, a mass of cloud sitting on the ground. The funnel, wrapped in rain, was invisible from this angle. But the telltale signs were present: a bright, cloud-free base to the right, which signaled an updraft so powerful that it swept falling raindrops back into the sky. It had grown into a monstrosity that looked big enough to swallow the whole world.

"Anybody in the city of Tuscaloosa, you need to be in a safe place right now!" Jason Simpson said on TV. "This is not a game. This is for real."

All across town, police scanners crackled to life. Firefighters, policemen, and EMTs froze and listened. The message seemed a time bomb.

Fire dispatch to all units. There is a large tornado that is on track to impact the city of Tuscaloosa in less than thirty minutes. Correction: less than fifteen minutes.

It was one of seven long-track tornadoes on the ground in Alabama.

CHAPTER 14

CORDOVA

4:56 P.M., APRIL 27, 2011—CORDOVA, ALABAMA

In a tiny town fifty miles north of Tuscaloosa, a woman stood under an awning, taking thoughtful drags from a cigarette. She noticed pink wisps that looked like cotton candy floating incongruously through the air. The sun was shining and the backlit raindrops quickly morphed into pea-size hail that peppered the ground. Wet-cotton clouds snuffed out the sun, and the sky turned green and jaundiced. The woman looked up with a thought she had never had.

If fear had a color, this is it.

The power was still out in Cordova. The two-block downtown had been gutted by the EF3 tornado that roared out of the pre-dawn. The fire station had been heavily damaged, and the trucks were stuck inside. No outside help had arrived, because most of the surrounding towns were dealing with their own storm cleanup. If more storms were coming, they did not know. They had no power. News came through the windows of passing cars.

The woman was taking a break from directing traffic when she noticed the shift in the wind. The lazy curl of smoke snaking from her cigarette vanished in a stiff breeze. More cotton candy rode in on the wind. She recognized this harbinger of danger: insulation.

Raindrops turned to leaves. Leaves gave way to objects.

"Mom! There's debris falling!" said a teenage boy.

"Stop playing!" said his mother.

The boy pointed at a tree branch drifting down from the sky, featherlike. What looked like a twig grew into a limb. In a blink, it became a full-size tree hurtling down upon them. As it hit the ground nearby, green lightning spidered out of the clouds and seized it like a hand.

The boy ran with another young man to the railroad tracks, the highest point downtown. They pointed their camera phones at the crest of a hill, knowing on some primal level that something was about to come over it. The trees on the hilltop began to bend and lean. And then some great, invisible force lifted the double-wide mobile home on the hill and flung it into the medical clinic across the street.

"Look right there!" a voice boomed above a chorus of yelling. "Look right there! Looklooklooklooklook!"

"That's it!" a woman yelled.

"Come on!" screamed another. *"Now! RUN!"*

Mothers shrieked in panic at their sons, who sprinted toward them. Firemen burst out of a camper—their temporary HQ now that the station was gone—and clambered into city hall. Next to the fire department's camper, in the old one-room train depot, the police dispatcher would not leave her post. Aware of the storm, she was sheltering in the bathroom with the dispatch radio, using the closed toilet lid as a desk to write notes in her log.

In the middle of the block, the twenty-one-year-old lieutenant waved everyone into the half-submerged basement of city hall, his voice cutting through the roar.

"Get in here! Get in! They comin'! *Get in!*"

He pulled the door closed just as the second tornado of his day charged through his broken town. This one was much bigger than the first. He pressed his phone's camera to a hole in the door. Outside, boards and branches hurled violently from right to left. Inside, the high-pitched whine sounded like a Shop-Vac sucking up gravel.

It plowed through town like a bush hog, bending steel I-beams like paper clips. The bank exploded. It decimated the Piggly Wiggly, scattering canned vegetables and bricks. It crushed half the church and spun the mansion on the hill off its foundation. It ripped apart a house and slung three boys and a mother two blocks.

Within seconds, the wind weakened, and flying objects slowed and drifted to the ground. Some of the rescuers felt the impulse to get outside and start digging for people. Others held them back.

"It's gone now. That's it. It's over."

"No, it's not."

"Nah. No no no no *no*!"

"It's calm! It's calm!"

"Did y'all wait for the center to go by?"

"That's right—I forgot."

The wind picked up again, flinging objects with equal force in the opposite direction. The core of the storm had passed over them, calm like the eye of a hurricane, and now the rear wall of the vortex was hitting.

Then they remembered the dispatcher who had refused to leave. They watched their camper sail away like a kite and crash into the building where she kept her post. A young fireman opened the door to go find her. His colleagues clawed at him, trying to stop him.

"No, get in! That's just the calm!" a female colleague screamed.

"I don't care! The camper's into the motherfucking building!"

He charged outside.

The woman screamed.

"No!"

CHAPTER 15

CODE GRAY

5:02 P.M., APRIL 27, 2011—TUSCALOOSA, ALABAMA

Druid City Hospital was under Code Gray. Patients resting on hospital beds had been rolled into the inner hallways. Those who could walk were ushered into the auditorium. Televisions in the lobby, emergency room, and inpatient rooms were buzzing with the news and weather. People on both sides of the white coat watched together as James Spann called out names of roads and landmarks in the path of the storm. The landmarks drew closer and closer.

The hospital disaster coordinator, Andrew Lee, had called Code Gray when he first saw the tornado on John Oldshue's LiveStream. His hospital was the only one in Tuscaloosa. The nearest facility of its size was an hour's drive away—on clear roads with no traffic—in Birmingham. Lee, a flight nurse and a meteorology enthusiast who closely studied the weather, had done everything in his knowledge to prepare for a catastrophic hit. When James Spann had begun warning of the coming storm last week, Lee had briefed his staff on Code Gray, the disaster plan for severe weather. The plan included four hundred and fifty premade medical charts with fake names, which would speed the admissions process and allow them to intake patients quickly, treating first and leaving the paperwork for later.

That was the count of his worst-case scenario, the most catastrophic event his imagination could grasp: a flood of four hundred and fifty patients, all needing urgent help at once.

He hoped it would not come to that.

■ ■ ■

Two blocks from the hospital, in the hallway of 31 Beverly Heights, Danielle, Loryn, and Will could do nothing more to protect themselves than they already had done. They had dragged the TV as far as the cord would stretch, so they could see it from their linen fortress. With pillows ready to cover their heads, they watched the blackness swallow their horizon.

"That is something significantly wicked on the horizon of Tuscaloosa and just about to move into the city," Jason Simpson said on the air. "It's large. It's violent."

Danielle feverishly texted her sister.

5:02	Danielle	There's a fucking huge tornado heading to downtown tuscaloosa
5:04	Michelle	I'm at my place and clay is on campus. so far we are ok. are you safe??
5:06	Danielle	Good good im at the house w/will and loyrn she's been in the hall since the cullman tornado im just getting sick w/this tornado its on the skycam on the news and its heading to downtown and campus

Michelle looked at the extra spaces, the misspelling of Loryn's name, and knew her sister was distracted and afraid. At least Will and Loryn were there beside her, so she was not alone. Michelle sat on her bed in her off-campus apartment, trying to study. But she could not shake off the feeling that crept into her stomach. This did not feel right. Michelle had never seen her sister afraid.

"This will be a day that goes down in state history," Spann said. "All we can do is pray for these people."

At 5:07 p.m., Spann experienced a rare few seconds of dead air, struck speechless by the second superstorm of his life, aimed at the heart of his hometown.

5:08	Michelle	oh my gosh! be careful!
5:09	Danielle	Its very big michelle u know how I dont get scared w/these but this is huge bigger than cullman

CHAPTER 16

ENTRAPMENT

5:09 P.M., APRIL 27, 2011—CORDOVA, ALABAMA

The tailwinds were still sweeping through when the volunteers poured out of city hall. Wearing navy blue Cordova Fire & Rescue shirts over ripped jeans and fireproof bunkers, they fanned out to search for survivors. Brett Dawkins, a twenty-one-year-old lieutenant on the squad, held his phone as he ran, still filming, capturing the moment in a perspective befitting pandemonium.

"Holy shit!" Dawkins yelled. "Our camper's exploded! There's nothing fucking left!"

The camper they had gathered in moments before—their tactical command center—was gone. Through the crack in the city hall basement door, they had watched as it tumbled down the street like a paper sack.

The responders scattered in all directions, looking for it. They ran quickly, taking in the scene as they went, peering in the busted-out windows of cars and trucks, listening for cries for help.

Cordova had lost to the morning storms much of the equipment it needed to respond to the crisis. The fire station had been demolished by the EF3 that hit town before dawn. The medical clinic near downtown Commerce Street was now gone. Unlike Tuscaloosa, Cordova had ambulance service and no hospital. The nearest hospital was around twenty minutes away in Jasper, the same town and the same hospital where eighteen-year-old James Spann had been sent with his amateur radio in the 1974 Super Outbreak.

"Jeff an' them was still in the Rebel Queen, wasn't they?"

Dawkins ran up the hill toward the only restaurant in town, across the railroad tracks, owned by family. It looked as if it had been struck by a wrecking ball. Inside it, his aunt and uncle had survived, holding on to an industrial grill that had stopped the imploding building from crushing them as it fell.

Nearby, at the United Methodist Church, the roof was sheared off. This church was the closest thing Cordova had to a community tornado shelter, its basement a refuge to the people of the small town. Inside it, dozens had survived.

People were spilling out of buildings and into the street, hollering, screaming, cussing. In the dizzying swirl of this new reality, Brett caught out of the corner of his eye a man running toward him, waving him down.

"Jackson and Bev are trapped," yelled the man. "The whole damn house is on 'em!"

The man was his uncle, Mike Van Horn, who had been crouched in a half-finished basement with his wife and grown kids when the house collapsed on them. Mike's daughter, Taylor, had made it out with her boyfriend, but his wife and son were still under the house.

Brett Dawkins ran to a truck with no windows but saw the roads were blocked with debris. Nearby, he found a tractor with the keys still in the ignition, and he drove it all the way to the fire station, clearing a little path through the rubble. At the station, he gathered equipment from the undrivable fire engines—extrication tools, airbags, and medical supplies thrust by the armful into paint buckets—and dropped them at the downtown pharmacy, which would become their triage spot.

Then he ran to dig his family out.

■ ■ ■

Under the house, it was dark and smelled of dust and wood and leaking gas. Beverly Moseley, fifty, was trapped under the floorboards, her right bicep pinned by the crushing weight of the house. She was sitting on the dirt, in the unfinished section of the basement, with her neck bent uncomfortably toward her chest by the unyielding wood of a floor joist.

On the other side of a crumbled support pillar, her arm was still wrapped around the shoulders of her twenty-one-year-old stepson, Jackson Van Horn, who was unnaturally quiet. Beverly's view was blocked by a heap of crumbled brick between them, but she could feel his hair and warm neck.

"Jackson?" she said. "Are you okay? Jackson! Say something to me! Please, Jackson, just say something!"

When the second storm came through, they had been ready. Though the power was out, they had a police scanner handy to listen for news of coming storms. They had crawled under the house and crouched in the four-foot-high crawl space, bracing themselves against four brick pillars that held the house up.

As the jet-engine sound of the storm had blasted their ears, a window had burst, spraying glass across the room. Then the house had lurched violently, shifting back and forth on the pillars.

"Lord Jesus!" Beverly had screamed, wrapping her arm around Jackson. "Keep us safe!"

The house had shifted on its pillars six feet to the right, turning square rooms into parallelograms. Then came a brief silence. Bev could hear the wind, but it sounded different, distant. When it roared again the house shifted in a new direction. With the third lurch, the walls and roof came down and they felt dust and rocks flying under the house, pelting them like mortar.

The floor joists thrust down upon Beverly's head, shoving her neck forward, pressing her chin into her sternum. She felt herself slowly suffocating, the sharp bend in her throat like a kink in a hose.

I am dying, she thought. *I am breaths away from dying.*

Missy, her big mutt, was on her lap, and yelping and digging frantically. When the dog broke free, Beverly was able to shift her body ever so slightly so that she could open her throat and breathe again. She tried to extricate herself, but she felt her arm pinned by a crushing weight.

"Baby!" her husband yelled. "Are you okay?"

"I am, but my arm's stuck," she said.

Mike Van Horn dug himself out and ran for help. Taylor and her boyfriend freed themselves and stood outside, holding each other and crying.

Mike had run toward downtown, calling for help.

"Help!" he yelled. "Bev's stuck! Help!"

That's when Mike saw his grown nephew running toward him.

■ ■ ■

Brett Dawkins was only twenty-one, the same age as his cousin trapped under the house. But people who looked at Brett saw the eyes of someone older. He had been the man of the house for as long as he could remember. His mother said he had met his daddy, once, but he could not recall a face. But he did remember the fire trucks that had wailed all through his childhood. Once, when he was three, he cut his hand on a broken bottle, sliced right through his lifeline. When a fireman came to fix up the cut, Brett looked up at him and saw the kind of man he wanted to be. After that, he had spent endless afternoons playing with a toy fire station, pushing the little red ladder truck through the dirt, glancing up whenever he heard a siren, looking for the heroes on the big red truck. When he grew into his first bicycle, his helmet had a little flashing light. He trick-or-treated in bunkers, fireman's pants, almost every Halloween.

When Brett turned fifteen he started coming to the real station with an uncle, who let him go on calls with the men. The boy would help unload axes and medical boxes on the scene, and later, roll up the big, flat hoses when they got back to the station. His strength did not go unnoticed or untapped. Brett had been an offensive lineman on the football team that went 15–0 for the first time in the history of Cordova High, winning the 3A State Championship that year, blowing everyone out of the water. He still had the build of a football player, and his broad shoulders served him well in his new occupation, lifting hoses at burning buildings.

Now enrolled at the Alabama Fire College, he worked shoulder to shoulder with men who had fought fires for decades. In a way, he had lots of fathers now, but they treated him as an equal. This was his family. His best friend, a young black man affectionately called "Chocolate"—his real name was Mike Simon—was the one he trusted most to follow him into a burning building. Both boys were strong of body and mind, and were known to keep their heads when things got real.

The house had listed to one side and collapsed like a cardboard box. The walls came to pieces as they hit the ground. Somewhere under this mess lay his aunt and cousin, and he quickly had to figure out where. Brett could hear Beverly yelling up through the floor. He followed his aunt's voice to a spot in the floor, revved his chain saw, and cut himself a manhole. As he peeled back the cutout, as if opening a trapdoor, light flooded into the basement, blinding Beverly briefly. He crawled into the darkness with a flashlight.

Crouching, Brett could see Beverly sitting awkwardly in the dirt, legs splayed out in front of her, neck kinked severely, right arm disappearing under a collapsed wall. Beside her, his cousin Jackson was slumped forward and motionless, chin pressed into his chest. The house was resting on Jackson's shoulders, his still body the only thing holding it off Beverly. His eyeglasses had slid to the tip of his nose, and one small drop of blood marked his cheek. His phone lay in his unfurled hand.

"He's gone," Beverly moaned. "He's gone."

She could not see him on the other side of the wall. She did not have to. Her arm was still wrapped around his neck, and she had felt him grow cold in her hand.

■ ■ ■

A couple of blocks away, other members of Cordova Fire & Rescue were frantically searching collapsed houses, the decimated remains of the Piggly Wiggly, and the blown-out storefronts of Commerce Street.

Firefighter Amanda Hodge was running toward the Piggly Wiggly when something on the ground caught her eye. It was a boy, curled up like a fetus. He looked about eight years old, and he was so caked with mud that his white skin looked brown. He blended right in with the brown debris. She must have passed him several times before she even noticed he was there.

Hodge ran and knelt beside the boy, feeling his neck for a pulse. Then she yelled for Dean Harbison, the fire chief and a paramedic, who drove the busted-up rescue truck with the EKG while she started CPR.

The boy's right shoulder was marred with a gaping hole, and from it a black streak marked the length of his body, all the way to his heel.

Lightning strike, she thought. *Lord.*

Hodge heaved over him, compressing his small chest as the chief hooked him up to the monitor. She prayed for a pulse. Maybe there was a chance they could bring him back. The chief did not see a heartbeat.

"Stop, Amanda, stop," the chief said. "He's gone."

But she could not stop. The firefighter in her knew, deep in her gut, that the boy could not be saved. But she was also a mother, and that part of her could not quit.

"Get me some water!" she screamed. "Somebody bring me some water!"

A firefighter brought her cup after cup. She was bathing him, washing the mud away. She knew this boy. One of the Doss brothers, Justin and Jonathan, who went to school with Amanda's own sons, Justin and Johnathon, a coincidence of names that would haunt her for months. She wanted to take care of him. This boy had a mother who needed him to live.

"Amanda, he's gone," the chief said gently. "Just stop."

"Dammit. Dean!" she screamed. "You can't stop!"

He understood. Chief Harbison had been a paramedic for eighteen years, and a father for nineteen. He knew as well as anyone that kids were hard to give up on. He let her work on the boy, perhaps longer than he should have. He let her choke on the sobs.

Then he made her look up and look around. There were others.

In the parking lot of the Piggly Wiggly lay the little boy's twelve-year-old brother, Justin. His body looked like a wet towel that had been wrung out, as if every bone in him was broken. They had been hiding in the house on the hill with a friend when the tornado obliterated the house, throwing them hundreds of feet.

Now their friend, sixteen-year-old Madison Phillips, was being carried up the hill from the Piggly Wiggly, unconscious, blood oozing through the bandages that wrapped his head. His mother, Annette Singleton, lay dead in a ditch.

▪ ▪ ▪

Trapped under the house with the body of her stepson, Beverly Moseley watched her nephew climb down with an armful of objects that struck her as so odd for him to be bringing that she actually heard herself laugh.

"What are you going to do with those pizza boxes?" she said.

They were not pizza boxes. They were air bags, and Dawkins placed them beneath points of the house that would hold. He connected them to an air compressor, and with an angry hiss of air, the house began to rise.

Brett pulled out the body of his cousin. He did not cry; the time for that would come later.

Jackson was gone. But in death he had saved a life.

■ ■ ■

It began to rain again, and there was talk of more storms coming. The rescuers kicked in the door of the vacant Miles Pharmacy on the corner of Commerce Street, where Brett had dropped supplies off, carrying victims there and laying them on the cool tile to keep them out of the rain.

In the town of around five thousand, four people were dead and eighty-six were injured, many of them needing transport to a hospital in Jasper or Birmingham. Chief Harbison called 911 and asked for any available help. Within minutes, several ambulances showed up and Emergency Management Agency staffers from other counties came to help Cordova. The chief paused to think how lucky they had been, to have the first tornado hit when and where it did. Had that first storm not torn through Commerce Street, the downtown would have been brimming with people at 5:00 p.m.—dozens of people would have been at the restaurant, maybe sixty at the medical clinic, dozens more at the Piggly Wiggly, the bank, and the shops.

CHAPTER 17

SLOUCHING TOWARD TUSCALOOSA

5:07 P.M., APRIL 27, 2011—TUSCALOOSA, ALABAMA

The sky above Tuscaloosa turned the color of a yellowing bruise. The birdsong stopped, and through the pregnant silence came the intermittent moaning of wind. The air held a charge. Now visible from the outskirts of town, the tornado emerged from the west. Even those who could not see it could feel its presence slouching across the horizon.

The dark column twisted down to the earth as the earth rose up to meet it. It plowed the verdant landscape, ripping up trees and chicken houses, grinding them up and spitting them out like shrapnel. Mesmerizing in its terrible beauty, it moved indiscriminately across the land, grinding at sixty miles per hour toward the city.

Across Alabama, people followed the black mass growing on their screen. In solid brick houses and double-wide trailers, in college dorm rooms and government projects, in church basements, corporate offices, and living rooms, people watched it unfolding, live. Through the unblinking eye of the rooftop camera, the people of Tuscaloosa saw death come into town.

They had been given sixty-four minutes of warning.

■ ■ ■

The rescuers of Tuscaloosa Fire Station No. 7 had been on edge all day. Their dispatch radio was oddly quiet. They had James Spann turned up in the background as they readied their medical kits, checking and rechecking their equipment. When they heard the pitch of his voice begin to rise, all heads swiveled toward the TV.

"Look at that thing—it's huge!" Spann said. "This is a very rare day. Reminiscent of the outbreaks of the seventies, the Super Outbreak of seventy-four."

The five men ran out the metal side door and into the engine bay, where two trucks stood by and pairs of yellow bunkers waited, puddled on the concrete. The men watched the blackness approach the southern edge of town, an industrial district filled with metal warehouses and boxy government buildings. The funnel was less than two miles away.

As the trees across Skyland Boulevard began to lean and sway, the firemen rolled down the metal door of the engine bay, protecting the trucks. Framed by the narrow windows, they watched grimly as flakes of drywall fell like snow on black asphalt.

"Everybody near Skyland Boulevard, be in a safe place!" Spann said on the station TV. "This is as violent a situation as you'll ever see."

The men ran for the bathroom. Drivers swerved off the road and banged on the station door. The firemen ran to let them in.

■ ■ ■

"Nobody should be driving!" Spann's voice boomed from the dashboard. "Everybody down there listening to me on the radio in Tuscaloosa, stop now. At the next exit, the next convenience store. Go into a business—they will let you in."

Two young men racing across Tuscaloosa ignored the voice on the radio and kept driving directly toward the darkness gathering in the sky. The twenty-five-year-old student behind the wheel, Ryne Chandler, had always wanted to see a tornado, ever since the movie *Twister*. He had no storm-chasing training and very little knowledge of meteorology. But he had lived in Tuscaloosa all his life, and he knew its streets as well as anyone. Well enough, he hoped, that he could find a quick escape route if this thing came their way.

Nate Hughett, his twenty-two-year-old friend riding shotgun, filmed the drive down Veteran's Memorial Parkway, pointing his camera west through the windshield. The rain had stopped, but the windshield wipers ticked back and forth like a metronome. Beyond them, the blackness rose from the treetops like a plume of smoke, indistinct but looming.

"This is a large wedge tornado," Spann's baritone boomed across the car radio. "This is making a beeline for downtown Tuscaloosa."

"That's exactly where we're going."

They were headed west on Veteran's, which turned into Fifteenth Street, a main thoroughfare through town. A few cars were still on the road, but most of them were headed rapidly in the opposite direction. A bolt of lightning lit the clouds as the amateur chasers passed University Mall. While they actually waited for the light to change at the corner of Fifteenth Street and McFarland Boulevard, Hughett's phone began ringing. Across the street, the Chevron station sign was still backlit, $3.69 Regular. In the passenger seat, Hughett set his camera on his lap, still rolling, to take the call.

"Hey. I'm good. Yeah, it's pretty big. Uh, I see something that looks like a tornado . . . Yeah. Okay, I gotta go."

They passed the neighborhood of Forest Lake and its ancient Druid oaks, Flowers Baking Co., and Fifteenth Street Diner. They could see the tornado hovering in the distance above the empty parking lot of TES, which Danielle Downs had left less than two hours ago. On the radio, Spann kept saying the tornado was headed straight for downtown, so they headed instead toward the interstate, where they could beat a hasty retreat.

As they changed direction, they saw the funnel emerge above the treetops, growing thinner and taller, spinning faster. Billions of flecks danced around it in the air.

"There it is! There it is!" the passenger said, the camera zooming in his shaky hand. "You can see debris in the air. That thing is massive!"

They headed on I-359, trying to get behind it. Now they could see it, clear and full, towering above the industrial rooftops, growing by the second. They were now directly in its path.

"We need to go faster. It's coming right at us!"

"Jesus!"

The engine roared.

"Never in my life will I see this again."

"Oh, my God . . ."

They pulled to a stop on the side of the interstate and watched it through the rear windshield.

The sky was black, the enormous mesocyclone rotating above like a giant malevolent planet. From this freakishly powerful storm, a dark funnel spiraled to the ground, now less than a mile away. Suddenly, it seemed as if some great dimmer switch had bled the light and color out of the sky, leaving every surface looking dark and slick, as if the world were sweating oil. The funnel grew before them, drawing them closer, luring them in.

The driver turned the car around.

"Chandler, do not go back that way!"

"Nate, film it."

"I am!"

"There's two of them."

"We need to go *that* way. Goddammit, go *back!*"

"We're fine. We're fine."

"Chandler, go the fuck back! I'm not kidding. We don't know if this thing can change directions. We're not experts!"

The driver jammed the car in reverse. They sped backward down the interstate.

"It's crossing the interstate right where we were."

Barely out of its path, the young chasers watched the EF4 tornado invade the city.

■ ■ ■

The tornado was a half mile wide when it entered Tuscaloosa. It barreled into the Tamko Roofing plant, inhaling nails and shingles and spitting them out. It slammed the Curry building, which housed the Tuscaloosa Emergency Management Agency (EMA), crushing steel-and-concrete walls built in the 1970s to withstand a nuclear fallout. Sheltering in an inner room, Battalion Chief Chris Williamson and Deputy EMA Director Billy Green saw the ceiling tiles begin to dance, and heard, through eighteen inches of concrete, what sounded like a jet engine. The Emergency Operations Center, which held much of the city's emergency rescue equipment, began to crumble.

Crossing I-359, the funnel toppled cars and semis, catapulting an elderly passenger—seventy-three-year-old Minnie Acklin—from her car at the Thirty-Fifth Street exit to the very spot where the amateur storm chasers had been driving just minutes before. The tornado's first victim, she left behind four children, eight grandchildren, and seven great-grandchildren.

The winds bent the steel beams of a warehouse and toppled the walls of a church. At the Salvation Army, thirty-five people sought refuge in the dining hall as the wind blasted open the doors and stripped away the roof. A steel building that crumpled like a wad of foil was hurled into the seventy-bed shelter, which collapsed upon the impact. An electrical substation twisted like a telephone cord, and the lights went dark across town.

▪ ▪ ▪

Without power, the hallway of 31 Beverly Heights was enveloped by silence. In the sudden absence of Spann's voice, in the void left by the whirring, buzzing things that fill the spaces between thoughts, the stillness felt thick and heavy, like being deep underwater. This kind of stillness is rare in our modern world, except when the power goes out.

Danielle, Loryn, and Will lay side by side in the silent hallway. All of the light had drained out of the sky, and their faces glowed blue in the light of their phones, the last lifeline. The world outside was a car wash, sluicing and swirling and gathering in a seething cauldron of shadow and light, water and wind.

Loryn dialed her mother.

"Mama, it's so black!" she said. "I've never seen anything like this!"

On the other end of the line, Ashley Mims could feel her daughter's fear. The sky above Wetumpka was still sunny and blue, but she could feel the storm roiling deep in her gut. She stood before the TV in the living room, phone to her ear, relaying everything she saw and heard. Before her, the funnel seemed to double in size. She knew without having to look at a map that her child was in its path.

On TV, Spann sounded defeated.

"This is something you pray you never, ever, *ever* see," he said.

Every cell in Ashley's body cried out in prayer. Choking on waves of panic and hope, she paced back and forth between the kitchen and the living room, praying to God and consoling her child. Her small children trailed her like lost puppies.

"Where's Sissy?" they cried. "Is Sissy okay?"

▪ ▪ ▪

About three miles southwest of Beverly Heights, children were still playing on the grass when the tornado blasted with bomblike fury through the government projects at Rosedale. Filled with shingles and scrap metal, the meat grinder shredded half of the fifty brick buildings that were home to many families. The sky rained cinder blocks and babies.

It swept through Charleston Square, a two-story apartment complex built around an inner courtyard with a pool and a dozen trees. On the second floor, a sorority girl sat on her bathroom floor, studying for a test. As the walls around her vanished, she was thrown like a rag doll through the air, her spine shattering upon impact.

In a 1950s cottage in the Downs, a mother rushed her daughter into a bedroom closet, setting two pairs of shoes inside.

"Come on, sweetie! Time to do tornado turtle."

As the walls began to buckle, Meredith Cummings lay over her little girl and searched her heart for the right thing to whisper, for words that would not haunt her daughter if they were her last.

Under the ancient oaks of historic Glendale Gardens, a white-haired woman sat in a chair in her closet, clutching a ninety-four-year-old christening gown, the one she had worn as a baby. Her neighbors grabbed their wedding album and held each other in the bathtub. Down the street, a woman clung to her big, white dog.

In a college house on Twenty-Fifth Street, a 220-pound Alabama football player gathered his brown-eyed girlfriend in his arms as they crouched in a closet with friends.

"Carson, I'm scared," Ashley Harrison told her boyfriend, Carson Tinker.

"We're going to be okay, Ashley," Carson said. "It's going to be okay."

■ ■ ■

In the hallway of 31 Beverly Heights, Loryn sobbed into the phone.

"I'm scared, Mama! I'm scared!"

"It's okay, baby," her mother said gently. "It's gonna be okay."

Loryn had Skyped with her mother that morning and, without makeup hiding her freckles, looked younger than twenty-one. Ashley imagined her firstborn child in the hall, a frightened little girl. She wished she had packed up the little kids and driven to Tuscaloosa. She wished they were all together. But thank goodness Loryn was not alone.

On the phone, Ashley heard a boy in the background.

"It's okay," the boy said. "It's gonna be okay."

Ashley did not know whose voice this was, but in it she could hear a boy who cared about her daughter. She also heard a slight catch, the sound of a young man trying not to sound afraid.

■ ■ ■

A mile and a half from Beverly Heights, the funnel was now a mile wide. The black vortex spun across paper-white sky, trailing tendrils of smaller funnels. It was so vast that, from a distance, it appeared to move in slow motion. But it was moving roughly a mile a minute, scouring its way through beautiful neighborhoods shaded by ancient trees.

The tall pines that gave Forest Lake its name began to writhe and twist. Trunks as big around as a man is wide snapped like pencils. Roofs began to peel away, and drywall ripped like wet paper. Windows shattered and broken glass flew in all directions. The wind whipped the little pond into a froth, and the earth itself trembled.

Inside a church, six students jammed themselves in a cinder-block closet. As the noise of ten freight trains hammered their ears, one young man began to pray. "Dear Lord . . ." was all he had time to say before the splinters of his sanctuary fell upon his bowed head, his plea engulfed by the roar.

In a little house off Fifteenth Street, three friends grabbed their dogs and hid under a mattress. Nearby, a group of students huddled in the crawl space under the building. In Cedar Crest, a college boy ran and hid in a closet. His three best friends did not follow. A metal sculpture shaped like a billowing quilt took flight and flew a mile.

A father herded his wife and two girls into the walk-in cooler of Full Moon Bar-B-Que, crowding in with a dozen employees. He tightened his arms around his girls as the walls of the restaurant buckled. A gymnast on the UA team was caught outside and pressed herself into the nearest doorway, trying to shield herself.

■ ■ ■

In the hallway, side by side with Loryn and Will, Danielle was so afraid that she felt sick. In times of trouble, she leaned on her faith. Her Joan of Arc medal dangled from a silver chain around her neck. On the back of the medal, three words were stamped:

Pray for us.

Will kept telling the girls it was going to be okay, whether or not he believed it. Raised to be a gentleman, he had come to this house to look after the girls. He thought of his mother, fixing dinner at home in Priceville. It looked as if the power might be out for a while, and he knew she would worry. He sent her a quick text to let her know he was okay.

5:12 Will This thing is huge. I'm fine

■ ■ ■

Less than a mile south, at Fire Station 2, the rescuers stood outside on the apron, eyeing the sky. Their colleagues at Station 7, three miles away, were already taking shelter. Located on Paul W Bryant Drive a mile from Bryant-Denny Stadium and the grassy Quad, Station 2 was bigger, with nine men on duty. They had readied their chain saws and paramedic kits and were waiting, antsy, for trouble to arrive. Through the doors of the station, propped open in the wind, they could hear James Spann blaring in the station lounge, where a few of their colleagues sat watching.

"Hey! There's a tornado down!" one of them yelled through the open doors to the men outside. "Y'all come in here and look—it's on TV!"

"TV, *hell*!" said someone in the engine room. "There it is!"

They watched it cut diagonally through the middle of the city. Some filmed it with their camera phones, transfixed by its awesome magnitude. Each minute brought it one mile closer, and in the time it took to draw a breath, it seemed to swell impossibly. Lieutenant Marty McElroy looked up from his camera, saw the blue flash of transformers exploding, and realized it was only four blocks away.

Oh, crap—It's coming right at us!

"Hey, man," McElroy yelled to no one in particular. "This thing's fixin' to get us!"

The firemen had made a pact to ride this thing out together in a place where the storm would take all or none. It had started as a joke—all for one and one for all—but in the end, they stuck to the plan. Pulling on helmets and turnout gear, they climbed into the heaviest vehicle of the fleet—Truck 32, the ladder truck—which they hoped was strong enough to survive a station collapse and heavy enough not to fly. The cab built for six was a tight squeeze for nine, and the men sat shoulder to shoulder in awkward silence.

Within seconds, the station began shaking, the doors of the engine bay rattling like an AK-47. Marty McElroy, an ex-marine who had been to war, was not afraid to die. What scared him was not dying but leaving behind a wife and two preteen daughters. *Am I gonna see my girls again? Do they know I love them? Who's gonna take care of them after I'm gone?*

"Hey, guys . . ."

It was Derek Riddle, the guy they always counted on to break the tension with a joke. Things were getting real, and they could use a good laugh to shake them out of this spell. The men waited for the punch line.

"Man, I love y'all," Riddle said gravely. "If something happens . . . you know I love you. And it's been good."

Silence.

"Shut up, Riddle," someone said.

They laughed.

And then they felt their ears pop.

■ ■ ■

Across the street from the station, at Druid City Hospital, the hospital disaster coordinator, Andrew Lee, was sitting in his office, on the phone with his wife. She and the kids were safe at the beach, but she was worried about him.

"I have to go," Lee told her. "It's right outside our window!"

He threw himself on the floor of the hallway and held on to the doorframe. Down the hall, in the emergency room, doctors and nurses presided over a battalion of stretchers and beds crammed into the innermost hallways. In one room a three-year-old girl who could not be moved lay immobilized on a ventilator. Two nurses, Sharon Oakley and Sharon Allen, threw their bodies upon her as the funnel appeared through the window. The double doors of the ER banged open as the wind funneled in, snatching pictures from the walls, sending patient charts flying. Everyone held their breath as they felt the cold fingers of wind wrap around them.

■ ■ ■

Half a mile north of the hospital, in Beverly Heights, the whipping trees swayed like reeds in a pond thrashed by the wakes of passing boats. In the dim hallway, Danielle, Loryn, and Will burrowed deeper under the blankets. The silence was broken now by flying objects pecking at the windows, branches crackling and popping like fireworks in the whistling rush of wind. Ancient trunks groaned in protest; naked boughs whipped violently, plucked bare by the inhalation. The atmosphere accelerated around them, singing the terrible truths of fate.

Surrounded by pillows, blankets, and friends, Loryn held the phone to her ear. Her pretty hazel eyes were red from crying. Her mother's voice rose with panic.

"Oh my God, baby, it's coming right toward you!" Ashley said.

"Get your head down! Get your pillows over your head—it's coming toward you!"

"I'm scared, Mama! I'm scared!"

"It's okay, baby. It's going to be okay. Just get your head down."

Every time Ashley Mims said it, she heard the boy say it, too.

"It's okay," Will said, Loryn's hand in his. "It's gonna be okay."

Ashley heard her daughter's voice once more, muffled by a pillow.

"Mama, I'm scared!"

Click.

The line went dead. Ashley's heart convulsed with terror.

At that moment, in the heart of the crucible, Danielle's phone lit up with one last message:

5:13 Michelle is it on the ground? That is very scary! I hope it just passes . . . i love you!

CHAPTER 18

THE TRAIN

People who have lived through a tornado say it sounds just like a train, a low and visceral rumbling that is felt as much as heard, a piercing roar that shakes walls and faith, the percussion of a billion things colliding.

When the winds died down in Tuscaloosa, the roar gave way to an awful, lonely silence. A mile-wide swath of emptiness stretched out to the horizon. The trees had vanished. The landmarks were erased. In their place was too much sky.

Everywhere in its path, people crawled out of the rubble and called for one another, shouting through the terrible silence.

The students who hid in the church believed that their prayers had been heard; their hiding place was the only fragment of building still standing. The mother who shielded her little girl peeked out of the closet and saw sky through the roof. The boy who ran into a closet in Cedar Crest crawled out and found his best friend dead in a tree; his other two friends, twenty-three-year-old art student Morgan Sigler and her boyfriend Blake Peek, would die of their wounds at the hospital. The family inside Full Moon Bar-B-Que was alive but trapped in the walk-in cooler. The student chasers who had driven directly through the storm's path realized they had cheated death; they turned the car around and drove up to the ravaged government projects of Rosedale, where a woman stumbled through the wreckage, screaming.

Somewhere under a mountain of rubble, a phone began to ring.

PART II

THE AFTERMATH

CHAPTER 19

THE RESCUE

5:19 P.M., APRIL 27, 2011—TUSCALOOSA, ALABAMA

Engine 7, Rescue 27, be advised, apartment 41 Bravo Rosedale Court, 41 Bravo Rosedale Court. We have a child cut and bleeding from the head severely.

Adam Watley was already on the way to Rosedale when the first call scratched over the radio. His gut had been speaking all day, and he was anxious to get to work. Like most paramedics, he was better at responding than waiting around for a crisis. He had watched this thing barrel into town from his second home, Station No. 7, the southernmost outpost of Fire & Rescue. Now, dressed in full turnout gear, he rode to the scene in the cab of Engine 7, facing backward. Out the window on his left, he could still see the funnel in the distance. It had barely missed his brothers at Station 2, near campus, and was now tearing through Alberta City. Headed northeast toward Birmingham, it was showing no signs of weakening.

Watley, twenty-seven, was part of a well-trained squad. Among the six men on duty at Station 7 was a driver with thirty years of experience and four paramedics, including an ex-marine who had served as a flight nurse during his tour of Iraq. This team had been together for only a few months, but they were as tight as a platoon. They joked that C shift was where they put the misfits who did not belong on A or B shift, and they answered to station names. Hail-ing from Chilton County, the peach capital of Alabama, Watley was known as Peaches.

In his seven years as a paramedic, Watley had seen a lot of things. Even though he had a two-year-old son who hugged his knees when he walked in the door, the prospect of responding to an injured child did not faze him. It was his job. And though he had watched the twister come through, he still expected, for some reason, to be attending to a minor head wound. Maybe some kid had bumped his head on an outdoor AC unit while running around outside, staring up at the sky.

Through his window, facing north, things looked relatively normal. As they neared the scene, the fireman on his right drew in a sharp breath.

"Rosedale's gone."

The truck rolled into the place where Rosedale used to be. What they saw looked less like a neighborhood and more like a landscape bombed into oblivion. His first thought was *Look at all those refrigerators.* They were the only recognizable objects, rising like tombstones from the rubble. The single-story brick buildings, once lined up in neat rows, were now scattered into mounds of boards and bricks. There were no buildings. No street signs. No landmarks. No trees. Gone, all those beautiful trees.

The big white fire truck became a lighthouse in this sea of devastation. People flocked to it, wading across swells of brokenness. They were bleeding, dazed, and covered with mud. Some were screaming. Others silent. The six men scanned the gathering crowd, more people than six men could possibly treat.

The captain grabbed his radio and called in the on-scene report.

> *Rosedale is completely demolished. We've got a lot of walking injured. We've got a lot of people that we are fixin' to try to find. We're gonna need any help you can give us.*

Across the torn landscape, a man staggered up, guarding his arm, which was bleeding badly. Watley moved to help him. Then he caught the eye of Nathan Moore, the ex-marine. Moore nodded subtly at Watley and cut his eyes away from the man.

"Hey—he's walking wounded," Moore said quietly. "Let's go."

Something clicked just then in Watley's mind. Today would not go by the book. No training, no textbook, no experience in his seven years as a full-time EMT could have fully prepared him for a moment like this.

About a hundred yards away, Moore spotted a woman coming toward them, hugging something to her chest. Moore waved her toward Watley.

What's going on? Watley thought. *What is this?*

As the woman drew closer, he saw in her arms a limp and lifeless bundle, tiny arms swinging hopelessly each time she took a step. The mother, in shock, placed her baby in his arms. A baby girl.

Watley looked at the baby and saw no hope. She was not breathing, and she had no pulse. Time slowed as his mind raced through the flow chart of triage. Somewhere in the rubble lay victims who still had a shot at living, but only if help came quickly. His training had taught him the cold math of triage: treat viable patients first. This poor child was not a viable patient. She had almost no chance of living, no matter what he did.

But how can you tell a mother that?

Watley did what he would want another medic to do if the child in his arms were his. He would try his best to bring her back, try until there was no sliver of doubt that nothing more could be done. He lay the baby gently on the back of the stretcher in Rescue 27, a lifesaving truck a little bigger than an ambulance.

As soon as he had laid her down, a man emerged from the crowd and presented a second lifeless baby. She looked younger than two years old. The man was not her father. He did not know her name.

"This come through my window," he said.

"What?" Watley said. "What do you mean?"

And then he understood.

Nothing good can come of this, he thought. *This snowball is headed to hell.*

Time slowed into freeze-frame.

The rescuers looked up from the infants and found themselves crushed by a gathering crowd. The firemen felt hands on them, heard desperate pleas for help. Triage had no meaning in moments like this. They had to help these babies before the world could be made right.

Doc, a fireman paramedic, climbed into the driver's seat of Rescue 27. The mother climbed up front. Watley bent over the infants, quickly checking their vitals, grabbing IVs, and preparing for intubation. He decided to start CPR on the drive across town to the hospital, which should take about seven minutes. Today it would take them forty-five.

As they began to leave, there was a banging on the truck. The back doors opened and Watley squinted into the daylight, his eyes adjusting to the silhouette of a man. His chest and abdomen were gashed and he was losing a lot of blood. In his arms was another tiny nightmare.

Watley moved instinctively to stop the bleeding, but the man swatted him away. The baby in his arms was not moving.

"Are you gonna help my baby?" he said. "Or do I just need to walk to the hospital?"

Watley placed the baby on the stretcher with the others. One, two, three little infants lined up in a row, like dolls, silent and still. The father climbed in and stood in the back of the rescue truck, holding on to the ceiling and bleeding. Watley closed the doors and got to work. As the truck pulled out of Rosedale, he caught a glimpse through the rear windows of the captain holding his radio.

■ ■ ■

The captain watched a third of his man power leave in Rescue 27. The rest of his men were scattered on the scene, searching and digging.

There were four of them left to attend to hundreds, everyone needing help at once. They could feel the crowd simmering, the agitation pushing toward panic. The captain's senses prickled.

One man leaned in aggressively, yelling.

The captain punched him, feeling the crunch of cartilage under his knuckles.

"I got to have some help!" the captain yelled.

Like a spell had been broken, the chemistry of the moment changed.

"What do you need?" the man said soberly. "You have to tell me. Tell me what to do."

"Get as many men as you can and go help these guys," the captain said.

He grabbed his radio and called again for backup.

Rosedale Command to dispatch. We've got several critically injured patients. We're gonna need several ambulances, as many as you can send down here. Also we're gonna need the gas company. We've got an open gas leak.

■ ■ ■

Four miles north, in Alberta City, the firemen of Station 4 emerged from the ruins of their station and stood scanning the landscape, searching for a landmark, a familiar sign of the place they had lived all their lives. All they could see in every direction was an ocean of debris, undulating in petrified waves. They inhaled the heady mix of gas and pine riding a choppy wind. All around them people emerged from crevices, moving in incessant, aimless circles of dreamlike disbelief.

The rescuers took a minute to process the gravity of what had just happened. Then they called in the on-scene report.

Dispatch, Station 4 was hit directly by the tornado. There's no buildings left in Alberta City. Our church is damaged. Our station is damaged. All members here are okay.

Copy, Station 4. Do you need medical assistance?

I don't but there's people screaming everywhere around here . . . We need to get absolutely as much help as we can get.

Their eyes were still adjusting to the new reality, like eyes adjusting to light. Minutes ago they had been four men praying under a mattress in a windowless bathroom. Heavy objects had drummed upon the station walls, first from the east, and then, after the calm, from the west.

It was like a space shuttle was launching directly above.

And then, silence.

They shoved open the door of the bathroom, blinking in bewilderment at the things they could now see. From the bathroom, they could see into the station's back bedroom. Through its sheared walls, they stared up the broken street. The things they should not be able to see stood out in arresting contrast to an impossible expanse of blue. That water tower, a mile or two up the road in the town of Holt, should be hidden by a wall of green. But the trees that had blocked it were somewhere else. All those trees, gone. It was dizzying, this feeling of too much sky, like diving one hundred feet underwater and looking up for the first time into the weight of all that blue.

Many of the houses and apartments, missing entire walls, presented the absurd impression of dollhouses, exposing the incongruously undisturbed contents of the private rooms inside. Beyond the ragged edges of shorn drywall, throw pillows rested on couches. Photo frames sat unmoved upon dressers. Dioramas of disrupted lives, the rooms' naked exposure testified to the fragile impermanence of the structures the residents had trusted to hide and protect them. Concrete and steel had crumbled like illusions.

Station 4 had been built in the 1950s as a bombproof shelter but was now gutted by flying debris. It had done its job and protected its men, but it would have to be torn down. The fire truck inside the engine bay was too damaged to drive. Even if the truck had been operable, they could not have gotten it anywhere through the telephone poles and live wires that lay strewn across the roads.

The firemen gathered armfuls of tools and medical supplies and marched out into the wasteland, not knowing what they would encounter. Right outside the station they found a grandmother and her tiny grandchild, dead, thrown hundreds of feet from their home. They covered the bodies with a sheet and a prayer and noted their location.

They heard a dog scratching under toppled walls, and they dug to free an elderly couple buried in their bathroom. Someone summoned them to the back of a pickup truck, where a woman lay struggling to breathe with a collapsed lung. A man volunteered to drive his truck on four flat tires to get her to the hospital. He made the trip again and again.

■ ■ ■

In Druid City Hospital, patients had opened their eyes to a blizzard of papers fluttering to the ground. The walls were still standing. They were still alive. As the power flickered and the generators kicked on, the room audibly exhaled.

The disaster coordinator, Andrew Lee, began running through the hospital, past caravans of gurneys and flocks of stunned nurses hunkered down in the halls. He met an ER physician doing the same, his white coat flapping like a cape. They ran downstairs, by the cafeteria, past three dogs with tucked tails, cowering on the tile. They burst out the south entrance, looking around wildly, expecting to find destruction.

They saw . . . nothing. The hospital appeared untouched. The only trace of the storm was a scattering of branches on the pavement. The men ran back up to the ER, which faces north, and came out the double doors. They felt sunshine on their faces. One tree limb dangled from a power line, beneath a sky showing patches of blue.

"It looks like we really missed it," the surgeon said.

What they could not see from their side of their building was the wake of destruction a few blocks from the hospital, the scar across the landscape that looked as if it stretched forever. This moment of misinformed hope would soon pass, but for fifteen minutes, the ER remained disturbingly quiet. No calls. No ambulances hauling in victims. The doctors and nurses readied their supplies and braced themselves for an onslaught of the wounded. Where were the patients?

Then the first call came in from an ambulance en route to the hospital. It was Adam Watley, aboard Rescue 27. He asked to speak with a doctor.

"I have three infants in full cardiac arrest," Watley said.

"Three infants?" said the doctor.

"All under the age of eighteen months. Full arrest. We are headed your way."

"What else do you have?"

"I don't know."

■ ■ ■

Engine 2, Engine 4, respond to 85 Cedar Crest. Eighty-five Cedar Crest. We have subjects trapped in a house.

Inside Station 2, on Bryant Drive, the firemen climbed out of Engine 32 and could see the destruction from their doorstep. The tornado had passed within a half mile of the station, and Tuscaloosa's ground zero—Fifteenth Street and McFarland Boulevard—was less than a mile from where they now stood.

"Hey, guys, it's bad," said Lieutenant Marty McElroy. "Time to get to work."

Reeling with adrenaline, they climbed back into the ladder truck and drove two blocks south before they realized that was as far as the roads would allow. So they set out on foot dressed in full turnout gear, carrying axes, chain saws, and Halligan tools. There was no room left in their arms for medical kits, but treating the wounded was, at this point, a secondary concern. Their first priority was freeing the entrapments, the victims buried and pinned beneath the crushing weight of collapsed buildings, their precious time ticking away like the clock on an activated bomb. If the firefighters did not dig these people out quickly, the mission of rescue would very soon give way to the haunting duty of recovery.

The neighborhood of student homes and small cottages two blocks east of the hospital, Cedar Crest, was crawling with people who had impossibly survived a direct hit to the shelled-out houses from which they now emerged. Some of the homes were flattened, and others had been stripped of their outer rooms, leaving only a ragged core. A few, on the outskirts, were battered yet standing. From one of the latter, an elderly lady walked out on her ragged porch and began calling out to the firemen.

"What's wrong, ma'am?" McElroy said. "Is everyone okay?"

"Yes, I'm fine," she said. "I need you to do something."

"What do you need?"

"I need you to put some plastic on my car. The tornado blew my windows out and I don't want the seats to get wet."

"Ma'am," McElroy said, with all the patience he could muster, "we'll be more than happy to do that but right now we have other people to check on. If we got a chance we'll come back."

"When are you going to be back?"

"Just as soon as we can."

As McElroy moved through the hardest-hit streets of Cedar Crest, it was hard to tell where one house ended and the next began. In his thirteen years of riding these streets on calls, he had memorized the details of every neighborhood, the shutters of this house, the colors of that one, but now they had all vanished. He looked around, trying to place himself on a map that had been ripped to pieces.

He followed the sound of someone yelling for help and saw the body of a young white male, college age, draped in the branches of a toppled tree. He guessed that the boy had died instantly. Gently, McElroy took down this boy and laid him on the street. This was someone's son, someone's brother, someone's best friend, someone's lover. It was UA student Scott Atterton covered up with a sheet.

"I got two more behind the house," a medic said.

A group of fraternity brothers came up to the firemen.

"What can we do to help?"

The firemen decided they could use a few more strong arms and took the young men with them as they swept the neighborhood, heaving toppled walls, lifting boards, and digging through mountains of drywall, chasing the muffled voices.

McElroy felt a hand on his shoulder. He looked up and met familiar eyes. It was an off-duty Northport fireman, a friend he had known all his life.

"Hey," the fireman said. "What can I do to help?"

"Hey, man," McElroy said. "Come with me."

■ ■ ■

A few blocks away, a college student woke up beside a chain-link fence outside his apartment. His ears were bleeding, and though the world sounded muffled, he could hear the shrill cry of a baby. Randy Robbins turned toward the cry and saw his neighbor and her baby, alive but battered. The baby's ears were gushing blood.

The image unleashed fragments of memory. The moments leading up to this rushed into focus, like fish surfacing in muddy water.

He remembered the wind knocking his backpack from his shoulder as he walked to his car from class. The sizzle and ding of a microwave pizza. The flurry of texts from his sisters, warning him of the coming storm. He had brushed them off as hysteria.

Robbins recalled closing the windows of his apartment as the trees bent like stems of grass. He remembered the searing pain in his eardrums. A scramble into the closet. The sound of drywall ripping. The rattle and yank of the doorknob in his hands, his tug-of-war with the wind. Being launched, along with the closet door. Sucked into the teeth of the storm.

He remembered being flung around on the ground by a lashing, whipping wind. The sound of hysterical screaming; the disturbing realization that the screams he heard were his own. He remembered raising his head in the lull and seeing a woman lying on her baby. Then the sprint, and the flash of pain in his foot as he threw his body upon them. The sting of flying objects stabbing his back. The belief, in that terrible moment of fury, that they were the last three people alive in this world rapidly dissolving around them.

Lying on his back, concussed and in shock, Robbins felt no pain. But when he slowly stood, he looked down at his body and saw bare skin shredded and bleeding. The tornado had ripped off his jeans and his shirt, had stolen his watch and his glasses. A three-inch shard of wood pierced the tender arch of one foot, and blood was pooling beneath it. A Bic pen was impaled in the flesh of his side. He wrapped his fingers around the pen and winced as he yanked it out.

Through his tender ears, every sound was muted, but he could hear a phone bleating nearby. Glancing around, he stared in disbelief at the phone ringing in his right hand. How had he not lost it?

"Randy?!" his sister said, breathless. "Randy?!"

"Kiki!" he said, a little too loud. "My apartment—it's gone! The baby is bleeding! I lost my glasses! My foot is bleeding bad! There are people stuck! I have to go!"

After crawling under his crushed pickup truck, which had landed in his living room, Robbins limped toward help on the arm of a friend. The only clothes that had not been ripped off were his boxers and the small, silver cross he wore on a simple chain. His foot, still impaled and bleeding, was wrapped in a neighbor's shirt. The man, whose name he did not know, had taken it off his own back. His good foot was tucked in a too-small loafer someone gave him to protect it from debris on the ground. He loaned out his phone, his only possession, to people who had lost theirs.

Robbins and his friend fell into step with an army of walking wounded. In the streets of Tuscaloosa, people shuffled and limped and carried one another to shelter, to the hospital, to a clean spot to sit. They merged with the ranks of instantly homeless, wandering the streets with glassy eyes and trash bags filled with scavenged things, wondering where to go.

As Robbins rode to the hospital in the back of a stranger's truck, he felt blackness bleeding into the edges of consciousness. He asked for a pen. On his forearm, he inked his name and his mother's number, so that if he lost consciousness before reaching the hospital, the nurses would know whom to call.

▪ ▪ ▪

At the hospital, victims came in waves.

The first came on foot and in the backs of pickups. They were rolled in on office chairs, carried in the arms of strong men or on ripped-off doors that served as makeshift stretchers. Throngs shuffled up like zombies. Some were screaming hysterically. Others appeared almost catatonic. They were broken and bleeding, hurt and mourning, experiencing every degree imaginable on the spectrum of human nightmare.

They were assigned to a premade chart with a name that could not be mistaken for real. Unknown Amsterdam. November November. Raja Ed Downtime (that was Randy Robbins). These preposterous names differentiated the 450 fake charts that the hospital staff had created ahead of time. In the golden hour after trauma, every minute makes a difference. By accelerating the intake process for hundreds of patients, the fake charts would save lives.

By the time the first ambulance arrived, the emergency room staff was already attending to fifty or sixty critical patients who had come on foot or in the backs of pickup trucks. That first ambulance was Rescue 27, from which Adam Watley had phoned as his driver navigated the many blocked streets on the way from Rosedale. The disaster coordinator, Andrew Lee, who was receiving patients in front of the ambulance bay, stepped up to Rescue 27's back double doors, painted in a high-visibility red-and-yellow chevron. He opened the doors to an image that would haunt him all his life.

Three dead babies.

On a normal day, the ER would have hemorrhaged resources to save the life of just one child.

Three kids, Lee thought, *you give everything.*

Today that was not possible, because it could have happened only at the great expense of dozens, maybe hundreds of viable patients, parents and children and siblings and lovers whose lives mattered no less, who could still be saved before their golden window closed forever. A female doctor bent over the babies, listening for a pulse. She heard nothing and wept.

At home, Lee had two kids of his own, both under the age of two. Inside him, the RN wrestled with the father. The nurse was trained to make calculated decisions through the unfeeling logic of triage. The father was steeped in emotion, driven by love. Lee knew, as any parent knows, that the death of a child will change someone's world forever. But if he harbored any wavering doubts about what to do for these three dead babies, Watley yanked him quickly back to their unrelenting reality.

"There are hundreds of people lying in the streets," Watley said. "We don't know if they're dead or alive. It's like that all over Tuscaloosa—it's gone."

"What do you mean, gone?" Lee said.

"I could see the hospital from Rosedale."

Lee rolled the babies into a dark, quiet room and covered them with a sheet. Two-year-old Zy'Queria McShan; Christian McNeil, fifteen months; and Ta' Christianna Dixon, eleven months old, were gone.

Someone said there was another storm coming.

CHAPTER 20

THE SILENCE

5:30 P.M., APRIL 27, 2011—STARKVILLE, MISSISSIPPI

Michelle sat on her bed in her dark apartment, fighting waves of panic and fear that broke over her heart in sets. She kept checking her phone, but Danielle had not responded. That was not like her. Michelle kept calling, but the phone rang and rang as she prayed for her sister to answer. The sound of Danielle's voice on the recorded message had, until now, felt comforting.

Michelle had not spoken with her parents yet. Ed and Terri Downs were taking cover in Priceville from the rash of tornadoes pounding north Alabama. The Tuscaloosa storm was raging north toward Birmingham, one of four violent tornadoes on the ground at this moment in the state. An EF3 was passing over Haleyville, with a trajectory that put Priceville in its path about fifty miles away. Ed and Terri Downs had lost power and had fled to a house with a basement. They did not know Tuscaloosa was hit.

In the lonely quiet, Michelle felt a cold heaviness pooling in the pit of her stomach, like ice water drunk too fast. Hope and fear dueled fiercely in her head.

Why hasn't she called?

The phone lines must be down.

What if her house was hit?

Everyone is checking in at once. The lines are overloaded.

What if she's lying somewhere in the street, unconscious?

Maybe she dropped her phone.

What if she's trapped under a house?

Her phone battery might be dead.

What if she's being rushed to the hospital?

She's probably busy helping someone else.

What if she's gone?

After twenty minutes of radio silence, sitting without power in a dark apartment, she could not drown the worry. An emotional storm raged on in her head, a deafening chorus of what-ifs, until she could not bear to wait any longer. She fired off another text to her sister.

5:33 Michelle are you ok?

Alone in the dark with her thoughts, she waited.

■ ■ ■

Danielle and Loryn's roommate, Kelli Rumanek, was still at Gorgas Library, where she had weathered the storm with her boyfriend, Eric Arthur, and a group of students hunkered by the checkout desk. In the dark, a student with a smartphone had read updates aloud as the storm blew by the hospital. That was just a couple of blocks from the house. The comforting weight of her boyfriend's arm on her shoulders felt like an anchor holding Kelli down. In the dim window light she and Eric exchanged worried glances. Danielle and Loryn were at the house, hiding under the stairs. Kelli knew this because she and Danielle had been texting each other all day.

Now neither roommate was answering.

■ ■ ■

Danielle's parents were still dodging their own storms in northern Alabama. Ed and Terri Downs were two of the six hundred thousand Alabamians without power. Around three hundred electrical towers had been blown down, and the Browns Ferry Nuclear Plant, not far from their home in Priceville, had experienced an emergency shutdown.

Ed and Terri Downs had taken refuge at Ed's parents' house, which also had no power. They did not have smartphones, and without them had no way to follow the storms online. Cut off from communication, they were dodging bullets in the dark.

They still did not know about Tuscaloosa.

■ ■ ■

Loryn's mother knew immediately that her daughter was dead. The second the phone went silent, Ashley Mims was seized by a stabbing loss, a visceral emptiness, as if a yawning black hole had opened up in her chest and swallowed the light in her world. It was as if, somewhere in the core of her being, a part of her was gone.

Still clutching her phone, Ashley walked out her front door, stepped off the porch and into the yard. In her mind's eye, she could see Loryn's face painted in clouds, white on white. Raising her arms to the sky, she felt a scream welling up inside.

"Oh, God—*no!*" she screamed at the sky. *"Don't take her!"*

She sank to her knees in the grass.

CHAPTER 21

UNDER SIEGE

5:40 P.M., APRIL 27, 2011—ACROSS ALABAMA

The Tuscaloosa EF4 was still thundering on the ground, tracking toward Alabama's biggest city. Now in sight of the live cameras mounted atop tall buildings in downtown Birmingham, it had grown into a wedge tornado that dwarfed the monster that had swallowed Tuscaloosa.

It was one of four.

Three other violent, long-track tornadoes were ripping through different parts of the state. The storm's fury was building to a crescendo. The radar was blooming with supercells and showing no signs of slowing down. Alabama was under siege by a fast-moving holocaust that lashed the state without mercy or discrimination.

The Hackleburg EF5 had narrowly missed Huntsville, a major metropolitan bastion of aeronautics and engineering—the home of NASA's Marshall Space Flight Center. It would kill thirteen people before it was done, and injure at least fifty others. The Cordova EF4 was petering out on Sand Mountain, fifty miles south of Huntsville, but the supercell would reorganize to bear a new EF5 that would kill thirty-five in northeast Alabama. An EF3 was on the ground in Haleyville, a town of four thousand in northwest Alabama, home of Guthrie's Fried Chicken and the first 911 emergency phone system in the country. A fourth long-track tornado, an EF3, had flattened Sawyerville and Eoline, two rural towns southeast of Tuscaloosa.

The meteorologist Jason Simpson looked closely at this last one. His eyes traced the storm's trajectory, and he saw that it was on track to hit the National Weather Service office in Birmingham, and just beyond it, his home. His wife, Lacey, had canceled her ultrasound appointment because of the weather, and was waiting out the storm there with their dogs. Their home, on the western side of a hill, did not have a basement.

6:16	Jason	get the dogs and go to Darryls right now do not wiat

Lacey Simpson saw the text and did not take any time to question it. She had weathered many storms before, almost always alone while her husband worked. Usually, when she heard a warning, her husband told her not to be alarmed. She grabbed their dogs and ran to the home of a neighbor with a basement. They had to get underground.

■ ■ ■

James Spann continued the warnings as the news desk patched in a call from Tuscaloosa.

"Let's bring in Mayor Walt Maddox," Spann said. "Mayor, everybody wants to know what has happened in your city. So tell us, what happened?"

"Well, right now we're in the incident command center and it appears that the damage is substantial."

"Can you tell us some of the hardest-hit areas?"

"Well, I caution, because these are the first reports and some of this may change, but it appears that the Rosedale community seems to be the hardest hit. We all know that our EMA in the Curry facility has been damaged . . . the East police precinct in Alberta has been damaged."

"How did the Tuscaloosa police headquarters fare? Because it looked like they were awfully close to this thing."

"It was awfully close. They seemed to fare pretty well. The PD is up and operational. The city is operational. We're at full go right now. Hopefully later tonight we'll have a better idea of what has transpired over the last few minutes."

"I've got countless mommies and daddies wondering how their kids are doing. Is there any damage on the campus there?"

"We've heard reports but they haven't been confirmed. One thing I've learned is that in any emergency what you hear in the first thirty minutes you have to caution taking as fact."

"There are no tornadic storms approaching Tuscaloosa from the west. I take that back, let's take a look at this one here. No signs of organization or rotation, so once we get through this last batch, you're going to be okay for about an hour."

"Thank you, James. You saved a lot of lives today."

CHAPTER 22

THE HOUSE

5:45 P.M., APRIL 27, 2011—TUSCALOOSA, ALABAMA

Across the river from Tuscaloosa, in Northport, Kelli Rumanek's mother, Dianne, emerged from her safe place, surprised she still had power and cable, and wondered if the storm had passed. Her landline began ringing. She had nearly gotten rid of it last month but was grateful today she had not. It was Loryn's father, Shannon Brown. He had been dodging other storms at his home in Madison, Alabama, and without power had not known about the Tuscaloosa tornado until friends began calling, worried about Loryn.

"Dianne, I can't get in touch with Loryn," Brown said. "Have you heard from the girls?"

"No, but I know Kelli's okay and she's on her way," Rumanek said. "Don't panic—there's been damage. But the phone lines are down, and no one's able to communicate. I'll just run over there."

"I hate for you to do that."

"No, I don't mind."

The weather in Northport had seemed so uneventful that Rumanek was not too concerned. Communication often fell apart after storms, and this was no exception. She kicked on a pair of flip-flops and got in the car, skirting downtown and campus by taking River Road. Everything at that end of town looked all right. She turned right on Helen Keller Boulevard, passing Baumhower's Restaurant, the labyrinthine sports bar where Loryn waited tables. But as she approached

University Boulevard, the roads were blocked. Not far from where Kelli and Eric had parked, she pulled over and left her car to continue on foot.

The first inkling of dread hit Dianne Rumanek at the corner of Beverly Heights. Was that the Lutheran church? She could hardly recognize it, splayed open as if by a giant ax. She flagged down a student with a backpack walking out of the neighborhood.

"Is everything okay down there?" she asked the kid.

"Everything but the house where the girls lived," he said.

"What?"

"Not the house where the girls lived."

"That's my house!"

■ ■ ■

Silhouetted by the wreckage of a fallen house, Kelli Rumanek blinked in confusion.

Where's my house?

Not a single wall rose from the ruins that filled the bowl where the house once stood. An ancient oak, so big it would have taken two people to hug it, had sliced the house in two. The second story had splintered and collapsed, crushing the first floor beneath it. The low point in the neighborhood was now level with the elbow of road.

"Oh, my God!" Kelli screamed. "They're in there! *They're in there!*"

She just stood there, shaking, crying, barely breathing, until her boyfriend ran up, breathless, and folded her into his arms. Kelli's legs gave out, and as she sank to the ground, Eric Arthur sank with her, guiding her fall, never letting go. He could feel her heart beating within her ribs like the wings of a wounded bird.

"Just breathe," he whispered. "Just breathe. Just breathe."

Eric held her, wishing he could crush out the sadness. As the magnitude of the moment washed over him, small details came into focus. The smoke and the splinters and toppled trees. The scent of pine and sulfur. The dying of the light. Kelli's tears hot on his neck.

On the ground beside him a playing card, ripped at one corner, lay facedown in the dirt. It was just one card, plucked from its deck by the storm and placed there like a message. Keeping one arm around Kelli, he reached down and flipped it over.

Queen of hearts.

He slipped the card in his pocket.

Dianne Rumanek ran up to find her daughter in Eric's arms, kneeling by a mountain of hopelessness.

There's no way, Rumanek thought. *No one in there could have survived.*

■ ■ ■

Loryn's mother, Ashley, kept calling her, but Loryn did not answer. At her knee, her youngest children were scared and crying. "Where's Sissy?" they demanded again and again. "Mama! Where's Sissy?" She pulled herself together, thought, *Who can I call to check on her?* Leah! Loryn's friend who worked with her at nearby Baumhower's.

"Baby, I was talking to Loryn and the phone cut off. I can't get her to answer. Where are you?" Ashley asked. "Are you okay? Are you with her?"

"No ma'am, she's at home. I just talked to her a little while ago. She was at her house."

"There was a boy with her. I think it's Dustin."

"I don't think it's Dustin. I just called him seeing if he'd heard from her. Miss Ashley, it went right over there. I can't get through. It went right over her house!"

"I know, baby," she said softly. "I saw it on TV."

Loryn's friends had been at work at Wings, a few blocks away on Helen Keller Boulevard.

Ashley Mims next tried Dustin, her daughter's good friend.

"Dustin, are you with Loryn? I can't get her to answer."

"No ma'am, but we're fixing to walk over there and we can't get through," he said, beginning to cry. "Miss Ashley, I'm so sorry! I'm so sorry!"

"Dustin, there's somebody with her. There was a guy with her. Who could it be?"

"I don't know, Miss Ashley. Steven's with me, and I've talked to Tribble and Sean, and it's not them."

They ran toward the house, climbing over trees and branches. When they got there, Dustin called her back.

"Miss Ashley, her car's not there," he said. "She must have left."

"No, she didn't leave. She's there."

"But her car's not here. It's not where she parked. I promise you she must have left."

"Dustin, she didn't leave. I'm telling you, she didn't leave."

It had been an hour, but it felt like minutes. Ashley paced the front yard, her kids trailing her, crying, "Mama, what's going on? What's going on?"

In Beverly Heights, Dustin realized he was standing in the wrong driveway. This used to be a vacant lot, and now it had a house on it. They ran around the ruins, yelling Loryn's name. No one answered. When he finally found Loryn's car, he didn't have the strength to call her mother. He called Ashley's husband, DeWayne Mims, instead.

It never dawned on Ashley to call her ex-husband, Loryn's dad, until his name lit up on her phone. Shannon Brown and his wife had been taking shelter from tornadoes passing near his home in Madison, a small town on the outskirts of Huntsville. The power was still out, and he had been unaware that a tornado had struck Tuscaloosa until his phone started ringing relentlessly. Everyone was worried about Loryn.

"I can't get Loryn to answer," Brown told his ex-wife. "Have you heard anything from her?"

"I was on the phone with her, Shannon, and the phone cut off," Ashley said. "I can't get her to answer!"

"She's fine," Shannon said. "She'll be fine. It's just that there's no phone service."

"I'm telling you the phones are fine. I was on the phone with Dustin earlier in her front yard. If that child was alive, I'd be the first person she would call. She would not let me worry for a second."

Shannon knew at that moment Ashley was right.

His father was already loading heavy equipment in Greensboro, about thirty minutes south of Tuscaloosa. A retired air force lieutenant colonel, Jerry Brown owned a tree-trimming service that helped clear the roads after storms. He had talked to Ashley and knew from the reports by Loryn's friends that trees had crushed the house.

As Loryn's Pop-Pop steeled himself for the saddest job of his life, his wife turned to him with tears in her eyes.

"Go get my grandbaby," she said. "Go get her."

CHAPTER 23

CHARLESTON SQUARE

5:55 P.M., APRIL 27, 2011—CHARLESTON SQUARE, TUSCALOOSA

Rescue 21, have a subject at Charleston Square. Are you at Rosedale?

We're en route to the Curry building. Where do you need us to respond to?

Charleston Square. Eight hundred Twenty-Seventh Street.

A young woman woke up somewhere outside her apartment, sprawled on her back, blinking up at the sky. The clouds were painted gray and green and blue and black, the colors swirling and bleeding into one another like a living watercolor painting.

Did that really just happen? she thought. *Am I in a dream?*

Chelsea Thrash did not know how long she had been lying there. As she surfaced into consciousness, the moments leading up to this stuttered through her mind. Sirens sounding and the trees outside the second-story apartment swaying. Stopping by the kitchen to grab a snack. Carrying notes into the bathroom and settling in to study on the linoleum floor. The cool porcelain of bathtub against her arm. A roar that shook the walls. Peeking out of the bathroom and seeing the front door flying off the hinges.

And then: blackness.

Now, lying flat on her back under the curdling clouds, she heard the world go oddly quiet. No cars. No hum of outdoor AC units. No voices. No wind. She wondered whether she had landed somewhere all alone, whether anyone else in the world had survived. She made a move to get up and look around.

Nothing happened.

She tried again.

Nothing.

Her legs would not move. She felt no pain. She felt . . . nothing. Something was terribly, horribly wrong.

Chelsea craned her head around, and it took a second to recognize the trashed inner courtyard of Charleston Square. Minutes ago it had been a lovely place, a giant grassy quad framed by a large two-story square of modest apartments. The centerpiece was a large blue swimming pool set in a lawn crisscrossed by concrete footpaths and shaded by clusters of trees.

Now it resembled those scenes on CNN of some distant, godforsaken corner of the earth where tanks roamed and suicide bombers blew themselves up. A section of the building was gutted, exposing bedrooms and living rooms in varying states of disarray. What was not shelled was utterly obliterated, the shredded remains smeared in an ugly white streak across the green lawn. Boards and drywall bobbed in the pool not far from where she lay. Chelsea could not feel it, and yet underneath her back lay a rock that had shattered her vertebra. Above her, a ragged tree raised its naked branches toward the sky like hands, as if to ask, "Why?"

She looked down to see what was wrong with her legs. Her shoes had vanished and her legs lay passively in the black yoga pants she had pulled on with a T-shirt that morning. Her legs appeared intact, but they felt strangely disconnected. Her brain kept willing them into motion, but they just lay there, aloof and inert, as if they belonged to someone else, someone who could make them move.

Voices began echoing across the courtyard as people dug themselves out of the shelled apartments. She was not alone.

"Help! I'm over here!" Chelsea screamed. "I can't move! *Help me!*"

Her phone was right there, within arm's reach, and she fumbled around for it. She knew the cell towers were probably down, that her call would never go through. But she dialed her mother anyway.

"Hey!" her mother, Kelle, said.

"I'm so sorry, Mom!" Chelsea said. "I lied to you! I'm sorry I lied! I was at the apartment . . . and it's destroyed."

She had told her mother that she was on campus, safe, when she had stayed in her boyfriend's one-bedroom apartment instead, while he went to work on campus. She had not wanted her to worry. She never thought this would happen. Not today. Not like this. And yet here she was.

"What do you mean? Are you okay?" her mother said.

"I can't move my legs! I'm so sorry! I lied, Mom. I'm sorry I lied!"

"You've got to get to the hospital," said Kelle, a surgical nurse who was on her day off. "Your dad and I are on the way."

■ ■ ■

At the far end of Charleston Square, two newlyweds crawled out of their bathroom to find every wall of their student apartment warped, torn, or missing. Water dripped through holes in the ceiling, and through the front door of their second-story apartment they could hear a neighbor screaming and crying. They looked at each other and filled the sinks and tub with whatever water was left in the pipes. Then they opened the door and realized how lucky they were.

Their corner of Charleston Square was the only section of the complex that still retained some semblance of a roof. Looking around them, they took in 360 degrees of chaos. Much of the complex was leveled to the foundation, and the massive oaks that had shaded the courtyard were splintered across the lawn. Muffled screams were coming from beneath great piles of rubble.

Derek and Susan DeBruin closed the door and rummaged through rooms that looked as if they had been hit by a hurricane, gathering first aid kits, headlamps, knee pads, gloves, and water. Derek, a grad student in higher education administration, was grateful he had taken a Wilderness First Responder course just a few months ago, a requirement for his summer job as a rock-climbing guide. He was still wearing his yellow mountaineering boots, which he had pulled on that morning to try out a new pair of crampons—the pointy metal spikes that would allow him to walk across a glacier. He kept the boots on as he and his young wife, Susan, began scrambling across precarious heaps of broken boards spiked with rusty nails.

Someone on the east side of the building was calling for help from the parking lot. Derek climbed over a three-foot wall of debris as Susan ran around it. In the parking lot they found three college students hovering over a figure sprawled on the ground. He ran to them and saw on the ground a blonde woman who looked a year or two younger than Susan, probably a fellow student. Her blue eyes were open but unseeing, pupils dilated, and when he pressed his fingers to her neck he felt her thready pulse slipping away.

Beside him, Susan did not see what her husband saw with a trained and clinical eye, that the extent of this woman's injuries was such that CPR was not possible. She only saw a beautiful young blonde woman, and a shirt that was ripped to pieces.

Derek looked up at the three students, two boys and a girl, standing over him, holding their breath. He had assumed they were the young woman's friends, but they did not know her, and yet they visibly mourned her loss. He asked them to go find him a sheet. He laid it gently over her body. Nicole Mixon, twenty-two, a junior in accounting, was an honor student and a member of the Gamma Phi Beta sorority. She left behind three younger sisters.

Charleston Square was now throbbing with people exhibiting a kaleidoscope of mental states. A hysterical woman emerged from the periphery, crying loudly and uncontrollably. Derek tried to help her, but he could not see an injury or understand what she needed. She kept trying to speak, but her words were strangled by sobs.

A group of college students from across the street came out and offered to help. No official responders had appeared on the scene, and suddenly Derek and Susan found themselves in the unexpected and precarious position of assumed authority. People looked to them for direction. But they were not authorities—they were graduate students and climbing guides. Maybe it was their gear that made them stand out in the crowd. Or maybe it was the way they walked with purpose, as if they knew what to do, and people were drawn to that comfort.

In the inner courtyard, Derek and Susan spotted a small group of men kneeling in the grass by a body. When they drew closer, they saw the body belonged to another college girl. She was lying supine, torso slightly twisted to the left. She was awake and coherent, crying into her mobile phone, apologizing to her mother.

Chelsea Thrash was scared but alert and oriented. Unlike the hysterical woman who appeared uninjured, this girl, though clearly hurt, was remarkably calm. Derek palpated her in a primary exam, noting extensive bruises and lacerations. Mud caked her skin and debris filled her hair, and she was visibly fighting pain. When he checked her spine his fingers found her lower back hemorrhaging badly. She said she could not feel her feet.

Spinal injury, he thought. *We need a backboard and an ambulance.*

It didn't take long to realize that if no responders had yet appeared on the scene, there was no telling when they might arrive, and this woman could not afford to wait. He and Susan could not carry her out alone, over these mountains of debris. They were going to need more strong arms if they were going to get her out.

As if summoned on cue, three strong men walked up. They had come to spread the word that Fire & Rescue was setting up triage at Mayer Electric, their place of employment, just a few blocks away.

"What can we do?" one of the men said.

"We need a backboard," Derek replied. "Something we can use to carry her and keep her stable. A door. A table. Find me something."

One of the men reached into the rubble, flipped a kitchen table upside down, and plucked off the legs as if he were pulling weeds.

Either that table is really cheap, Derek thought, *or you are really strong.*

Derek guided the men through the delicate process of logrolling Chelsea carefully onto her side, taking great care not to twist her spine. They slid the makeshift backboard under her hip and shoulder and rolled her back upon it. Now they needed to make sure she didn't roll off.

"I need pillows, towels, some kind of padding," Derek said.

Derek rolled a towel and wrapped it around Chelsea's neck, stabilizing her cervical spine, then used pillows and linens to pad the gaps between her body and the tabletop. He strapped her body to the table with belts and bath towels torn into long strips. Then eight strangers and neighbors each grabbed an edge of the table and carried her over the debris.

As they crossed the parking lot and neared Tenth Street, a man drove by in a 1970s pickup truck with his wife and two children riding shotgun. Two older kids were sitting in the bed of the truck, which was loaded with every possession the family had salvaged from their home.

"Do y'all need a ride?" the man asked.

"We don't need a ride," Derek said, "but she does."

Without question, the man unloaded the back of his pickup truck and dumped his things in the street. The men gingerly slid Chelsea and the table over the rusty tailgate and secured her in the back.

"I have room for two'a you guys," the man said.

Two men from Mayer Electric climbed in and directed the truck to their parking lot, where the ambulances were shuttling load after load of people to the hospital.

Derek and Susan had turned and started back into Charleston Square when two students approached them in the parking lot, clutching an infant.

"We just found this baby in the rubble. It's totally fine."

■ ■ ■

The responders of Rescue 27 set up a makeshift morgue in the back of Mayer Electric, because people kept bringing them bodies. There was nothing they could do but set them aside and pull a dirty sheet over them as they turned their efforts back to the living. The dead came to them pitifully, on tables, in the arms of family, one in a dirty rolled-up carpet.

By now they knew that the Curry building, their Emergency Operations Center, had been destroyed, and with it most of the emergency supplies they needed to work through this. Mass casualty trailers with backboards and stretchers, C-collars and bandages, were now buried or swept away. FEMA disaster trailers with medical supplies, blankets, and water were crumpled up and discarded by the wind. The tools they needed for digging and prying—gone.

They improvised, ripping T-shirts to make tourniquets, fashioning splints from scavenged two-by-fours. They found a pickup truck with keys dangling in the ignition. It had blown-out windows and four flat tires, but it served as a makeshift ambulance.

Rescue 27 had run out of medical supplies long ago. Its compartments were completely bare, not a single bandage left. Now it became a shuttle bus, carrying loads of the walking wounded to the hospital. Adam Watley and his crew packed them in like cordwood—ten, twelve, fourteen at a time. This was not patient care. It was hauling live bodies. The rescuers had long since given up on operating by the book. The book had no chapter about days like this.

As Watley returned to Mayer Electric for another busload, his next patient arrived on a table, numb and motionless from the waist down. Chelsea Thrash looked at him lucidly, her blue eyes brimming with pain, and he saw in those eyes a calm that gave him the first hope all day. There was nothing left on the truck with which to treat her, but if he could give her one thing, it was time. He turned to the driver.

"Let's run this hot!"

The lights flashed and the sirens wailed as Rescue 27 sped to the hospital, this time hauling only one patient.

This one, Watley thought, *just might make it.*

CHAPTER 24

BEVERLY HEIGHTS

7:00 P.M., APRIL 27, 2011—PRICEVILLE, ALABAMA

Fixing supper in her kitchen, Will's mother looked up and turned to her husband, Darrell.

"It's not like Will not to call me," she said. "Something's wrong."

Jean Stevens had dialed her son's number again and again but kept getting that unfamiliar beeping. She had assumed that the lines were down, but now she was starting to worry.

She turned on the TV, to newscasters talking feverishly. There were three big ones on the ground in Alabama right now. The biggest one of the day, an EF5, was in the northeastern corner of the state, claiming twenty-five lives. Between shots of a radar showing multiple storms, the news was flashing scenes that looked as if they came out of a horror film.

That's Tuscaloosa? She felt an icy hand squeezing her heart.

Will had gone over to Danielle's house, that much she knew. They decided to call Danielle's parents but did not have the number. What was Mr. Downs's first name? They couldn't remember, so Jean dug through last week's mail to find Michelle's wedding invitation.

"Have you talked to Danielle?" Darrell asked Ed Downs.

"No, we haven't talked to her today," he said. "But her landlady called and said there had been damage to the house."

Jean and Darrell felt a surge of panic. They got in the Tahoe with Will's eighteen-year-old sister, Taylor, and hoped they could make the two-hour drive to Tuscaloosa on a quarter tank of gas.

As they sped down the interstate, Darrell dialed Will's best friend, Rand Hutchinson. They had played ball together since fifth grade, and Rand lived across town from Will in Tuscaloosa.

"Hey, man," Darrell said. "Have you talked to Will?"

"No, I haven't talked to him. But I'll see if I can get ahold of him," Rand said. "His apartment was nowhere near the storm. He'll be fine."

"I got word Will wasn't at his apartment," Darrell said. "He went to Danielle's."

"I don't know where that is. Do you have an address?"

"Thirty-one Beverly Heights."

Rand hung up the phone and pulled up the map on Google.

Gosh, that's a lot closer than I thought.

He texted Chase Martin, a mutual friend who had played football with them at Priceville High.

"Swing by here," Chase said. "I'll ride with you."

Nearly every street was blocked. They made their way down McFarland toward Fifteenth, staring in awe at the wake of this massive force, noticing puzzling details. A whole wall had been rent from the gas station at the corner of Fifteenth and McFarland, but there sat an undisturbed shelf of food, every bag of chips in place. How could that even be possible?

Like many others, Will's friends found a way to circumnavigate the city, passing busted stoplights, dangling wires, cops and fire trucks driving every which way. Near the church, the trees blocked their path, so they parked in a ditch and walked in.

Police stopped them at the entrance to the neighborhood. They were not letting anyone in. Rand began to pace and worry and wonder. Fear of the unknown roiled in his gut. Rand and Chase leaned against the truck, thinking of ways to get to the house. Out of nowhere, a stranger wielding a giant chain saw ambled up to them.

"I overheard you talking to the police," the man said. "Carry this chain saw and tell them you're going back there with the tree service to clear the roads."

The stranger nodded at the logo on Rand's shirt: ACE TREE SERVICE. His buddy's company. It was either dumb luck or providence that he had happened to pull that one on today.

"Thanks, man," Rand said, accepting the offer. It had never occurred to him that angels carried chain saws.

Rand and Chase walked into the neighborhood unquestioned. As they hunted for 31 Beverly Heights, they grew more and more disoriented, looking for points of reference that no longer existed. There were no street signs, and in some places it appeared there were no streets.

They spotted a track hoe pulling debris off a house.

"I'm trying to find 31 Beverly Heights," he told the operator. "I've got a good friend there. I'm trying to find him."

"I don't know," the man on the track hoe said. "There's a possibility there are three people in this house."

"Okay," Rand said. "I'm going to look around."

He walked up to the end of the driveway and noticed, hidden by the branches of a fallen tree, a mailbox without a number. He swung open the metal door and looked inside. The sticker said: 31.

His insides sank.

No. It can't be. This house is destroyed. Maybe it's not really them. Maybe there's a chance. His truck's not here.

Just as that glimmer of hope crossed his mind, the man from the track hoe walked up.

"Hey, man, I found your buddy's truck," he said. "It's parked over on the side of the road."

He had walked right by it, hidden by fallen trees. His phone rang and a knife twisted in his gut. It was Darrell. His best friend's father. Who did not know. Who could still hope, for a few more precious minutes, that his son was still alive.

If I answer this phone, what am I supposed to say?

He let it ring.

■ ■ ■

Michelle, distraught, called her father to see whether anyone had heard from Danielle. He had not. He had warned the girls to take shelter as he watched the two nasty-looking supercells spiral across the radar around 4:07—one headed for Starkville, the other for Tuscaloosa. Now he consoled his youngest daughter with the reasonable likelihood that Danielle was not able to get in touch because cell towers across the state were blown down.

Michelle dialed her sister's number again. At first the tinny song of Danielle's ringback tone—"Don't Stop Believin'," a favorite '80s song by Journey—sounded almost hopeful. But eventually her calls went straight to voice mail. Without Internet access, she felt starved for information, so she called her uncle in Florida.

"I can't see anything—we don't have power. Mom and Dad don't have power. Danielle's not answering. Can you look?"

"I'm sure she's fine," he said, trying to calm her. "She was in a safe place."

Michelle then called Cheryl Singleton, a cousin of theirs in Shalimar, Florida. Cheryl posted a message on Danielle's Facebook wall, hoping that a friend would see it and give them some details.

6:50	Cheryl	Ok sweetie, please please call somebody, the family is worried bout you, we have all heard of the tornadoes in Tuscaloosa and nobody can get ahold of you. Call us please . . . love you!

After work, Clay arrived at Michelle's apartment to check on her.

"Let's just get on the road," she begged Clay. "Let's go find her."

As a meteorology student, Clay knew that this was not a good idea.

"If she was hit, we don't need to be in the way," Clay said. "There are all sorts of people out there to help them, and we don't need to be in their way."

They agreed to drive to Tuscaloosa at first light. They downloaded a photo from Facebook and created a missing-person flyer. Next to her photo, Clay carefully wrote Danielle's name, height, age, and eye color with a marker. They would tack them up on telephone poles if that's what it took to find her.

Michelle did not want to be alone, so Clay took her to his apartment. His power was out, too, and the candlelight flickered upon the faces of people who would not normally be at Clay's place. Michelle struggled with the cognitive dissonance of staying here, doing nothing, in this warm, safe place, while her sister was somewhere out there alone in the dark.

They were standing in the kitchen when Clay's phone rang. It was Michelle's father. The kitchen grew silent as everyone cleared out, giving them space.

"Hey, Mr. Downs. Have you heard anything?"

"I just got a call from Kelli's mother," Ed Downs said. He paused a long time. He was calm, but Clay heard his future father-in-law cracking. "They just started digging through the rubble."

Michelle read Clay's face and came apart. He hung up and repeated what her father had just said. They sat on the kitchen floor for a long time. Michelle imagined the worst. She felt the ground truth, the ice water pooling in her stomach once again. Clay held her. He searched for words that didn't feel hollow, something that could bring her comfort that didn't feel like a lie.

"No matter what, she's going to be okay," Clay said. "If she's here or if she's gone—she'll be okay."

■ ■ ■

Dusk dropped like a curtain on Beverly Heights. The moon had not yet risen, and through the black-velvet darkness, lights that once had been hidden by trees now winked from distant hills. Chain saws growled and generators roared, yet underneath the surface noise prevailed an empty silence. Without the enclosure of trees, the world seemed wide and lonely.

Kelli Rumanek had been calling her roommates' phones, hoping the ringing would help the rescuers find them. Now she sat in the street, numb with shock, watching firemen swarm over the house, their yellow bunkers glowing like bees against the abstract canvas of devastation. Eric was glued to her side and her mother was on the phone.

Rob Rumanek, her older brother, had joined them at the house, which had once been his house, the backdrop of his college years. Rob stepped back and surveyed the car bumpers protruding from beneath felled trees, hidden by sprays of branches. That was when he noticed a third vehicle, a beige truck no one recognized. Dianne Rumanek realized with horror that a third person, unknown, lay under her house. She had been bracing herself to call two sets of parents and deliver the worst news of their lives. She had no idea who this third person could be. She fought another wave of vicarious nausea on behalf of this new set of faceless parents, who would soon have to grasp the unthinkable.

The rescuers' headlamps bobbed through the dark as they canvassed the house, guiding the driver of the track hoe that rolled over the debris on tanklike treads. On the end of a giant mechanical arm, a clawlike bucket gingerly plucked off layers of walls and roof. The digging was slow and laborious. Phantom shadows danced in the headlights of parked vehicles casting their brights upon the house. As one of the walls was lifted, Rob Rumanek glimpsed something that his sister should not see.

"Mom, they're dead," he whispered fiercely. "You need to get Kelli out of here. She doesn't need to see this."

Dianne saw it and agreed.

"I can't leave!" Kelli protested. "I can't leave!"

"I'm a nurse, and I'm stronger than you," Rob told her. "I can help them. I'm not leaving until they come out."

Kelli's boyfriend and her mother guided her out by the pale light of their phones. Rob, an outline of black on black, stood under the moonless sky.

In the dark, peeking out of the rubble, was a single, shoeless foot.

CHAPTER 25

TWILIGHT

7:00 P.M., APRIL 27, 2011—ACROSS ALABAMA

The storm was far from over. It was twilight now, and the chasers had abandoned the roads. Chasing at night was dangerous and pointless, and filming it was impossible; even if they were able to catch a tornado, they would not be able to see it until it was perilously close. Across the state, rescuers looked over their shoulders for the next one. Damage reports were fragmented, contaminated with the rumors and misinformation that infect communications during the first twenty-four hours of a crisis.

"The reports are very troubling," Spann said on TV. "The bottom line is, we don't know how many people have died," he said. "We don't know how many people have been injured at this phase. It takes the first light of day the next day to see the severity of this whole thing."

Even as Tuscaloosa tried to save itself, the atmosphere above Dixie Alley continued to convulse. Impossibly, the Tuscaloosa tornado had strengthened as it left the town, bringing down a steel train trestle spanning Hurricane Creek, ripping thirty-four-ton steel trusses from their concrete anchors and flinging them up the hill. It had flattened tens of thousands of trees and charged through a coal yard, where it derailed twenty-nine of thirty-one coal hoppers poised on the railway. People saw a thirty-five-ton coal car lofted and heaved nearly four hundred feet. The Tuscaloosa storm widened as it crossed I-65 and approached Birmingham's financial district, where workers had watched through the glass of the high-rise towers as it approached. It had grown to a mile and a half wide.

The monster tornado missed downtown Birmingham by less than four miles. But as it passed through the northwestern outskirts of the city, it left whole communities mirroring the scenes from Tuscaloosa. These communities—Pleasant Grove, Concord, McDonald Chapel—had already witnessed the terror of previous storms: an F4 that killed twenty-five people in 1956; an F5 that killed twenty-two in 1977; and another F5 that killed thirty-two in 1988. This EF4 would bring them to their knees all over again.

But a few miles northeast of the city, eighty miles from where it began, the Tuscaloosa tornado mysteriously faded out. The town of Center Point was spared. This single tornado killed sixty-five and injured more than fifteen hundred. The villain of the outbreak, the tornado upon which the national media would focus it overshadowed all the rest. But it was just one of sixty-two tornadoes that would pummel the state on this record day. It was not the largest tornado of the day. It was not the most violent. Nor was it the most deadly. But it had hit the largest population center affected by this outbreak, and for that, it would be the one that took root in collective memory. But many people—even those in storm-struck areas—would somehow lose sight of that tornado's context within a greater outbreak. Before the night was done, eighteen more would follow. Including four more its size, or bigger.

Now, at 7:00 p.m., ten miles after the Tuscaloosa tornado dissipated, its mother supercell regained its strength and spawned a deadly twin. A second tornado grew even more rapidly than the first into an EF4 with 190-mile-per-hour winds and a funnel that lurched toward Georgia, trampling the chain of small Alabama communities that lay in its path—Argo, Shoal Creek, Ohatchee, Forney. In Shoal Creek, it killed a man who left behind ten children and a wife. In one house, a couple hid with their sixteen-year-old daughter as the roof popped off and bricks came swirling around and around.

■ ■ ■

Families who have lived through tornado season for generations have passed down many folk beliefs about twisters. Some of them are even true.

A lot of the dangerously inaccurate wives' tales concern beliefs about geography. Many people believe that tornadoes will never cross a mountain, that "they bounce around in the valley like a pinball." Others say they will not cross certain rivers, or hit big cities. Some swear they follow the interstate.

If only tornadoes were so discerning. The strong and violent ones tower tens of thousands of feet in the air. Topography may influence the likelihood of tornadoes forming in certain locations, but once one has formed and grown into a thirty-thousand-foot giant, minor topographical variations could not possibly change its path. Tornadoes have climbed mountains, danced across lakes as waterspouts, and pummeled great cities.

People believe that tornadoes always follow the same routes, year after year, and decade after decade, as if following a highway or a valley, or both. And sometimes they do, but not for the reasons people believe. Tornadoes do appear to follow certain mountains, such as the Appalachians, and certain interstates, including I-20/59 between Tuscaloosa and Birmingham. But as with the old Statistics 101 example of ice cream sales and drownings increasing every summer, it would be incorrect to assume a causal relationship. Tornadoes typically travel northeast—the direction of most weather—and that is the same direction these mountains and that interstate also happen to run.

People claim that tornadoes "skip," when in fact they merely weaken and strengthen (no one knows why). They believe they move erratically, but tornadoes generally move steadily northeast, which is why most maps of tornado tracks look like parallel scratch marks. They rarely veer south or west. One notable exception is the El Reno, Oklahoma, EF5 tornado that killed the scientific storm chaser Tim Samaras and his son on May 31, 2013. Samaras, a researcher attempting to place probes in its path to measure the inner workings of tornadoes, fled south to escape the path of the oncoming tornado, a 2.6-mile-wide monster, the widest ever recorded. It made an unusual U-shape dip southeast that put Samaras and his son right in harm's way.

Many say you should open the windows in a house to equalize the pressure, let the wind flow through. Not true—most homes have enough air leaks to do that, and the force of the wind is what destroys a house, not unequalized pressure. "Don't worry about equalizing the pressure," instructs a NOAA treatise on tornado myths. "The roof ripping off and the pickup truck smashing through the front wall will equalize the pressure for you."

They also say you should hide in the southwest corner of your basement, because the house will fall northeast. But houses collapse—from falling trees, cars, or debris—and do not necessarily collapse in any given direction. The best place is under a stairwell, in a tiny, innermost room such as a closet, or under a sturdy table or workbench in the basement.

A great number of highly educated people believe that tornadoes do not occur where they live. Unless they live in Antarctica, they are all wrong. "This comforting myth can kill you," wrote the meteorologist Chuck Doswell. "Tornadoes have been observed on every continent and in every American state at every hour of the day and in every month of the year."

Across Alabama, people reacted—or did not—based on what they believed. For some, it made the difference between life and death. For others, it was a matter of luck.

■ ■ ■

7:50 P.M., APRIL 27, 2011—NATIONAL WEATHER SERVICE, BIRMINGHAM OFFICE

The Birmingham office of the National Weather Service found themselves in the path of a storm. The small government office had been running wide open, on all cylinders, since 3:00 a.m. NWS Meteorologist in Charge Jim Stefkovich had never seen his staff working with such focused intensity as he had today. They had issued nearly fifty warnings so far, and the next one would place the polygon—the projected path of the supercell—directly over their office.

In a rare step away from the radar, the staff of the National Weather Service left their stations and filed into the office safe room. A concrete-reinforced box designed to withstand violent weather, it was also the break room, with a fridge, coffeemakers, and a small plastic lunch table. The heavy metal storm door swung shut with an ominous boom, and someone latched it. On the other side of the door, the forecast room sat silent and empty, radars flickering unwatched. Their colleagues in the Atlanta office had taken over the reins.

The fiftieth tornado of the day, an EF5, was moving through the northeastern part of the state, destroying two hundred homes and claiming thirty-two more lives in and around the small town of Rainsville. Its path, thirty-four miles long, was one of the shorter of the long-track paths, but it left an astounding wake that revealed the mysteriously acute selectivity of tornadoes. Foundations wiped clean of all debris were found within eighty feet of trees that had kept their leaves. A school bus was thrown and shucked from its chassis. At one home, an eight-hundred-pound safe, bolted to the foundation, was ripped free and thrown two hundred yards, its locked door blown open by the magnificent winds.

Meanwhile, tornado number 51, the twin of the Tuscaloosa storm, was billowing through the blue twilight above Ohatchee, coming over black hills like smoke rising. More than a mile wide, it stayed on the ground for seventy-one miles, killing twenty-two and injuring at least eighty-one.

It approached Piedmont, Alabama, a part of the state that has a long history of being unlucky. In its path lay a church that had seen far more than its fair share of sorrow.

"Anybody near the Goshen United Methodist Church, be in a safe place," Spann said. "Anybody affected by that 1994 Palm Sunday tornado, be in a safe place—*now!*"

■ ■ ■

The Palm Sunday tornado was one of the most tragically memorable storms ever to strike Alabama. Twenty-nine tornadoes had torn through five states on March 27, 1994, but it was the one most people remember because it struck a church during Palm Sunday services.

Goshen United Methodist Church sat on a rural road in Piedmont County, a redbrick sanctuary with around a dozen wooden pews and a tall, white steeple pointing skyward like a compass needle. There was no sermon that day, because it was the day of the children's play, a Palm Sunday drama about the Passion of Christ. The children walked around the pews waving palm branches in a gesture of welcome. The church was packed for the special performance.

"Have any of you seen this many children in church on a Sunday morning?" Pastor Kelly Clem asked the congregation. Two of them were hers.

There were 142 people at Goshen that day, as many as the church would hold. It was rainy, and someone was meeting people in the parking lot with umbrellas and walking them in.

The man playing Jesus was about to come out with the cross. His crown was made of real thorns and the pastor warned him to be careful, they could cut. The power went out and the lights went dark, and the children sang louder through the thunder and rain. The drama onstage was so captivating that it kept the darkness in the window at bay.

Then a window broke and the peace was shattered. People ducked, screamed, and ran as the winds tore into their church. The pastor ran toward her four-year-old daughter, Hannah, and saw her running toward her, hand in hand with a friend. In an instant, everyone flew in different directions. A boy looked up and saw a black cloud with cars and pieces of houses hurtling inside it. The white steeple was sucked off the roof. The wooden pews were ripped up and thrown. It knocked children out of their Easter shoes.

Something struck the pastor in the head and she fell, hitting her shoulder and breaking her arm. She was the first to stand up and behold her church transformed into a battlefield. Her altar was buried under a mountain of bricks, her people covered in dust. She could not tell the living from the dead, and as she looked up at where the roof should be, there was nothing left but sky. She prayed the deepest prayer she had ever prayed in her life:

Help!

She found her four-year-old daughter unconscious under a pew.

"Mama's right here," she said, patting her tenderly.

A rescue worker came and took Hannah away. The pastor did not know whether her child was alive or dead. And not knowing gave her the presence of mind to continue being a pastor. She looked down and saw her dirty robe and remembered it was her duty to shepherd her flock through this valley of death.

Twenty people died in the church that day. Six of the dead were children. One of them was Hannah.

It was hard to see this and not question God.

"This might shake people's faith for a long time," the minister said as she mourned her daughter's death. "But having your faith shaken is not the same as losing it."

The believers of Goshen United Methodist picked up the pieces of their broken church, leaned on one another when they felt their faith slip, and rebuilt their sanctuary with the help of donations from all around the world. When they opened the doors of their brand-new church, they invited James Spann to the pulpit as their first guest speaker.

"If you're looking for a theological explanation as to why this happened, I'm not your guy," Spann told them. "I'm just here to love on you and encourage you."

The burning question in everyone's heart was *Why?*

"You've got the wrong question," he said. "It's not '*Why?*' because you will never get an answer at this time and place. It's '*What?*' What can we learn from this? How should we respond? What can we do to take this and turn it into something positive? It's biblical, when something good comes out of bad things."

■ ■ ■

At 8:12 p.m., the fifty-sixth tornado of the day, an EF4, tore up the beautiful lake houses of Lake Martin, taking seven more people from this world and injuring thirty more. After forty-four miles, it came to an end at 9:09 p.m. This is how the superstorm ended in Alabama. But it continued its rampage northeast.

CHAPTER 26

THE SEARCH

7:44 P.M., APRIL 27, 2011—FD STATION 1, TUSCALOOSA, ALABAMA

Alberta Command, we just had a report that in Beverly Heights, we're trying to get a better location, that there are two 1089s at that location. Can you advise me how you want to handle that? Or do we want to send the PD unit?

Rescue 23 to Alberta Command. Hey, we're right here close to Beverly Heights. We're gonna swing in there and check it out. I've got seven men with me.

A volunteer with a chain saw, Joe Chastine marched into Beverly Heights beside the six men of Rescue 23. To him, these firemen looked as if they belonged on some calendar. He did not look like them, but he had worked as a paramedic thirty years ago, and now he swung hammers, building houses with tools they might need at a time like this. He had found his way to Battalion 4, asking if they could use a good man with a chain saw and a truck full of hardware. And of course that was just what they needed. Much of the equipment they needed to dig for survivors was out riding around on other trucks, or buried under the ruins of the Emergency Management Agency. The battalion chief shook Chastine's hand and sent him along with Rescue 23 on a call to Beverly Heights.

Chastine was not sure whether it was instinct or providence that had led him that morning to buy a chain saw he could not afford. The five-thousand-dollar insurance check he had in his pocket was meant to fix his roof, which had been damaged by the April 15 tornado. He expected his wife to give him grief about buying a thousand-dollar chain saw. And rightfully so. But if it could help save a life, it was worth the money and the grief.

Chastine now lugged his chain saw into a neighborhood choked with fallen trees. Some of the trunks were so big around that the thirty-six-inch saw could not clear them in one swipe. In the distance, another volunteer with a backhoe was clearing the roads, making a path for the rescuers. The man was Loryn's grandfather.

■ ■ ■

7:50 P.M.—WETUMPKA, ALABAMA

Ashley Mims's house flooded with family and friends from church, who swept in like a tidal surge of love—cooking, cleaning, and fussing over the children. Ashley and her husband hurriedly packed their overnight bags for a trip to Tuscaloosa. They were eager to leave, but the weather had made its way east by now and they would have to drive west, straight into its teeth.

On TV, James Spann called out the name of their town.

Wetumpka was under a tornado warning when they pulled out of the driveway. Ashley stared out of the passenger window, past raindrops that danced along the glass and glittered in the headlights of passing cars. On Highway 82, MONTGOMERY FIRE & RESCUE trucks zoomed past them at an urgent clip, headed west toward Tuscaloosa.

Go get my baby, Ashley thought. *Go get Loryn.*

Down the road from Ashley's house, in the neighboring town of Eclectic, four died. A twenty-three-year-old mother of two was thrown a hundred feet from where her home had been. Her five-year-old niece was tossed across the road. In the same trailer park the sixty-seven-year-old woman who drove the school bus for Elmore County held her grown daughter in their trailer. Their bodies, still clutching each other in death, were found fifty yards away.

■ ■ ■

8:04 P.M.—BEVERLY HEIGHTS, TUSCALOOSA, ALABAMA

We're at the house in Beverly Heights. We got one fatality and two unaccounted for. It's totally collapsed. If we can get the TRT rescue over here to Beverly Heights, we're gonna need the camera off of that truck.

It was night now, and the moon had not yet risen, so the Technical Rescue Team could see only what the pale ellipses of their headlamps could illuminate. Jagged edges protruded from dark shadows, and the surroundings were cast in black and white, as if color itself had been sucked away.

The men made out the silhouette of a massive root ball. The ancient oak attached to it had been dropped on the two-story house like a sledgehammer. The walls had fallen in, and the two-story home pancaked under the impact. Under thick layers of shingles, beams, and drywall, the lonely foot protruded. There was only one way to get to it, and that was to go in from the top down.

They dug down through the layers, cutting and prying, descending like cavers through sedimentary layers of roof, wall, and floor. A responder crawled into the excavated cavity, where he could hear the muffled sound of a mobile phone. It was not an ordinary ring but a country song. He did not listen to country music much, but the radio stations in Tuscaloosa mixed in a little pop-country, and he recognized it. As the tragic refrain played over and over in the dark, he knew without wondering that the caller on the other end of the line was somebody's mother.

I'd be doing the very same thing, he thought.

Steve Stewart had a daughter at the university, the same age as the girl he was digging for. This moment stuck in his heart like a splinter that would never dislodge itself, one of the sharpest details among many blurry memories of that day.

It could have been her. That parent could have been me.

On the other end of the line was Ashley Mims. When other people called, Loryn's phone played Beyoncé. But when her mama called, it played a bittersweet ballad by Miranda Lambert.

> *I thought if I could touch this place or feel it*
> *This brokenness inside me might start healin' . . .*
> *Out here it's like I'm someone else*
> *I thought that maybe I could find myself*
> *If I could just come in I swear I'll leave*
> *Won't take nothin' but a memory*
> *From the house*
> *That built me*

A woman's voice sang wistfully into the dark.

The rescuer heard the voice, and it guided him.

■ ■ ■

Will's family pulled into Tuscaloosa just as the fuel light went on in the Tahoe. They had seen no lights from the interstate since Bessemer, and now in the middle of McFarland Boulevard the blue lights of a police car stabbed through the dark. Darrell braked and rolled down the window. The officer tried to turn him back.

"We're going," Darrell said in a voice that no reasonable man could contest. "We're trying to find our child."

The cop waved him through.

They crept along McFarland, able to see only what their headlights illuminated in front of them. The farther they went, the more littered the street was with dirt and branches and what looked like torn bits of paper. They drove in silence. Words felt superfluous. They were all feeling the same thing.

At Druid City Hospital, they entered a vortex of fragmented information. They asked whether they had registered William Chance Stevens, but nurses with shell-shocked eyes explained that the incoming flood of patients had been assigned charts with fake names to expedite their intake. The staff had prepared 450 of them in advance, as part of their disaster plan. They ran out of charts in two hours.

Just blocks away, at 31 Beverly Heights, Will's friends waited. How long had they been there? Four hours, maybe. They had lost all sense of time. In the place of time was the ebb and flow of emotions: devastating cycles of grief and numbness. Now the reality of it was setting in as they watched the rescuers peeling back walls.

A great mechanical arm was combing away the debris, layer by layer. Phantoms danced in the shadows.

"We need everyone who is not a state employee to back away."

In a circle of spotlight, the final layers of wall and floor were slowly lifted. The rescuers heaved a toppled refrigerator and found what they had been searching for.

The three bodies were huddled together in a tangle of blankets and pillows. Will had thrown himself upon the girls, shielding them, as the house came crashing down. They had done everything right. But when the giant oak sliced through the house, not a single wall stood. They did not have a chance.

The rescuers gently pried them apart.

From the road, Rand and Chase watched a tall and lanky boy being carried over the ruins in a sheet, held at the edges like a hammock. They laid the body gently on a driveway a discreet distance from the road. A police investigator looked up, walked over to Rand and Chase, and sat down.

"Gentlemen," homicide investigator Terry Carroll said softly. "I understand you're friends with the deceased."

Rand swallowed and looked at the ground. *Wow. He said deceased.*

"We cannot one hundred percent identify these bodies. They don't have IDs."

Rand looked up. The investigator met his eyes with a square and heavy look.

"I want to ask you a serious question," he said. "Would you be willing to ID these bodies?"

Rand looked at Chase. Chase looked at Rand.

"Yeah," Rand said slowly. "I just want answers."

The investigator held out his digital camera.

It did not look at all like Will. But Rand saw the Priceville *P* on the front of his T-shirt and knew then his best friend was gone. It was the darkest moment of his life.

"Yeah, that's William Chance Stevens," Rand said. "Birthday December twenty-third, 1988. That's my buddy."

Rand sat in the street and put his head in his hands, crying as if he had not cried in years, squalling like a baby. Around him, the chain saws, the generators droned on, oblivious to his loss.

"Is this real, Chase? Is that really Will?"

"Yeah," Chase said. "That's Will."

Once he dried up, Rand spent a long while thinking. How was he going to tell Darrell? How do you call your best friend's dad and tell him his son is dead? There are no right words for times like this. Rand paced for twenty minutes in front of the house, mustering the courage. Finally, he dialed Darrell's number.

"Hey, Darrell," he said hoarsely. "Where are you?"

"Drivin.' "

"I think I found Will. He didn't make it."

"How do you know?" Darrell's voice was clipped.

How do you answer that? Rand took in a shaky breath.

"I saw him."

"Do you know it's him?" He was trying to hold it together in front of his wife and daughter. "A hundred percent?"

"Yes, Darrell. I know it's him. I identified him for the police officer," Rand said. "I will not leave this spot until you get here."

■ ■ ■

Loryn's father, Shannon Brown, arrived just in time to see his daughter pulled out of the house. She was the last one out. That was just like Loryn, he thought. He could almost hear her voice:

Daddy, I'm not coming out till you get here.

The investigator held out his camera.

"Yeah," Shannon said. "That's my child."

The pixels of the tiny screen shaped the awful, inescapable truth.

There she was, the girl who had changed his world as soon as she had entered it, squirming and squalling in his giant arms, twenty-one years and thirty-nine days ago. There was the toddler who cheered him on from the sidelines of Alabama football games, her pigtails in bows, crimson skirt flouncing. There was the little girl who walked on his back in bare feet after practice, her tiny toes easing the knots in his shoulders. He saw the growing girl who helped him press his hands into the cement in front of Denny Chimes, the Alabama football walk of fame. The girl who returned to that spot as a young woman in a houndstooth coat, kneeling for a photo beside her daddy's name. He saw the young lady who posed for a picture at Disney World with Jessie, the redheaded cowgirl from *Toy Story*, after whom she named the sprightly mare she loved to race around barrels in the yard. He saw the twenty-one-year-old college student who slept in his number 75 football jersey and wore it with a skirt to football games. He saw the young woman who should be walking across the Quad to class at the University of Alabama this fall.

The defining moments of Loryn's past, present, and future all swirled together and slipped through his hands like water. Shannon Brown could not hold back a grief so vast that it seemed to fill the sky. The men working in Beverly Heights paused as they heard it echoing through the black night, the sound of a father's loss.

■ ■ ■

A block away, just outside the neighborhood, Darrell Stevens got out of the car. His wife, Jean, her eyes red and raw, stayed in the car and stared through the glass at her husband's lips moving silently at the officer. She watched Darrell return, walking through the headlights with a hopeless curve in his spine, an awful emptiness in his eyes.

"It's not good" was all he could manage to say.

Will's best friend, Rand, watched from the shadows, wondering what he should do. He saw his best friend's father sag, as if someone had opened a valve and all the hope holding him up had leaked out. Rand had been waiting for his best friend's family, leaning against his truck on the roadside, watching for their Tahoe. Chase had gone home, but Rand's sister had come to give him company and support. When she drove up, he had hugged her tighter than he ever had. Now he watched from a distance a family whose world, like his, would never be the same.

What do I do? What do I say? What would Will do if it were me, and that was my dad? Rand thought. *He'd go over there and be the best friend that he was.*

Rand walked over and embraced Darrell like a man. No words were necessary. The two men cried and held each other up.

Jean and Darrell wanted to see their son. Rand led them through the lonely dark, down a road flanked by stacks of trees piled and shoved to the side. The air smelled dank and earthy, and the road felt textured underfoot, crusted with mud, broken twigs, and tender leaves crushed into the pavement.

Rand introduced Darrell to the investigator, who held out his digital camera, the little screen glowing like a flashlight. Darrell bent his tall frame over the two-inch display and looked with stabbing pain on the face of his only boy.

"Yeah," he said slowly. "That's my son."

"I'm sorry for your loss," the officer said.

Jean looked at the photo and saw through the stubble, the manly jaw, to the boy who once fit in her arms. The boy who wore a path in the lawn between home and his grandparents' house, running there every day. He always had to carry a little something back home—a stool, a pan, a bag of potatoes. The stool he had carried home as a toddler was still in a corner of her living room. All the memories came at her at once.

"Why! Why did this happen?!" she screamed so loud she thought her voice might shatter. "Why did this happen?"

But even drowning in grief, she thought she saw on Will's face a tiny smirk.

He has seen his Nana. He's with her now.

They had lost Nana eighteen months ago. Will had taken it hard. Those last few days, as Nana slipped away, Will sat all night in a chair by her bedside, watching over her until dawn. One morning when he went home to shower, she passed quietly. They buried her in the church cemetery, where each of them had a plot waiting. Just three days ago, after Easter services, they had stopped by as a family to visit and remember. Leaving her grave, Will had turned to Darrell with a sad smile.

"Daddy," he said. "What I wouldn't give to see Nana again."

Jean believed his wish had come true. That brought her comfort.

Will's younger sister, Taylor, moved to look at the camera, but Rand caught her shoulder and gently pulled her back.

"Sweetheart, you don't need to see him," Rand said. He didn't want that picture to steal from her the image of Will living.

Taylor heard in that moment her brother's voice. Her last memory of Will was Easter Sunday. They had gone to church, visited Nana's grave, then joined the extended family over at Paw Paw's house for a big lunch. Before he had left for Tuscaloosa, they had said good-bye in the living room. He had picked her up in a hug so big her feet flutter-kicked the air.

"I love you!" He would not let her down until she said it back.

"Well, I guess I love you, too," she said with a huff that made him smile.

That had only been three days ago, but now it felt like forever. As her parents talked quietly with the investigator, an ambulance slammed its doors and drove off. They watched it go in silence, taillights vanishing into the night. The world as they knew it continued to unravel at every seam.

Jean felt her head go light and her legs grow weak, and she melted onto the ground. She sat there in the street, too stunned to cry. She just wanted to go home. Looking around at this new and awful world, a world without Will, she noticed his beige Ford F150 peeking out from beneath a bouquet of green. A heavy limb had crushed the rails of the bed, but the cab looked survivable, one window blown out. She walked slowly to Will's truck, knowing she would find the doors unlocked and his wallet on the seat. That was Will. So trusting. Even when he knew he was not on the farm. She held the wallet, fingering the smooth black leather embossed with the University of Alabama seal.

The weight of reality crushed her. What were the chances he would be here, at this house, at this fateful moment? At the only house in the neighborhood that looked this bad? What were the chances?

Chance. It was Will's middle name. Born two days before Christmas in 1988, William Chance Stevens was their miracle baby after eight years of trying. "We're gonna name him Chance," Darrell had said, "because I may not have another chance to have a child."

They did in fact have another child, a sister for Will named Taylor. A quick-tempered brunette, Taylor Stevens knew exactly what she thought and let it be known. Will teased her that she was born without a filter. Will almost never got mad. Even-keeled and easygoing, he had the soul of another generation.

Rand finished knocking the broken glass out of the driver's-side window, and Taylor crawled into her brother's truck and sat behind the wheel, wishing she could drive it back in time to the days when

Bubba was alive. That's what she called him, even though he didn't look much like a Bubba.

The investigator wrote down the Stevens' name and phone number, said he would call them when they were ready to release Will's body. It was well after midnight when they started the drive home. Taylor lay down in the backseat, curled up around Will's pillow, his wallet in her hand.

■ ■ ■

As Will's family drove home on I-20/59, among the first lights they saw from the interstate were those of the Wingate, Danielle's hotel, where Ashley Mims had taken a room on the second floor. She could not sleep.

She had been told that she could not see Loryn's body until morning and had been tempted to spend the night in her car in the parking lot of the VA hospital, where she would be allowed, at 8:00 a.m., to enter the morgue and see her child. But her friends and family had talked her into getting a hotel room where she could shower and go through the motions of getting some rest. By coincidence, she had chosen the Wingate, not knowing Danielle had worked there.

In her room, Ashley sat quietly in a stuffed chair by the window, staring out into the night, seeing only her daughter's face. In her mind's eye she could see Loryn as clearly as if she were painted on the clouds, white on white—the vision she saw in the sky outside her home right after the phone cut off. She had begged her daughter not to go. But she knew at that moment it was over. And now the only thing she could do was sit in the dark and beg the dawn to hurry.

She passed the time by reliving their last, perfect weekend, replaying each moment over and over, as if the act would record every detail indelibly in her memory. Loryn singing into the steering wheel as she drove home to Wetumpka that Thursday before Easter, bursting in the front door like a happy tempest, going to pieces when she found the house empty.

Loryn had cooked them all tacos that night, adding too much water to the taco mix so the meat came out a little bit soupy. Anna and Holly fought over whose turn it was to sleep with her, and little Anna won out. It was a tight squeeze in Anna's skinny twin bed, but Loryn loved snuggling with her sisters so much that it did not really matter.

On Saturday they went to see about a horse. Loryn's older horse, Prissy, needed company, and they had looked at a sprightly chestnut mare. The girls took turns galloping in pairs through the fields and woods, around the small pond in back of the house. Ashley filmed Loryn racing barrels in the field beside the house. She rode Western, in jeans, boots, and a T-shirt, her long, brown hair sailing behind her.

On Sunday, after church, Loryn made them take family pictures until everyone's cheeks ached from smiling. She herded them around the yard, the girls in their gleaming white dresses and worn cowboy boots. She had them pose with the horses, by the pond, together and apart, orchestrating the perfect family portrait.

"Holly, fix your hair!"

"Anna, you're not smiling!"

"Parker, you've got to smile. Everyone look—Parker's not smiling!"

The pictures!

Ashley thought with a jolt that they might be lost to the storm. Loryn had taken the memory card back to school and posted a few on Facebook. But that memory card with all the rest—it had to be somewhere under that house, mixed up in all that rubble. They would never be able to find it. But they just had to. Those photographs were all they had left of their last precious day together.

The photographs and the note. Every time she left to go back to school, Loryn loved to sneak into the hallway and leave a little note on the chalkboard that hung on the wall. That Sunday, she wrote:

I love you!

To the moon and back, Ashley thought, completing the sentence her daughter had said ever since she was little. When it came time to head back to Tuscaloosa, Loryn pulled out of the driveway and drove slowly down the road along the front yard, as Anna ran barefoot beside the car, waving. Loryn rolled down the window, pointed to the sky and delivered her parting line:

"To the moon!"

■ ■ ■

In Priceville, Danielle's family slept fitfully. Her father, Ed, had fallen asleep in a chair by the phone, waiting for a call that never came. He had not heard from Kelli's mother since eight or nine o'clock, when she had called to tell him that the house had been hit, that the rescue workers were on site, and that they should wait to come until morning.

Terri finally nodded off despite the gospel music that had been playing in her head since the hour of the storm. It was the strangest thing. She had never really listened to gospel, such a contrast from the solemn hymns that sighed from the organ of the Catholic church. She found it curious but not unpleasant. It drowned out the ringing that filled her ears most days, damage from working around humming electronics. But this evening she felt ensconced in a cone of silence, with no background noise to interfere with this strange and enchanting music being piped into her head.

At 1:00 a.m. an African-American woman's voice, robust and lovely, blasted her awake. It was soulful and powerful, with a crisp and joyful chorus. Her husband, Ed, heard nothing. But Terri could hear it as clearly as if this woman were belting it out in her room. She turned to her husband.

"Let's go."

CHAPTER 27

THE UNTHINKABLE

4:45 A.M., THURSDAY, APRIL 28, 2011—TUSCALOOSA, ALABAMA

A mile-wide gash bisected the city. Along it, more than 1,200 homes had been destroyed, and another 1,612 homes damaged. More than twenty thousand Tuscaloosans lived or worked along this path, and more than twenty-five hundred families were now homeless. The sewer plant had been hit. The water system had failed. The death toll was unknown. From the look of things, it had to be staggering. Would there be fifty? One hundred? Five hundred bodies? It would be days before they knew for sure. Refrigerated trucks were standing by to catch the overflow from the morgues.

The situation almost seemed like nature's cruel joke, as if the tornado had chosen its path with wicked intent, destroying the very things the city needed to respond. The EMA headquarters were demolished. Much of the city's heavy equipment for removing debris was totaled. Two communications towers were crushed. There were broken gas lines, water lines, and power lines citywide. The hospital was overwhelmed by several orders of magnitude. The agencies that came to aid in times like this, the Red Cross and the Salvation Army, had taken a hard hit themselves.

Search-and-rescue teams all over town were changing shifts. The surface victims had all been swept to the hospital, and now the primary search was under way, the hunt for buried victims in the closing window of time in which they might still be alive. The missing-persons list was growing into the hundreds, and the mile-wide corridor of devastation was six miles long.

The search was methodical and tedious, covering a grid drawn over a map of the city, each box crossed off as it was cleared. It was also dangerous. Some structures teetered on the verge of collapse, and the blanket of debris concealed perils underneath. One fireman stepped onto a patch of rubble that gave way under his boot like a trapdoor; had he fallen into the swimming pool beneath, his heavy turnout gear would have dragged him to the bottom like an anchor. With the chaos and ruptured communication lines, teams found themselves searching areas they did not realize had already been cleared. The body count and missing-persons lists were riddled with duplication.

But crisis is a catalyst for courage, and teams of responders from all parts of the state drew together like bands of brothers. Driven beyond exhaustion by adrenaline, they crawled over a thousand felled trees and lifted ten thousand splintered boards.

At a lonely intersection, a single police officer from another city waved traffic through. Friends had arrived to help.

■ ■ ■

6:07 A.M.—DRUID CITY HOSPITAL, TUSCALOOSA

The staff at the hospital had been working for twelve solid hours on patients who had arrived in droves, bleeding through the hallways, waiting in a wounded, pitiful line that stretched out of the ER's sliding glass doors and into the parking lot. Babies had been lost and found. No one had any idea how many patients they had treated, or even the real names of the ones in the beds. Organizational procedures had gone to hell.

But help, too, had arrived in droves. Off-duty doctors and nurses showed up for work, as did medical professionals employed somewhere else. A group of students from the Capstone College of Nursing arrived and offered to pitch in. Just shy of getting their licenses, they could not legally treat patients, but Andrew Lee put them to work in other ways. He handed them babies, told them to walk the halls until the babies reached out for a parent. More than a few families reunited this way.

They did not stop to eat, but strangers kept them fed. A box of Little Debbies landed like air-dropped emergency munitions, and the staff had passed them hand-to-hand in the hallways. A woman brought an SUV filled with deli sandwiches. Pallets of water and Coca-Cola appeared in an endless stream. The pace slowed a little as the evening wore on, but the doctors and nurses braced themselves for another wave of patients chasing the dawn.

As the sun peeked over the horizon at 6:07 a.m., the disaster coordinator, Andrew Lee, took an elevator to the seventh floor to look out on the city. He joined about a hundred others pressed against the glass, gaping at the ragged corridor that stretched out in both directions.

It missed the university by a mile.

It missed the hospital by less.

▪ ▪ ▪

In the lobby of the Wingate, guests milled around the continental breakfast bar like refugees. They lingered by the flat-screen TV, where live images flashed in awful succession, tiny thumbnails of the giant horror unfolding just a few miles away. The hotel's ninety-seven rooms were all booked with a motley mix of people: families who had crawled out of ruined homes, parents searching for their college kids, emergency workers from other states, news crews from around the world. Some guests had lost every possession they owned. Some had lost even more.

Ashley Mims glanced at the news as they passed through the lobby. On it, she saw a mother waving a photograph of a pretty brunette, a university student around Loryn's age. The mother had been up all night, searching in the dark for her daughter. Ashley felt chords of empathy quiver in her chest.

■ ■ ■

The day after the tornado hit, Danielle's sister rode quietly in the passenger seat on the drive to Tuscaloosa, next to her fiancé at the wheel. Michelle had brought the stack of missing-persons flyers they made last night. Outside it was cooler and drier than yesterday. Mississippi's eastern plains were lush with trees filling out, unfurling new leaves, stretching skyward with the hopeful, effervescent green that is the color of spring in the South. It was a beautiful day, but she could not shake the black dread that coiled in her belly like a viper.

Her parents were driving south to Tuscaloosa from Priceville, and her father called and talked quietly with Clay. They agreed to meet up at Druid City Hospital, where they hoped to find Danielle. Ed Downs was wary of what they might see there, and he worried about Michelle seeing it.

"Don't let Michelle go in the hospital," he told Clay. "Whatever you do, keep her outside."

Around eight o'clock, Ed and Terri Downs pulled off the interstate and became ensnarled in traffic on McFarland Boulevard, where emergency vehicles were fighting their way through a river of gawkers. Throngs of onlookers dumbly waved smartphones at the people lifting boards. A responder in steel-toe boots looked at all the flip-flops and shook her head.

■ ■ ■

The Veterans Affairs Medical Center stood like a sentinel in an out-of-the-way part of town where most students never ventured. Built in 1932, it was a beautiful structure, the centerpiece of a campus of medical buildings on 125 wooded acres. No longer a hospital or emergency facility—it had stopped performing surgeries and taking inpatients many years ago—it now provided outpatient care and housed a nursing home. It also had the largest morgue in the city, with bays for forty bodies.

At the entrance to the VA lobby, a pretty blonde woman with a clipboard stood in front of the sliding glass doors. A VA administrator and a former RN, Connie Booth was prepared for an influx of veterans. Some would be newly homeless and might need a place at the Red Cross shelter, which was being set up in the auditorium. Others might have lost their medicines and need a new prescription. Some might be injured and come to the VA for emergency care, even though the city's only operating ER was just a few miles away at DCH.

Before she saw a single veteran step through the sliding doors, she felt a tap on her shoulder. She turned with a smile to a young face pale with panic.

"There's a family here," the young employee said. "They're looking for their daughter's body!"

Booth stared back at her, uncomprehending, as the ambulances began arriving.

Bodies? Why are they bringing us bodies?

She soon learned that the VA was the city's official morgue, as laid out in the mayor's new emergency plan. Her morgue already contained about a dozen bodies that had been brought in overnight. A temporary morgue, a trailer cooled to frigid temperatures, was on its way from Montgomery. A temporary morgue? How many casualties were there? No one could even guess.

A police officer dropped off a stack of color photographs documenting each recovery. Taken on the scene before bodies were moved, they were gruesome and disturbing, like something from a crime scene investigation. As a nurse, she had seen death before, many times, but she blanched as she looked at these photographs.

I can't show these to a parent!

Booth called her staff photographer, a young woman who was only twenty-five, who took pictures of ribbon cuttings and smiling veterans. This girl had never seen a cadaver. But she did not hesitate when

Booth explained what she needed to do. They gathered in the morgue with a group of VA nurses who were equally inexperienced for the task at hand, and equally willing to rise to it. All the women agreed: They had to clean up these bodies before the families arrived to claim them.

The women wiped blood from faces, combed leaves out of hair, and closed unseeing eyes. In acts of unflinching compassion, they did their best to wash away the horror, to make these people recognizable to their families. The young photographer took care to approach each body from the angle of least offense. With some, she focused on jewelry and clothes, avoiding the faces.

It was a ghastly task and an unexpected gift. They did it to preserve dignity. And to spare the families from seeing something that could never be unseen.

■ ■ ■

Loryn's mother and stepfather arrived at the VA at 8:05 a.m. They were among the first to begin the unthinkable process of identifying their daughter's body. Ashley and DeWayne Mims were ushered into a private room, where a social worker spoke with them. Ashley described, in great detail, what Loryn was wearing yesterday morning on Skype. She had not straightened her curly hair and was wearing a Big Daddy's Fireworks T-shirt from last summer.

The social worker handed them a photograph taken at the scene. The body was in rough shape. Sharp-edged objects hurtling through the air at two hundred miles per hour had penetrated tender skin and bone. It was hard to see past the injury, to imagine the face that once was.

Ashley wanted to see Loryn, to touch her skin and feel her hair, but was told they weren't letting people see the bodies. They would have to ID her by photograph. Ashley found this unacceptable.

"I am not leaving Tuscaloosa," she said, "until I touch my child's body."

A nurse walked her to the morgue, a cool, open room with white walls and floors, and one wall of forty small, metal doors. They had placed the black body bag on a gurney and stepped back to give the mother a moment alone with her child.

Ashley stepped up to the poor battered body, searched its broken features for the face she knew, but could not see her daughter. The truth hit her like lightning.

That's not Loryn.

Beneath the brown, curly hair was a broken neck and a face scrambled beyond recognition. But the hue of the skin was untrue. Could it be the pallor of death? No. No. This figure was too petite. No. And a tattoo snaked down one shoulder and arm. Definitely, no.

"That's not my child."

Her heart surged with hope. Maybe Loryn was still out there somewhere, unconscious but alive. Maybe she was at another hospital. Maybe there was some mistake. Of one thing she was certain: this was not her daughter.

The nurses tried to comfort her. They gently acknowledged her reaction. Denial: the first phase of grief. It takes time to set in, to accept the unacceptable, to face the crushing truth. They had faced grieving parents in other disasters. They had seen this all before.

"She doesn't have a tattoo," Ashley said.

A lot of students got tattoos their parents didn't know about, they said, nodding kindly and knowingly.

Ashley shook her head, gently adamant. She had seen that shoulder four days ago, bare and tanned and glowing under the white strap of a Sunday dress.

Tattoo or no, she knew what a mother knows without question.

"That's not my child."

It had to be, they said. This was the only Caucasian female in the morgue that had not been claimed by a family. The others were ready for transport.

Then there must be some mistake. She needed to see the other bodies.

That wasn't possible, they said. The bodies had been claimed.

But the love of a mother is a powerful and implacable force.

At last, they agreed to show them another photograph. This body had been claimed, they said, by a family who had identified her in an e-mailed photograph. Arrangements had already been made to have her shipped home to another state.

Ashley told them again what Loryn had been wearing, and exactly how her hair looked. But she could not bear to look at another body if it did not belong to her child. So her husband, DeWayne, went into the little room with the nurses and looked at all the photos. He picked one up.

"Yeah," DeWayne said, "that's her."

The nurses gasped when Ashley walked into the morgue.

"She must be yours," they said. "You look just like her."

This time, when the zipper parted it revealed a girl intact. Without makeup covering up her freckles, she did look like her mother. Her hair was just as Ashley described—tight brown ringlets pulled from her widow's peak and scrunched into a bun. There were little shards of Xbox tangled in the curls. Ashley snipped a few locks and tucked them in her purse.

Ashley bent over her sweet child, touching her face, stroking her hair, caressing her cold, stiff arm. To Ashley Loryn looked like she was sleeping, except for a single drop of blood that had dried upon her cheek. Ashley took her finger and wiped it away. Loryn's hand was clenched, as if she had something in it. Ashley uncurled her fingers to find it empty. But she noticed Loryn's fingernails were broken off at the quick. She must have been holding on to something, tight, the moment she died. Whatever that was, it was gone.

■ ■ ■

After fighting through traffic, detours, and roadblocks for an hour, Danielle's parents had advanced about two miles, to University Mall in midtown. Terri Downs called Danielle's landlady, Dianne Rumanek, for directions to the hospital.

"Dianne, we're in town. The police say we need to go to DCH."

"You need to go to the VA. That's where Loryn's mother identified her body."

Terri felt a fluttery, screamy thing beating in her chest.

"A body?"

Dianne froze with the phone to her ear. She thought they already knew.

"Ed—" Terri cried, choking on the scream.

▪ ▪ ▪

Michelle and Clay arrived at DCH to find the parking lot full and parked on the ramp. Ed and Terri were standing outside the ER. As soon as she saw them, Michelle began running. But as she neared, she saw her father's face. Ed shook his head slowly. The eyes that smiled when his mustache didn't looked sadder than she'd ever seen.

"Dad, no!" she cried. "No, Dad! No!"

As she came to pieces, she heard Danielle's voice in her head.

Michelle, stop. Can't you see him?

She looked up and saw her father crying.

Her dad, who could fix anything.

Look at him. He can't.

▪ ▪ ▪

At the VA morgue, the Downs family showed the staff the flyers Michelle had made. Terri pulled out a file of identification papers, including a handprint. But there were questions to answer, and waiting, and more waiting. The Internet was down, and the computers were slow. The waiting was absolute torture.

A counselor pulled them into a little side room and asked them what they remembered about the afternoon of the storm. Michelle shared their text messages and the feeling in her stomach when the silence began.

"I heard gospel music," Terri said.

"Danielle listens to gospel!" Michelle said.

"Since when?"

"She does! She likes listening to it—it calms her down."

A staff member left the room and returned to hand a photograph to Ed. He looked at it, and something inside him broke like a plate of glass.

He laid it on the waiting room table. Michelle grabbed it, studied it, and came apart. Clay held her silently.

Terri felt as if she had been shot point-blank with a missile, opening a gaping hole in her chest that people could see right through.

"I want to see the body," said Terri, her voice husky and low.

Like Ashley, Terri was told that a photo was all that she could see. The caustic reaction of grief and anger brought her to a boil.

"We're not leaving till we see Danielle."

Then came a team of new officials with another round of questions. What did they remember about Danielle and her whereabouts yesterday? Did she have any identifying marks? Tattoos? Scars? Notable jewelry?

"Michelle, what was the necklace that Danielle always wore?" Ed asked.

"Joan of Arc."

Like a key, her patron saint unlocked the door that led them to Danielle.

The family walked into the refrigerated room and gathered around the gurney. The black bag parted to reveal the angled chin, the smooth skin, the lips that they would never again see curve into a smile.

Danielle looked like herself, and didn't. Her hair spilled back from her face in a light brown halo. Her eyebrows, crisp and angular, had just been waxed for the wedding, and they pinched together above her closed eyes in a way that made her look grumpy. Her face was bruised and puffy. It looked to her mother as if someone had spilled grape juice concentrate on her right cheek, leaving a purple stain. A pink tuft of insulation was caught in her hair. Terri reached over and tenderly pulled it out.

Ed beheld his daughter with a military stoicism and a deep, dark sadness in his eyes. Michelle's eyes became waterfalls, and Clay pressed her to his shirt to catch them. Terri felt the fluttery-screamy thing come fiercely alive inside her. The family clutched one another and wept.

Before they left, Terri ran her hands over Danielle's forehead. Her skin felt smooth and cool. She leaned in and smelled her hair. Underneath the smell of freshly shampooed hair was a scent so dear and singular that it exists one place in the universe. It is something every mother knows by heart: the scent of her baby's head.

▪ ▪ ▪

Ashley Mims had heard that Danielle's parents were here, and she waited for them to finish the awful duty she had also just done. She watched the Downs family walk back into the lobby, sharing the pain they now felt. She rushed to Terri and hugged her. In the hallway of the VA hospital, two mothers who had never met before embraced each other's agony, forever sharing an intimate, terrible bond that no one else could ever understand. There are no right words for times like this, and few were said. Instead, there was the feel of warm arms, hot tears mixing cheek to cheek.

As they prepared to leave, another anguished mother arrived at the morgue. Ashley recognized her as the woman she saw that morning on the news, the desperate mother waving the photograph of her beautiful missing daughter. It was the mother of twenty-one-year-old Ashley Harrison, who had been ripped from the arms of her boyfriend, Carson Tinker, and thrown hundreds of feet to her death in a field.

Oh, I feel so sorry for you, Ashley Mims thought. *I'm sorry you have to feel like me.*

The woman and her husband disappeared into the little room. Through the walls they heard her scream.

▪ ▪ ▪

Danielle's family was still at the VA as Ashley Mims sifted through the ruins of 31 Beverly Heights, searching for artifacts of Loryn's life. It was high noon, and to Ashley, the world around her seemed unnaturally bright and crisp, every color more vivid, every smell more intense—natural gas commingled with pine and azaleas. Even the trees that had fallen on the house seemed fresher and greener than before.

Members of the UA baseball team had gathered in front of the house across the street, where one of their teammates lived. He had watched through the window as 31 Beverly Heights exploded under the giant tree. His team came over to help him clean up, and they noticed the family weeping as they searched through the ruins across the street. The team walked over and asked how they could help.

"There's a white dress," Ashley told them. "We'd like to bury her in it. Can you help us find it?"

It was the dress she had worn to church on Easter. Loryn had been going to that church since she was five years old, and dreamed of being married there. Loryn would make one final trip down that aisle. Ashley wanted her in that white dress.

The players joined the families like a team of archaeologists, digging and sifting through the sedimentary layers of rubble. They lined up like a fire-bucket brigade, passing Loryn's wardrobe, piece by piece, to the street. Dresses paraded over the rubble in a colorful stream of patterns and colors and shapes. One of the baseball players paused and looked up between dresses.

"This girl liked clothes," he said.

Ashley smiled. "Yes, she did."

Loryn's paintings landed in the neighbor's yard. Her necklaces were found splayed in the street.

A member of the baseball team, the pitcher, lifted a white sundress at last and held it up for Ashley Mims. It was streaked with red Alabama clay, but that did not matter. It was the dress. She would never, ever forget how beautiful Loryn looked on that day in that dress.

"Thank you so much," Ashley said through the tears. "Thank you."

The white dress lay silently in the backseat as Ashley rode home through the yellow afternoon light to a house filled with friends who had been cleaning, cooking, and doting on the kids. They had kept Holly, Anna, and Parker at bay, preserving what few hours remained of life as they had always known it. Church ladies met visitors in the driveway, whispering over the casseroles: *They haven't told the kids.*

Ashley could not let them hear it from anyone else. She had to be the one to tell them, even if she did not yet know how. She could not imagine anything harder than what she had just done.

Except facing the future.

In less than a month, Loryn was supposed to be getting on a plane for her first big trip. She was going to tour Beverly Hills with her aunt, then embark on a two-week wandering road trip across the great wide country, to all the places she had never seen, and the places in between. They had booked her flight on April 26, the night before the storm. In July, the whole family would drive to Florida for a beach vacation. Oh, how she loved the sugar-white sands and bath-warm waters of the Gulf.

Ashley realized the beach would never look the same. She would always see the empty place in the waves where Loryn should be playing. It was where Loryn became a child again, digging for sand dollars and gathering shells, her little sisters trailing her like ducklings, copying everything she did. On their last trip to the beach, Ashley snapped a photograph of her three girls doing handstands on the hard, wet sand. The waves swept into three sizes of handprints, washing them all away.

■ ■ ■

Danielle's friends and colleagues had begun to worry. It was not like her to go MIA. She was the cool head in the crisis, the starter of the phone tree, the one counting heads. She was exactly the person you wanted to be around at a time like this. She would know what to do and say.

At TES, Danielle was the only one who had not come into work. Even though her field placement had ended on Tuesday, she would have been among the first to show up to help, no phone call required. Her absence was a palpable void; today was all-hands-on-deck and they needed her desperately. Every time the front door opened, her colleagues glanced up, hoping to see her walk in.

At the Wingate, the front-desk staff had begun to suspect that something was terribly wrong. On the night of the storm, a lady had called and asked for her parents' phone number. Giving it out was against hotel policy, but the measured desperation in this woman's voice had been reason enough to break the rules. Her friends and colleagues had been calling her all day, but no one had been able to reach her. They had been in touch with her parents, who had not heard from her either. Now, as the hotel throbbed with guests in varied stages of crisis, the phone call came. Danielle's good friend Chanel Chapman was working her third shift in two days when she picked up the phone.

"Wingate, how may I help you?"

At first there was silence on the other end of the line.

"Is this Chanel?" the man said.

"Yes sir," she said. "Is this Danielle's father?"

At first, she got excited. They must have found her. But his long pause turned that feeling inside out. She was crying before he spoke again.

"She's gone," said Ed Downs.

"She's gone? What do you mean?"

"They found her and her friends under the house. As soon as we know anything else, we'll let y'all know."

Chanel opened her mouth, but nothing came out. She turned to her colleague, another friend of Danielle's. The friend read her face and began to cry as Chanel mouthed the words.

"That was her father."

■ ■ ■

Loryn's family had gone home by the time the Downs family arrived at the house late that afternoon. Many of the roads were still blocked, and they parked nearby and hiked their way in, crossing the railroad tracks that bordered the back of Beverly Heights. The tracks, no longer cloaked by trees, now lay naked and exposed in the sun.

It was a beautiful day, and the sunshine seemed incongruous with the death trap that lay beneath. The giant tree that guillotined the house had sliced right through Danielle's room. On one side of the tree her grandmother's bed lay smashed, part of the bedpost slung into the street. On the other they found her Disney movies, scattered like playing cards. Danielle's stuffed pink hippo was stuck in a tree, ripped and bleeding stuffing.

Michelle scrambled onto the second floor, which was now the first floor, and began filling the drawers with the things she found—clothes, jewelry, movies, a throw pillow with a purple flower.

Acts of kindness condensed from the air, like rain. Strangers dropped off cases of water. A group of men had driven three hours with hunting ATVs. Four men they had never seen before cut up trunks with saws and formed a chain, passing armfuls of Danielle's things over and out of the house. People walking by gently offered whatever they could.

"Do you need anything?"

"We don't have any gloves."

"Here, take these."

A young woman from the Highlands, the adjacent neighborhood, gave Terri the ponytail holder from her hair and brought a tray of water. A student who went to college in another state offered to let them store Danielle's furniture at her parents' house, one street over, to keep it out of the rain. They were grateful for all the kindness. Several men, whose names they would never learn, carried the big things to the storage room. They would come back down with a trailer. By the time they were done, dusk had draped itself over the house. They were too exhausted to drive home.

The Wingate was booked, but Danielle's friends had held two rooms for the family as soon as they had heard the news. As night settled over the scrambled city, they made their way to the little franchise by the interstate, where the wall-mounted AC units hummed white noise.

As they walked into the lobby, Terri looked drained and on the verge of breaking down. Danielle's friends rushed over and embraced her. Family, friends, and colleagues stood in a giant huddle, exchanging more tears than words near the front desk where Danielle should be standing. Michelle had once surprised her with a visit, hiding behind the customers until Danielle looked up and said, "May I help you?" Danielle had squealed and fanned her cheeks with her hands in shocked delight, her mouth forming a little *O*.

Exhausted in every way imaginable, they surrendered to the numbness of sleep.

■ ■ ■

Ashley and DeWayne Mims took the kids into their room and sat them down on the bed. Ashley held Anna, the littlest, on her lap. Holly, the middle child, sat beside her. Parker, the oldest, stood.

They knew. Ashley could see it in their faces. They knew.

Her husband was the one to say it.

"We found Sissy."

Holly's face brightened with relief. "Oh, good!"

"When is Sissy coming home?" Anna said.

DeWayne sighed. This hurt as much as anything.

"Baby, Sissy's not coming home," he said. "Sissy's in heaven. She's gone before us. She's waiting on us."

They screamed and cried and clawed at their faces, doubled over with pain. Ashley hugged the girls to her chest, feeling Holly shaking with sobs. Anna moaned pitifully. Parker walked to his room, sat on his bed, and stared out his window.

■ ■ ■

It was close to midnight when Brian Williams, the anchor of *NBC Nightly News*, checked into the Wingate.

A little more than twenty-four hours before, Williams had been on a plane to London Heathrow Airport to cover the wedding of Prince William to Kate Middleton. After landing, as the airplane taxied to the gate, he checked his BlackBerry and saw that the death toll from the outbreak was eighty-three. By the time he reached the baggage claim, it had risen to 172. On the drive into London, he asked the driver to pull off the highway while he joined a conference call with NBC News in New York. Which story was more important?

"Go home," said NBC president Steve Capus.

The car turned around and drove Williams back to the airport. He landed in Birmingham after ten o'clock and drove to Tuscaloosa along a dark interstate. He noticed the air smelled wet, and of pine. He came upon a tangle of cars twisted near an underpass, guarded by a lone Alabama trooper.

When Williams checked into the Wingate, one of the only hotels that had power, the hotel manager approached him and his crew and said that the hotel "has been touched by this tragedy." The manager told them about his front-desk clerk, working her way through college at this interstate hotel.

When Williams learned that the girl's parents were at the hotel, he thought of his own twenty-three-year-old daughter in New York, and what he would say when he e-mailed her tonight from his room. The feeling moved him to write about it on a blog post that caused other fathers around the country to pause and tear up as they imagined their own daughters. Among them was the meteorologist Jim Stefkovich, who closed the door to his office at the National Weather Service in Birmingham, put his head on his desk, and wept. Ed Downs, who was at this moment sleeping almost exactly one floor beneath Williams, would not see the post until three years later. He, too, would cry.

"Just a nice kid, not from a fancy family, but wanting a degree from Alabama and doing the work it requires," Williams wrote. "She's someone's pretty, lovely angel, and one man just a few floors below me is coming to grips with the fact that his life will never, ever be the same."

CHAPTER 28

GRADUATION DAY

FRIDAY, APRIL 29, 2011—TUSCALOOSA, ALABAMA

Danielle's family checked out of the Wingate and thanked the staff for the room, and for the tears they had shared. Today was Michelle's college graduation from Mississippi State. Clay and his mother would be taking photos and cheering from the bleachers. Ed and Terri drove home to plan a funeral.

Before they left, Michelle wanted one more walk through Beverly Heights. She gingerly stepped through the splintered two-by-fours, shredded drywall, and soggy insulation, hunting for more relics from her sister's life. She searched for photographs, clothes, jewelry. Lifting a blanket of insulation, like the batting of a quilt laid bare, she found the ceramic picture frame, painted with pink daisies, that had rested on Danielle's nightstand. It held a photo of two sisters in front of a waterfall, smiling into the sun.

The clothes hamper was still in the closet, filled with shirts that still smelled like her sister. On a shoe rack hanging on the back of the closet door, Michelle noticed a pair of kitten heels. A birthday gift from a friend, they were the color of morning sunshine, with pale blue stripes and a flourish on the toe. Danielle called them her "happy shoes." Michelle longed to keep them—they were cute, they fit her perfectly, and they were Danielle's—but she had other, bigger plans for them. She found a pair of earrings and tucked them in her pocket.

These things were just things, but they were more than things, because they felt like a part of Danielle.

Among the last and most precious things she found was a whiteboard. On it was a Bible verse in Danielle's hand, written in purple dry-erase marker. Every letter remained intact, and when she found it, Michelle believed Danielle had left it for her to find:

> *We are hard-pressed on every side, but not crushed,*
> *perplexed, but not in despair;*
> *persecuted, but not abandoned;*
> *struck down but not destroyed.*
>
> —2 Corinthians 4:8

■ ■ ■

In the skies above 31 Beverly Heights, a little before noon, the President of the United States gazed out the window of Air Force One. From high above, the tornado's path looked like a brown smudge through a pointillist painting, an eighty-mile scar across the verdant land. People scattered through the interrupted streets of a broken city like ants rebuilding a hill.

Air Force One landed at Tuscaloosa Regional Airport, a two-runway operation with no commercial flights. Wearing slacks and a light button-down shirt with no tie, President Barack Obama climbed down the steps of his plane hand-in-hand with First Lady Michelle Obama. At the bottom, they shook hands with the governor, the mayor, and their wives.

The roads had been cleared for the motorcade, and people paused from their digging and hauling to rise up and catch a glimpse of the President. The limo passed slowly down Fifteenth Street. To the left, Forest Lake sparkled like a diamond in the dirt. Once hidden by ancient Druid oaks that shaded its homes like lacy parasols, the small lake was one of the few recognizable landmarks left in a featureless mess. Those giant oaks were snapped at the trunk, as if cut by a giant

Weedwacker. Across the street, the tiny cottages of Cedar Crest were mowed down, one yard indistinguishable from the next.

The limo stopped in Alberta City, where the President and First Lady emerged to walk a raggedy stretch of Seventh Street. It was seventy-five degrees and muggy, and the politicians had all rolled up their shirtsleeves. They paused to speak with a group of residents standing atop a crushed house and met the principal of Holt Elementary School, which was now functioning as a shelter and aid station. Principal Debbie Crawford had been at the school with her school nurse for the past forty-eight hours. The First Lady hugged survivors, and the President held a two-year-old girl who no longer had a home.

The President had declared Alabama a major disaster area on Thursday night. The total death toll had reached 333, including those who died when the outbreak began to the west on April 25. Alabama's death toll had now reached 247. Fifteen hundred people were staying in sixty-five Red Cross shelters, 654 families had been displaced from government housing projects—and that was only a fraction of the number of people who were suddenly homeless. The missing-persons list had grown to 454.

"I have never seen devastation like this," the President said before he left Tuscaloosa.

But in the devastation he noticed something else, a universal truth that echoed across tragedies.

"When something like this happens, people forget all their petty differences . . . and we're reminded that all we have is each other."

■ ■ ■

Clay and Michelle Downs loaded the shoes, the earrings, the photograph, and the whiteboard in the car and drove back to Starkville in time for her graduation from Mississippi State. She had long been looking forward to this day of celebrating milestones and accomplishments. She and Clay were graduating on the dean's list. Her parents would have beamed with pride, but they were picking out a casket.

Michelle slipped on her black cap and gown, put on Danielle's earrings, and slid her feet into the happy shoes she had found in her sister's closet. She would wear them for the most important walk in her life—until the one next week that would take her down the aisle of a church.

After the storm, the University of Alabama canceled commencement ceremonies and postponed them indefinitely. Michelle hoped to be able to walk on her sister's behalf, to receive the diploma that Danielle had struggled so hard to earn. But just in case that did not come to pass, Michelle decided to cross her own stage in Starkville holding the framed photograph that she had dug from the rubble, the one that showed the two of them smiling in the summer sun.

Now, as she sat in the rows of robed graduates, she held the photograph in her lap, studying their faces until they grew blurry. Her blue eyes were red and puffy, and she ached with the greatest hurt she had ever known. Yet somewhere deep inside her sprang the inner well that Danielle had divined, the strength she did not know she possessed until her sister showed her it was there. From this source she summoned a genuine smile as the officiant called Michelle Kathleen Downs to walk across the stage.

It was a short walk, but in each step was a thousand journeys, a thousand acts of courage and faith. One more step into a future without Danielle, one step further from this awful past. One breath, one step, one day at a time. For some things in life, there is no way around—you have to go through them.

Michelle raised her chin and smiled through the tears as she walked in her sister's shoes.

CHAPTER 29

THE WALK

SATURDAY, APRIL 30, 2011—PLEASANT GROVE, ALABAMA

The crack of a bat and the arc of a ball into the bright green of the outfield made the storm seem like a horrible dream. James Spann watched his thirteen-year-old son, Ryan, sprint across the field in his baseball whites. Here was a little pocket of normal, a rare moment of escape from the aftermath that would haunt the state for months. These were Spann's happiest times, with his wife by his side and his son on the field doing what he never got to do with the father he never had.

▪ ▪ ▪

Fatherhood nearly filled the void that Spann's father left behind. Nearly. Three decades after the man walked out, Spann found his house in Huntsville and went knocking on his door. Now thirty-seven, and a father himself, Spann still had questions. He still had anger. He still had a tiny shred of hope that he might find a father.

The man who opened the door that day looked nothing like the memory. He was old and drunk, and filthy words spilled freely from his lips. He had never told his son he loved him. He did not say it now.

And yet, deep in the old man's eyes, Spann glimpsed the dad of his youth. Small memories broke free from some buried place. Going with him to the circus in Montgomery. Their fishing trip in Georgiana. Small things. Big truths. And suddenly, the anger slipped away.

Spann called him sir, and spoke of faith.

"The least I can do is forgive you," Spann said. "I need to say that to you, and you need to hear it."

The old man rambled and cussed, and did not seem to hear it. He drank his beer and urinated in his own front yard. James turned and left, still fatherless; sad, and yet at peace.

A year later, he learned the old man had died, alone, in some facility.

■ ■ ■

After the game, the Spanns climbed into the black 4Runner for a drive into the disaster zone. From a part of town where the landscape allowed them to forget what had happened, they drove west, squinting into the sun, to a place where the trees were bare and twisted. Blown-out windows stared back at them like vacant, haunted eyes. Under their tires, gritty pieces scattered in the streets. The air smelled of death, and pine.

"This is the edge of the storm," James said quietly.

In the passenger seat, Karen Spann felt her soul ache. She was not sure what was drawing her so desperately to this area, but she needed to be here. Officials recognized James behind the wheel of the 4Runner and waved him through the blockades.

Pleasant Grove was a suburb of Birmingham that had been hit by the same tornado that had ravaged Tuscaloosa. Southwest of the city, it was an old-fashioned blue-collar neighborhood of modest homes and beautiful hardwood trees. Home to ten thousand residents—generations of coal miners, retired teachers, and working families—it was a place where people sipped lemonade on the porch in the afternoons, where on Friday nights in the fall, fight songs played by high school marching bands could be heard filtering through the woods.

Now all that was gone. The Spanns drove slowly through the streets of vanished neighborhoods. The car rattled and shook as the damage grew more grotesque. In the backseat, Ryan quietly took it all in. James had briefed his son about what he might see or encounter.

At the breakfast table with Karen, James Spann had finally broken down. She had not seen her husband cry in years. He told her about horrible things he'd seen that she would never write down or speak aloud. Yet they'd broken her heart and become part of her, even though she only saw them through her husband's eyes. She was grateful for the tears and for his honesty.

Go ahead, she thought. *Get it out.*

But then he was needed on the radio, and he went upstairs to the War Room to take the call. Hearing his voice on the radio, no one could have known how much he had been hurting. That was her James.

Now as they entered the devastated neighborhood, James remarked on how the cleanup had progressed, but Karen wondered how it possibly could have been worse. It looked as if the mouth of hell had opened up, spewing death and brokenness everywhere. The odor that hung in the air seemed the saddest smell in the world, a combination of sick and sweet, foul and musty. It was as if the air itself mourned the horror of it all. And yet the sky seemed almost obscene in its clear blueness, just as it had been days before when a breeze had carried the scent of blooming jasmine and freshly mowed grass.

"Leave your cleats on," James told Ryan as they stepped out of the car. "Look down. Always look down when you walk."

They tiptoed through devastation so vast and incomprehensible that it was hard to process—twisted cars and broken dishes, books and sinks, toilets and clothing, pictures and papers and purses and luggage. They stepped over family portraits and a life insurance policy. Karen wept over the remnants of a crib, a doll tangled up in the insulation, a stuffed animal lying in broken glass—hoping that somehow, somewhere, the baby was fast asleep in its mother's arms.

As she walked, Karen wrestled with dissonant emotions. There they were, uninvited, walking through the ruins of strangers' lives. She felt as if they were trespassing through someone else's sorrow. As they passed sad-eyed people picking through the carcasses of their homes, she held back, respecting the invisible walls of privacy. A few wanted to talk, and she listened, knowing that part of healing lies in the telling and the hearing of stories.

James looked through the eyes of a meteorologist and saw in the wreckage a few signs that gave him hope: the interior walls and closets still standing, the safe places he always rants about, ragged but intact. Among the twisted metal and fallen walls, they saw a closet filled with clothes, hung tidily on their racks, as though somehow immune to the winds. Karen noticed her husband's posture lift as he took it in, because it meant that someone could have survived there. He documented a few such places with his phone. Karen took only one photo the entire day: a magnolia blooming from the rubble.

SATURDAY, APRIL 30, 2011—TUSCALOOSA, ALABAMA

One of the rescuers, Shannon Corbell, who had helped recover the bodies from 31 Beverly Heights, had never been involved in search and rescue. A tree maintenance supervisor for the Tuscaloosa Department of Transportation, Corbell was accustomed to dealing with trees, but not trees that crushed houses and killed people. Strong and stoic, he did not ordinarily show emotion, but having just seen bodies and babies who had flown through the air, this hit him pretty hard. He called his girlfriend, who lived in Georgia. They were supposed to head out on vacation this week, but they decided to spend their vacation together, helping Tuscaloosa.

Corbell's girlfriend, Tracy Sargent, was a professional K-9 handler for search, rescue, and recovery dogs. In her twenty-three years of work, she had been on hundreds of searches and seen them end in grisly, terrible ways. Tuscaloosa would be no vacation, but she loved her work and lived to help in times precisely like this. She loaded her Suburban with search-and-rescue gear and called her two K-9 partners, Cinco and Chance, who bounded into the car, eager to do their job.

Sargent joined thousands of volunteers pouring into Tuscaloosa. Police officers and firefighters and EMTs drove emergency vehicles from several states to work side by side with their overwhelmed brothers. A team from Montgomery Heavy Rescue was searching the west side of town, working its way east. Prattville was searching Alberta east to west. Louisiana Task Force One jumped in with the Technical Rescue Team, helping search precarious structures. There were six hundred National Guard members on the ground, guarding neighborhoods from looters and helping direct traffic, and five hundred more were on the way.

Some 850 volunteer civilians registered with the city on Friday, and 1,350 more signed up Saturday—individuals, whole families, church brigades. A couple with nine kids sorted donated clothes in Holt. A mother with a three-month-old baby drove in from North Carolina. Medical students came down from Philadelphia. An arborist from Tennessee climbed trees and doctored broken limbs. Fraternity brothers grilled burgers and pushed old ladies' garbage cans up their driveways. People noticed the mayor on the ground, pitching in, when the cameras were not present.

The city of Tuscaloosa had come a long way in the past seventy-two hours. Thirty-nine bodies had been found. More than seven hundred people reported missing had been located, but 570 were still on the list. The hospital had treated at least eight hundred people, though the exact number would never be known.

But there was still a long, long way to go before the city came close to feeling normal.

The tornado's six-mile blitz through the city put twenty thousand Tuscaloosans directly in its path. Even more were indirectly affected—more than twenty-three thousand city residents still had no power. City crews had pieced together seven garbage trucks from the wrecked EMA building, but the trash trucks, which haul away brush and large garbage, were not even close to salvageable.

"At the beginning of this cleanup, it's going to look like we're throwing rocks at a battleship," said Tuscaloosa Mayor Walt Maddox.

"But we're out here, and we're moving. And it's going to take some time, but we're going to cross that finish line."

■ ■ ■

Will's father stood at the edge of the house once again, feeling just as lost as before. Darrell Stevens never received a phone call with the news that Will's body could come home. Frustrated, he and his daughter drove back to Tuscaloosa, hoping to find at 31 Beverly Heights a few of Will's things, and some answers. There would not be much to find, since he had not lived in that house, but Taylor desperately wanted to find her brother's laptop, which held all of his photographs, papers, and notes, and the backpack he always carried.

Will's truck was undrivable but not totaled, so Darrell Stevens had brought the flatbed truck to haul it back home to Priceville. The truck reminded him of the conversation they had that Sunday before Will left.

"Hey, Dad, can I take your truck?"

Will loved his dad's red 4WD dualie, a larger and beefier version of his own truck. Darrell let him take it to school from time to time, but this week he needed it on the farm. He agreed, on one condition.

"Tell you what I'll do, son," Darrell said. "Your last class is Wednesday. I'll let you drive my truck back down there if you'll come home after your last class."

"Nah," Will said. "I want to stay down there."

"That's the only way you'll get to drive my truck. If you'll come home after your last class and bring the truck back."

"It costs too much. And I've got things I want to do and things I need to catch up on."

Darrell thought about that now. If only Will had changed his mind. But thinking like that was useless now. It would not bring Will back.

He could still see Will's wiry silhouette in the front yard, where he had stood talking with a friend hanging out of a pickup truck window as he paused on the street to say hello.

"I guess I'm gonna leave," Will said, poking his head in to say good-bye.

"You still got the option of driving my truck," Darrell said, "if you bring it back Wednesday."

That was the last time Darrell Stevens saw his son alive.

Will's best friend, Rand Hutchinson, had come to Beverly Heights with his parents to help the Stevens family. Rand remembered seeing a sports bag sitting on Will's passenger seat Wednesday night. It was gone now, and his train of thought pulled him down the steep, rocky slope of anger. That someone would steal from a dead man.

Beverly Heights was filled today with people helping with the cleanup. A group of volunteers approached them, asked how they could help.

Taylor had not eaten in two days and was desperate to find the only thing of Will's that would be here.

"I'm trying to find my brother's laptop," Taylor said.

The family set them to work, knocking away walls with axes and shovels. After twenty minutes one of the volunteers walked up to her.

"Is this what you're looking for?"

She hugged it and fell to the ground, crying.

But they still could not find Will.

A man who lived down the street heard about their situation. He came down to see what he could do.

"Is there anything I can do for you?" he asked Darrell Stevens.

"You can help me find my son. We're not leaving Tuscaloosa until I find him."

"They may have taken him out to the VA hospital," the man said. "Do you know where that is?"

"No."

"Come on. Let's go."

Tommy Wagner drove Will's father to the VA and waited as he was taken into a little room, where a series of nurses and doctors asked questions about Will. He knew they were doing their best, but he was tired of questions. He wanted answers.

"Why can't you just let me look at him?"

"It's against policy," a nurse said. "Can you give me some specific markings on his body?"

"He has a scar on his chin and on his left elbow. He just had surgery."

"Yes," she said. "I think we have him."

She left the room and came back with a folder in her hand. She sat down and handed it to him.

"Whenever you're ready, you flip that open and tell me if that's your son or not," she said. "Just take your time."

Darrell flipped it open. The three words that once had brought him joy now unleashed a torrent of pain.

"That's my boy."

▪ ▪ ▪

Will's body beat them home, arriving at the Priceville funeral home before the Stevens family rolled into town. The pastor phoned to tell them.

"Will's home."

The owner was a family friend whose kids grew up playing baseball with Will. He faced death every day in this line of work, but this kind of death, like a rosebud cut and withered before it could bloom, was the saddest kind of all. When they met to discuss the funeral arrangements, he left the room three times to compose himself.

The soonest they could bury Will was Tuesday, but they could not bring themselves to put him in the ground on his grandfather's eighty-sixth birthday. Paw Paw's heart was already broken. The morning after the storm, Darrell, Jean, Taylor, and two of Will's aunts had walked over to his house to tell him.

Wayne Stevens was sitting in the den, reading the paper, when through the front window he spotted them walking slowly across his front lawn. He opened the front door and they all filed in and sat down without a word. Darrell pulled up a chair right in front of his father, sat down, and looked into his eyes. It was a long five minutes before Darrell could choke out the words.

"Daddy," he said, "we lost Will last night."

The old man thought the top of his head would come off.

Paw Paw was hard of hearing and sometimes asked a question more than once, but he recalled with utter clarity the very last time he saw Will. It was just days ago, on Easter Sunday, when the family had come over for supper. After the meal, Will had stayed with Paw Paw a good long while. They had always been close, and that had not changed when Will went off to college. When he got ready to leave, Paw Paw drew from his wallet two crisp hundred-dollar bills and held them out to his grandson. Will thanked him but waved the bills away.

"I don't need 'em," he said.

Paw Paw thought about that a lot. He kept those hundred-dollar bills in his wallet for a very long time and could not bring himself to spend them. He told the story more than once to family and friends.

"That was the kind of boy Will was," he would say, walking that line between laughter and tears. "When I was that age, if somebody had held out two hundred-dollar bills, I'da grabbed 'em hand and all."

Paw Paw had seen a lot of things in his life. He had seen Pearl Harbor engulfed in flames. He had seen a small town spring up around his rural farm. He had weathered many storms in his long life. But he never dreamed he would outlive his grandson. That was the hardest thing he had ever done.

When the Stevens family went to the funeral home to make arrangements, they discussed whether to open the casket. The director tried to look at his friend's son with an unbiased eye. Will's bones were shattered, and his body had swelled from the trauma so that he looked as if he'd gained a hundred pounds, which obscured his chiseled jaw.

"If it was my child," he said, "I wouldn't."

It was agreed.

The family stood to leave.

"Make sure Will's got his socks on," Jean said softly. "He's got cold feet."

The man went into the back and sat with Will, just sat there beside him, for a very long time. When it came time to prepare him, he noticed something curious. The palm of one hand was imprinted with four tiny half-moon marks.

The mothers were the ones to figure it out.

Loryn's nails had been broken off at the quick by whatever she was holding fiercely in the last moments of her life.

It must have been Will's hand.

CHAPTER 30

CHANCE

SUNDAY, MAY 1, 2011—CHARLESTON SQUARE, TUSCALOOSA

Tracy Sargent and her rescue dogs had been clearing neighborhoods on the west side of town when they were called to Charleston Square. The stump upon which Chelsea Thrash had been found, paralyzed with a broken back, sat in a sea of brokenness. Debris still lay in petrified waves as far as the eye could see. Clearing it away seemed as impossible as emptying the ocean with a spoon.

Teams of rescuers had been searching this spot over and over for the past five days. No bodies had been found since that of Nicole Mixon, who had been discovered within the first hour. But on the scene was a father who said his son was buried somewhere under all that hopelessness.

"I know he's here," he told the rescuers.

Sargent went to the back of her Suburban, retrieving gear from a long, black box. While her dogs rested in the air-conditioned car, she donned her technical rescue gear in a routine that rarely deviated: helmet, headlamp, goggles, gloves, backpack. In the pockets of her thick, black work pants she placed bottled water and rubber balls for the dogs. Under sunglasses and the brim of a ball cap placed under her safety helmet, it was hard to see the beautiful woman underneath. The blonde ponytail that trailed down her back was the only thing that made it easy to spot her in the crowd.

As Sargent walked to the back door of the driver's side to get her dogs, an officer caught her attention. He nodded at a man who had been sitting in a chair under an umbrella at the foot of a mountain of rubble that towered like a levee, two stories high. Clean-cut and muscular, with close-cropped hair, reading a book with composure that seemed out of place in this armageddon.

"We're going to do everything we can do to find your son for you," the officer told the man. "We're going to keep searching until we find him."

The man looked at Sargent, who nodded respectfully. She noticed his kind, sad eyes. What struck her most about him was the stoic patience that was so different from the response of all the bereaved parents she had met in her twenty-three years of search and rescue. She read his face and inferred that he had come to accept his loss, and in that acceptance was a glimmer of peace in a time of great chaos and horror. The man was sitting about sixty feet from the spot where his son's apartment had stood. All that was left of that apartment was an empty concrete slab.

The boy's mother and older brother were sitting nearby in chairs that strangers had brought to them, along with small kindnesses—water and food—to bring them some small comfort.

This family embodied every reason that Sargent had devoted her life to this. It wasn't what she did. It was who she was. She had spent decades proving her strength and capability to male colleagues who would have liked to see her fail. But underneath the callus on her psyche that protected her from this reality, her heart was not jaded. No matter how many grieving families she encountered, she asked herself how she could help each family through their vortex of hell. She believed that if she did her job with skill and compassion, this nightmarish moment of awful discovery would inevitably change their lives, but not necessarily come to define them. If she ever stopped believing that, she would find another job.

Sargent turned toward the levee of debris. As she scanned the terrain, she mapped out in her mind the downstream areas, where the wind had shoved the building and everything in it. That was where she always started, at what she called the high-probability areas.

First she called Cinco, a German shepherd as black as a moonless night. Nearly six years old, Cinco was all she could ever want in a K-9 partner, a combination of unwavering loyalty and uncanny intelligence. Slow and methodical in every search, extremely consistent, he was born with a work ethic most humans could not match. Cinco had come into her life shortly after the death of Logan, who had been killed in the line of duty as he had searched for the remains of a little girl in Georgia. The dog had slid down an embankment and under the wheels of a passing car. He died in Sargent's arms. The only good thing that had come out of it was Cinco, a pick-of-the-litter puppy whose name she had chosen before the birth of his litter on Cinco de Mayo, 2005. As she trained him, Cinco showed a precocious talent and love for his job. When he turned twelve months old, he passed certification tests for tracking, search and rescue, and cadaver search in a single week. He had since been on hundreds of searches, on live national TV, and in movies.

Now Sargent took Cinco to a neutral zone, a place in the grass free of any debris, with no likelihood of remains. This was the first step of the search.

"Tracy, what do you need help with?" said Brian Phillips, the lieutenant with whom she and her boyfriend, Shannon Corbell, had been paired on a search team.

"You and Shannon's sole job is to protect these dogs from vehicles," she said.

"What do you mean?"

"When we're searching an area, you stand by the road. You need to make sure there's no traffic coming. And if there is, you stop it."

The two-story hill of debris towered above them, a twisted amalgamation of trees and boards, walls and roofs. Men in green jumpsuits and red hard hats were crawling all over it, searching for the body that had evaded them, as it had other rescuers, for days. From a distance they looked like fire ants swarming over a kicked-over anthill. A yellow track hoe was parked on top, plucking and digging with the metal spork angled from the wrist of its long, jointed arm.

Sargent asked the men to come down from the debris mountain and the track-hoe operator to stop. The scene grew silent, except for the dog's footsteps and her breathing. All eyes were trained on Cinco.

"Hunt!" Sargent said.

Cinco raised his nose to the wind and his black ears perked up as he searched the atmosphere for a scent that he had been trained for years to distinguish from the scent of rotting food or animal remains. He trotted past a shredded wall to a concrete slab and sat. This was his "alert," his signal to Tracy that this was the place where he smelled death. It was the precise location where Nicole Mixon had been found five days ago, a responder said. Sargent tossed Cinco a ball, his reward for the job. After he played with it for a minute, she took it away.

"Hunt!" she said again.

This time, the jet-black German shepherd tiptoed up the mountain of debris with deliberation and restraint. Sargent followed him, walking along the foot of the mountain. About two-thirds of the way to the top, he stopped and stuck his head in a hole. Then he raised it, looked at Sargent, and sat.

The whole process took about twelve seconds.

It felt to Sargent as if the air had been sucked out of the area, as if everyone present had been holding their breath and suddenly inhaled. Most of the observers did not know what it meant. But they knew it meant something.

Cinco got his ball. His game was over.

Now it was Chance's turn.

A honey-colored mix between a yellow Labrador and a golden retriever, Chance was younger, faster, and eager to please. He had come to Sargent as a puppy, after a family rejected him for chewing on things and left him at a shelter. Someone at the shelter noticed something special about this dog and asked Sargent to evaluate him. He was just four months old, but they were right. This dog was fearless, agile, and smart.

Chance worked faster than Cinco. Where the serious German shepherd was calculating and methodical, the Lab-retriever was a bundle of instinct and athleticism. Chance fared better in debris piles because of his long legs, sure-footed confidence, and fearless sensibility. He was born to do this.

"Hunt!"

The small crowd of responders watched in total silence as Chance went to work. He had been kept around the corner and out of sight, and had not observed Cinco doing his search. Chance bounded up the debris with the agility and speed of an antelope. Without hesitation, he ran to the very spot where Cinco had alerted, and sat.

The silence was palpable as everyone strained to hear what Sargent whispered to Phillips.

"The dogs are telling me there's something there," she said quietly. "The track-hoe operator needs to remove debris exactly where the dogs sat."

The great machine rumbled to life through the eerie silence and removed two or three scoops of debris with great caution. The crowd murmured, and the energy focused on that one spot was so thick you could have poured it in buckets.

Phillips raised his hand.

The track-hoe operator stopped.

The investigator leaned forward, straining to see what might be hidden there. When bodies are swept into the debris ball of a twister, they become part of it. Coated with dirt, they are hard to distinguish from their brown surroundings. Phillips stared deep into the puzzle and saw what few people would be able to see. A face, smeared with mud like a camouflaged soldier, emerged from the rubble, as if surfacing from deep water.

Phillips stood, turned toward Sargent, and gave a thumbs-up.

A collective surge of relief filled the air, the mission finally accomplished. It gave her chills. This father's five-day nightmare of waiting had come to an end. The rescuers removed the last branches and boards and lifted the young man from the rubble. Four men carried him, each supporting a limb, and laid him on a clear spot of ground.

Two CSI guys in dress pants walked around the mountain.

"You have found him," the father said.

"Yes, we found him."

The father asked to see him. Usually, this is discouraged. It can be gruesome, haunting. This is why rescuers often make families wait until the emotionally antiseptic setting of the morgue, after the bodies have been cleaned up. And sometimes, that is why they push the photograph.

But the father needed to see his boy. He told them so, and sent his wife and oldest son away. Given his composure and what he had endured, giving him a moment with his son on the scene was the only right thing to do.

The father knelt by his boy, took him in his arms, and wept with grace and dignity. He told him that he loved him, and that he would miss him. He held his son with such tenderness, with such unconditional, absolute love, that it made some of the grown men turn away and scrub imaginary dirt from their eyes.

Marcus Smith was a twenty-one-year-old student, a bright young man from Richmond, Virginia, with a broad smile and his father's kind eyes. A junior at the University of Alabama, he had been on track to graduate next spring with a business degree. His Sigma Pi fraternity brothers knew him as a genuinely happy, humble guy who was as passionate about church as he was about sports. After Wednesday night services at Northwood Church of Christ, where he sat with his girlfriend in the third or fourth pew, he would join his church buddies for a game of basketball. Every Friday afternoon found them playing football at Snow Hinton Park. The last Sunday before the storm, he taught a Bible study at a member's home and spoke about putting God first.

Marcus Smith had been in his apartment talking on the phone with his girlfriend when the phone went dead on Wednesday afternoon. She drove there to check on him and had helped the firefighters search.

Today every rescuer who had been to Charleston Square felt a great burden lifted, knowing the son who was lost for so long had been found. He was the needle in this citywide haystack.

His father, Robert Smith, thanked the men, who were startled by his graciousness; they were doing their job, but in his eyes they saw an arresting reminder of exactly why they did that job.

The rescuers would speak of this moment for years.

He had been waiting there for four days.

CHAPTER 31

THE WAKE

2:00 P.M., SUNDAY, MAY 1, 2011—HARTSELLE, ALABAMA

On the drive to Danielle's visitation, Kelli Rumanek wore a new black dress, one of the few items of clothing she now owned. Her mother was at the wheel and her boyfriend in the back, and their presence was the only thing keeping her on the solid side of a precipitous ledge.

Kelli was not okay. She had come home to find her roommates dead under her devastated house. She had no doubt that the horror of this would haunt her for the rest of her life.

At first she had shut down, her eyes absent of tears, her body frozen by a numbness that made her catatonic. Underneath that deceptive stillness, fear and anxiety pounded within her. When something tripped the fuse, her heart would flutter, her eyes would dilate, and her breathing would grow shallow and rapid. Her mind would race with a million fears, founded and unfounded, until she shut down again.

Her mother and boyfriend had whisked her away to Atlanta for a couple of days to get her out of Tuscaloosa, a beloved hometown transformed overnight into a minefield of sights, smells, and sounds that triggered flashes of terror. Arresting and visceral, the flashbacks would accost her like muggers leaping from the shadows of her mind in unexpected moments. A conversation, an object, a memory was all it took to unleash them.

She had not wanted to go back to the house, ever. Not until it was an empty slab.

"Kelli, you have happy memories there," Dianne said. "Your life is there. We need to go."

"No."

Dianne knew she could not force her daughter, but she felt it was important for her to go. She knew that Kelli would find at least a few mementos that conjured happy memories. If she could salvage a few pieces of her past from under that house, maybe the house, and the past, would not become haunted.

Kelli finally relented. When they got to the house, the hallway was visible, and the girls' clothes fluttered silently in their closets. Kelli's brother crawled into the voids and called out, asking what he should be looking for.

"Can you get my necklaces?" Kelli said. Handmade in Uganda, they were not worth much, but they were a hundred happy moments of her first big trip abroad, strung together on a bit of string.

"I can see them, but I can't get there," he said. "They're under something."

"What can you see?"

"I'm just gonna grab stuff."

Her brother crawled out clutching a shirt. It was a man's Hawaiian shirt, patterned with brown palm fronds on a black background. It was her boyfriend's shirt, and Kelli hated it, thought it was as ugly as homemade sin. But Eric loved it. She didn't have the heart to throw it away, so she had hidden it deep in her closet.

"Hey!" Eric said. "I thought I lost that shirt!"

For the first time in days, Kelli found herself laughing.

They salvaged a bedside lamp that had belonged to her grandmother, with a Tiffany-style stained-glass shade that somehow escaped a single crack. Her brother found a little tie-dyed scarf tied in a heavy bundle.

"It's my rocks!" she cried, weeping as if they were diamonds. "My Uganda rocks!"

As they left, Kelli turned to her mother and admitted that she had been right.

"I hope I never have to come back here again," she said. "But I'm glad we came."

Now, as they drove to Danielle's visitation, she wondered whether she would feel that way again. Kelli was not sure she could bring herself to go in. She did not know how to face her friends' parents. She felt a great, heavy guilt about being at the library instead of at the house. She feared being identified as the one who did not die beside her friends. Every time she watched the news she feared seeing her home on CNN. This unrelenting, ominous feeling of dread pervaded her days and consumed her thoughts. When she walked down the street, she felt certain people could see her guilt, branding her indelibly as if with a scarlet tattoo.

They arrived in Hartselle around two o'clock and were among the first in line at Danielle's visitation. Kelli began to unravel in the parking lot. Her pupils shrank and her breath grew quick and shallow. She fought the terror of being recognized, of being known as The One Who Lived.

"Honey, you don't need to do this," Dianne said.

"I've got to do this!" she said. "You have to go first."

As they stood in the receiving line, Kelli fought the urge to run. And when they finally stood face-to-face with Terri, Ed, and Michelle, she felt the terror squeezing her throat. She thought they would hate her for living.

Terri turned to Kelli with a flash of recognition.

Kelli braced herself.

"Oh, sweetheart!" Terri said, hugging her hard. "Thank God you're okay!"

Kelli broke open then, and all the sadness spilled out onto Terri's shoulder in a glorious rush of sobs and release. Her dead friend's mother held her up, held her with love and no need for forgiveness.

"There's a reason you survived," Terri said. "You've got to live your life for the three of them."

Dianne Rumanek stood speechless beside them, in awe of this

woman showing such grace and dignity as she prepared to bury her child. There had been moments when Rumanek felt so grateful Kelli's life had been spared, but that gratitude came laced with guilt knowing others had not been so lucky. Later, Dianne pulled Terri aside and thanked her.

"I watched you give my child her life back," she said. "I'll never forget that as long as I live."

"Dianne, the pain in that child's eyes," Terri said, "I did what any mother would do."

"You did what any mother would like to *think* that they would do."

■ ■ ■

The funeral home scheduled an early viewing, because the director did not know whether or when the power would be restored, or the air-conditioning. Terri worried that there were not enough flowers. Without power, the florists had watched their inventory wilt in the heat. Clay's family made up for it with photographs. As mourners waited in an hour-long line that led to the closed pastel casket, they walked through twenty-four years of memories curated with great care. A slide show flashed through Danielle's life in snapshots, and Clay's sister had included messages written by friends and family on her Facebook page. On a table, notebooks, journals, newspaper clippings, and photographs formed a mosaic of her childhood and youth. Danielle as a baby, then as a toddler holding her baby sister. In her soccer jersey, on bended knee. Standing in the yellow prom dress she helped buy with McDonald's wages. High school graduation. Making goofy faces with Michelle.

A middle-aged man who only knew her from the Wingate looked sadly through the portrait of a life cut short. Flipping through her high school yearbook, he began weeping for the umpteenth time since he had heard about her death. On the page, she shared where she thought she would be ten years after graduation. Danielle wrote, *Married with at least one child. Graduated from college and helping people for a living.*

That sounds about right, thought Joe Kryzkowski.

Joe was a customer and a casual friend who knew Danielle from the Wingate. He stayed there during his business trips to the Michelin tire plant. Joe remembered the first time he met Danielle, during one of his first stays at the Wingate. She was in training under a manager, but she projected a natural friendliness with everyone who walked in the room. As she typed his information during check-in, she noticed his address was in Decatur, not far from her hometown.

"What part of Decatur?" she said brightly.

Joe immediately grew suspicious.

Why is this cute girl striking up a conversation out of the blue?

She looked about the same age as his daughter. Joe was the kind of man who did not open up to strangers, and he responded aloofly to her friendly overtures. But Danielle had a gift for breaking down walls with her unrelenting friendliness. When Joe realized this girl was not flirting, he lightened up. They soon learned that they belonged to the same parish and had several friends in common.

Joe became one of her favorite regular guests at the Wingate. She always gave him the best room, and he liked to pick on her by ringing the front desk bell obnoxiously. Whenever she saw him coming, she would run and snatch it away, laughing. Even when she claimed to be in a very bad mood, she was kind. And blunt in ways that he came to appreciate. Danielle called him out whenever he said something cynical, and she taught him the value of laughing at the absurdities of life.

When he heard through the grapevine about her death, Joe found himself bewildered by the unexpected emotions that accosted him. He did not think he knew her well enough to grieve this much. Needing someone to talk to, he called his ex-wife, who was as puzzled as he was by the magnitude of his feelings.

"Joe," she said, "I've never heard you cry before. Just what did this girl mean to you?"

That question haunted his thoughts for days. He had known her for only a year and a half. They were casual friends, and nothing more.

He saw her, at most, once a week. And yet, he felt the crushing sadness of the void she had left in the world. He puzzled over it for some time.

What did Danielle mean to me? Why have I been so torn up?

After considerably more self-examination than he was accustomed to, he came to several answers. Danielle surfaced in his life at a very tough time, when he did not even realize how much he needed a friend. When she asked "How are you?" she was one of the very few people in his life who cared to hear the *real* answer. Most people hear, but they do not listen. She did. And beyond that, she cared. They had shared many thoughtful conversations about life, and she always gave surprisingly salient advice for someone half his age. Just as her yearbook suggested, she was born to help others. She was special. More than that, she made everyone around her feel special, too. As Maya Angelou wrote, "I have learned that people will forget what you said, people will forget what you did, but people will never forget how you made them feel."

The fact that Danielle had so much to give the world, and died so young, in such a horrible way, shook him to the core. It made him think of his own mortality and the value of true friends, so few and so fragile. Danielle had cracked his cynical shell and freed a long-dormant part of his heart that had been afraid to love. He reflected on this and wrote a long essay about it, and shared it with her family. In it, he shared a great and vulnerable conclusion that helped her family comprehend the subtle ways in which she helped others:

> *I think the main reason I have reacted so was because her death forced me to admit that I love her. Not in the romantic way, but in the "This is truly my friend and I would do anything for her because I know she would do anything for me" way. And, when you think about it, how rare is that?*

■ ■ ■

Joe Kryzkowski was one of 350 people who consoled the Downs family with poignant testaments. For three hours they absorbed a thousand hugs, ten thousand tears, and a million kind words. No parent ever imagines such a day, but Ed and Terri found themselves moved and humbled. With each hug, Terri felt a little bit stronger.

Even in the midst of their infinite sorrow, Ed and Terri had the chance to catch a glimpse of their daughter through the eyes of the world. That she had meant so much to so many different people revealed a side of her they always knew, but now they cast it in a new light. She truly had made a difference. She had not died on the cusp of a life of service; she had already lived one. And for this she would be remembered. With that knowledge came the very start of healing.

There is no getting over this. There is only getting through it.

▪ ▪ ▪

Kelli Rumanek felt that she could breathe again for the first time in five days. Terri's words had released the chains of fear and guilt that held her psyche hostage. That moment was the first step on a long and treacherous road through grief and recovery. With this influx of oxygen came new strength that surprised both Kelli and her family.

"I am not sure what I expected, but I am so glad we came," Kelli told her mom. "I think we can still make it to Loryn's visitation."

"Really?"

"No, Mom. I feel better!"

"Well, okay!"

They left one funeral home and drove to another, 170 miles away.

PART III

THE RECOVERY

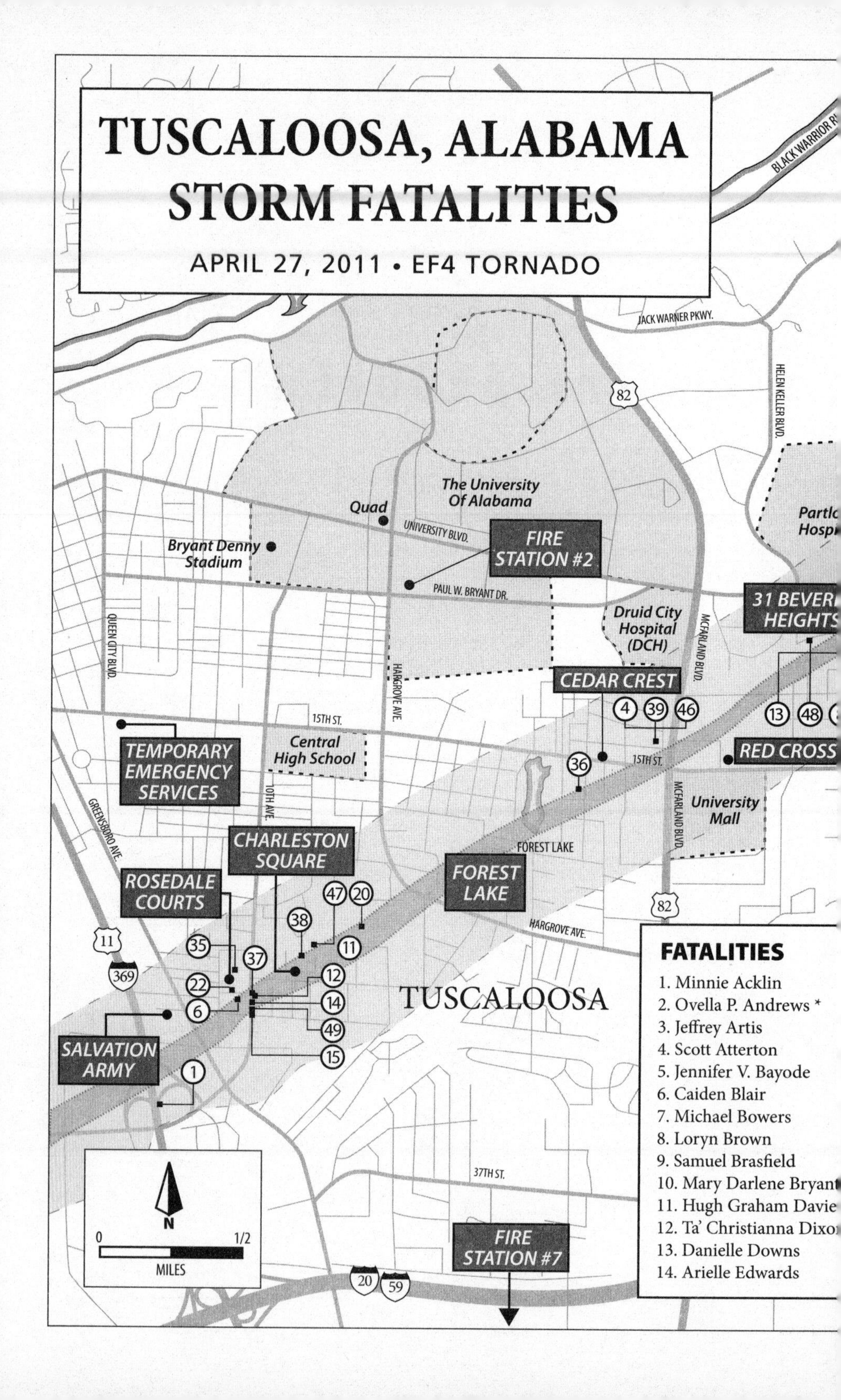

TUSCALOOSA, ALABAMA
STORM FATALITIES
APRIL 27, 2011 • EF4 TORNADO
BLACK WARRIOR R
JACK WARNER PKWY.
HELEN KELLER BLVD.
82
The University Of Alabama
Quad
UNIVERSITY BLVD.
FIRE STATION #2
Bryant Denny Stadium
PAUL W. BRYANT DR.
Druid City Hospital (DCH)
MCFARLAND BLVD.
CEDAR CREST
QUEEN CITY BLVD.
HARGROVE AVE.
15TH ST.
Central High School
TEMPORARY EMERGENCY SERVICES
10TH AVE.
GREENSBORO AVE.
CHARLESTON SQUARE
ROSEDALE COURTS
FOREST LAKE
University Mall
RED CROSS
31 BEVER HEIGHTS
Partl Hosp
11
369
SALVATION ARMY
TUSCALOOSA
37TH ST.
N
0
1/2
MILES
FIRE STATION #7
20
59
FATALITIES
1. Minnie Acklin
2. Ovella P. Andrews *
3. Jeffrey Artis
4. Scott Atterton
5. Jennifer V. Bayode
6. Caiden Blair
7. Michael Bowers
8. Loryn Brown
9. Samuel Brasfield
10. Mary Darlene Bryant
11. Hugh Graham Davie
12. Ta' Christianna Dixo
13. Danielle Downs
14. Arielle Edwards

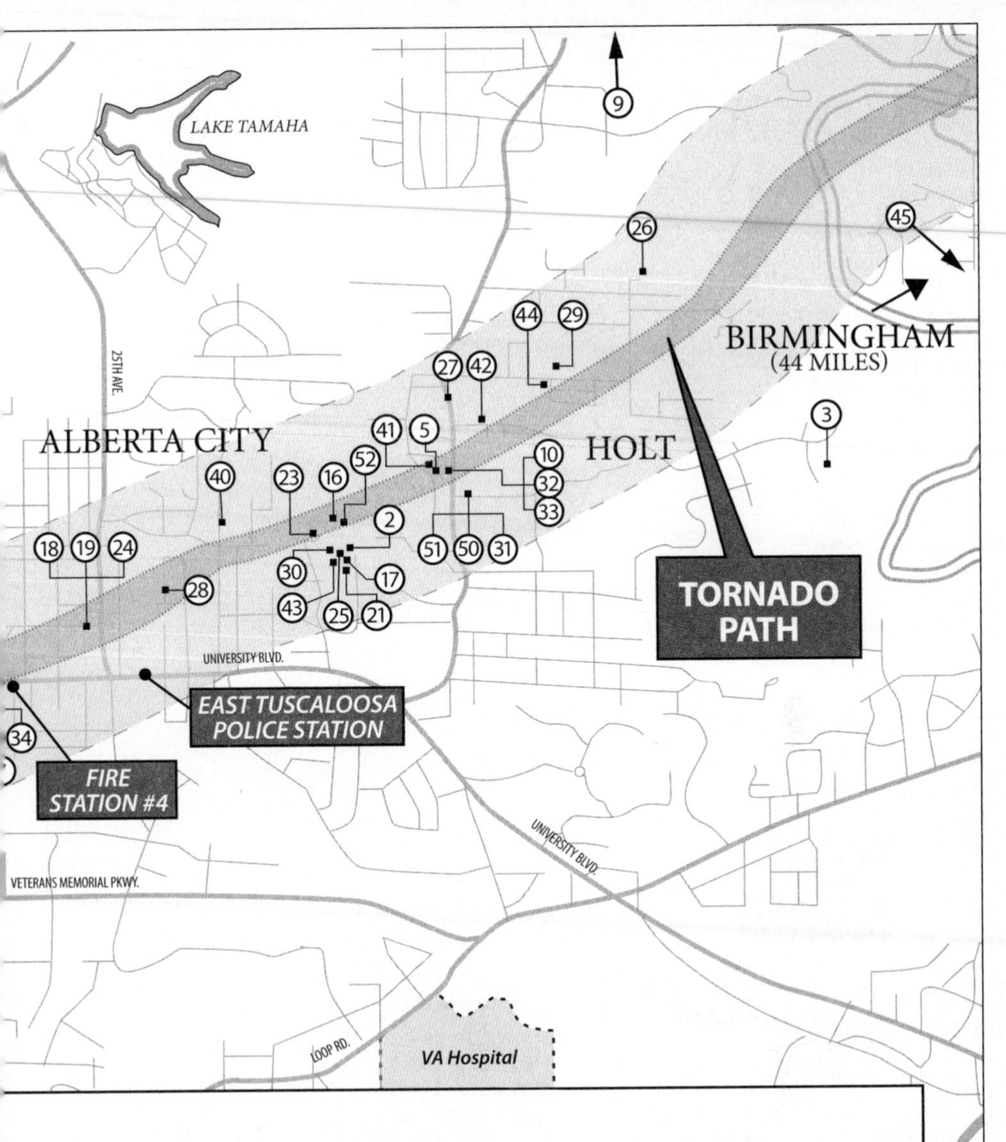

15. MaKayla Edwards
16. Melgium Farley
17. Thomas Hannah*
18. Cedria Harris
19. Keshun Harris
20. Ashley Harrison
21. Robert Gene Hicks*
22. Shena Hutchins
23. Carolyn Ann Jackson
24. Jacqueline Jefferson
25. Leota Jones*
26. Helen Kemp*
27. Thelma May Bennett Krallman
28. Tennie Mozelle Lancaster
29. Davis Lynn "Gordo" Lathem
30. Lee Andrew Lee*
31. Velma T. LeRoy
32. Dorothy Lewis
33. Thomas D. Lewis
34. Yvonne Mayes
35. Christian A. McNeil
36. William R. McPherson*
37. Zy'Queria McShan*
38. Melanie Nicole Mixon
39. Perry Blake Peek
40. Lola Pitts
41. Terrilyn Plump
42. Kevin V. Rice, Sr.
43. Colvin Rice*
44. Annie Lois Humphries Sayer
45. Judy Sherrill
46. Morgan Marlene Sigler
47. Marcus Smith
48. William Chance Stevens
49. Justin Le'Eric Thomas
50. Patricia Hodo Turner
51. Willie Lee "Trey" Turner III
52. Helen Wurm*

* Subsequent deaths attributed to the storm

CHAPTER 32

PICKING UP THE PIECES

AFTER THE STORM—ACROSS THE SOUTH

Little pieces of Mississippi fell on Alabama. Alabama rained down on Tennessee. A flock of blue jeans from a plant in Hackleburg flapped forty-six miles and landed in a field. Photographs from Phil Campbell fluttered down over Lenoir City, Tennessee, 280 miles away. Across the South, bits of lives that had ridden the winds were picked out of azaleas and barbed-wire fences.

One of them was a memory quilt that flew over two counties and landed in a muddy backyard in Athens, Alabama. When she found it, Leah Meyer saw through the rips and stains, saw the life unfolding in photos—a baby, a little girl in a pageant, a teenager playing basketball. The bobcat emblem was a clue that led to Phil Campbell High School, seventy-five miles away. Leah ran her fingers over the embroidered name—*Carrie Lynn*—and knew she had to find her. She posted a photo of the quilt on a Facebook page that served as a giant lost-and-found for belongings taken by the storm. And then she waited.

It was like this all across the South, as people helped victims pick up the pieces of their lives. Friends, neighbors, and perfect strangers did not wait for the many agencies that were on the way with help. As soon as the winds died down, they started rescuing one another.

In a trailer park in Holt, Angie Hays lay under a collapsed wall, trapped with her son and daughter-in-law. The wall was pinned by a water heater and a double-door fridge, and they pushed in vain. Hays cried out for help.

She could not see help coming. But she will never forget its voice.

"Just keep hollerin'!" the voice boomed. "I'll find you!"

"I'm right here!" she screamed. "Someone's standing on my leg!"

"Good—it's me," said the voice. "Hold on a minute. I'll get you out."

The voice belonged to Robert Reed, a man who had seen the inside of a Mississippi prison, but started over in Crescent Mobile Home Estates. At first, the neighbors, black and white, had eyed him with suspicion. His hard work and pretty landscaping had won them over. Now he was the manager.

Huddled in the bathtub with his fiancée and kids, Reed had flown through the air, grabbing for the children, and landed in a field. He threw himself on his daughter as an airborne truck grazed the back of his neck. Afterward, he plucked an air-conditioning unit off his fiancée's head, and once he saw she was alive, he ran to help others.

Within minutes he had dug out twelve people.

■ ■ ■

The days that followed were fueled by volunteers with coolers.

Even as relief trucks filled with cans of beans and shelf-stable meat rolled into every battered town, so did a battalion of Junior League bakers, backyard chefs, and Samaritans armed with spatulas. They rolled into town after devastated town, towing grills the size of campers.

Cooks of all stripes tied on their aprons, stepped up to the plate, and filled it. They were faith groups that set up buffet lines under tents in church parking lots. Families from small towns that had been spared. Professional chefs who offered free meals at their restaurants. Students who fired up their backyard grills and cooked all the meat from their neighbors' melting freezers. When the parking lots were filled with trucks and tents, they found a flat spot on the side of the road and held a cardboard sign: FREE FOOD!

They did it because food is love. Because they knew that dragging branches and lifting boards could not be done on an empty stomach. In the South, food and tragedy are sisters. And while the instinct to feed others in a crisis may not be strictly southern, what they prepared, and how they did it, may be the region's finest recipe.

Some ills in this world cannot be cured by a chocolate cake with buttercream frosting. But that cake, and the compassion baked into it, may be more beautiful than any cake that graced the cover of a magazine. It was what Rita Trull could give of herself, and she joined a few friends from a small-town church on a drive to Smithville, Mississippi, devastated by an EF5. From the looks of the spread in front of her, she was not alone in her ability to help, and cope, through baking. When she put out a call for help after the storm, the answer came strong and sweet:

"I said, 'I need some cakes for these people!' I had twenty-one cakes come to my house."

In Tuscaloosa, a man with a grill and trailer loaded with groceries tried driving into Alberta City. The National Guardsmen stopped him at a roadblock—only residents were being allowed in. So the man found a grassy median by the river and parked his grill in the middle of four-lane Jack Warner Parkway. People saw him and honked and pulled over to help. Before long he was feeding the National Guard. They got him into Alberta.

He set up his tent in a strip-mall parking lot, a staging area surrounded by devastation. Soon he had neighbors. The tents sprang up like wild mushrooms after a rain, and together they merged into a phenomenon that felt like the cross between a food court and a melting pot. The Germans from the Mercedes plant brought a cooking team that built burgers like a well-oiled assembly line. An army of Baptists teamed up and did prep work. The Methodists were in charge of deliveries. A group of Muslims grilled side by side with football coaches. The only walls between them were built out of clear stacks of cases upon cases of water. Their culinary resourcefulness knew no limits; if it didn't move, they grilled it.

"Hey, Coach, d'ya think we can grill this?" asked a man, holding up a giant soft pretzel.

"I dunno. Do you?"

"What the heck, let's try!"

In the storm-whipped town of Vilonia, Arkansas, two thousand volunteers showed up to pitch in. The Senior Citizens Center became the headquarters of help, and those who ran it—retired teachers, moms—somehow found a way to feed twelve hundred people three square meals a day.

In the fable of Stone Soup, a broth that starts with one boiled rock is proven to feed a village—when each villager chips in one ingredient. Vilonia saw that happen, as the meals came together like a town-wide potluck. The elementary school gave sausage and biscuits. The bank donated a near half-ton of meat. Ten flats of milk arrived from the grocery store, unbidden. The brand-new Mexican restaurant fed everyone and charged no one. The ice-cream company brought freezers and an eighteen-wheeler packed with ice, a giant community fridge where people saved food from their powerless kitchens.

Some people cried into that first hot meal, because it tasted so good, so normal. No one saw even close to the bottom of the barrel, much less had to scrape it.

"I had twenty-five cases of hamburger meat in the fridge trailer, and I went in there the other day and there were still twenty-five cases, even though we've been going through it every day for two weeks," said Sandy Towles, a retired teacher who volunteers at the Senior Citizens Center. "People just keep bringing us more to serve. It's like the proverbial loaves and fishes."

Vilonia's victims were soon feeding its volunteers. Miss Dollie Pruett, in her midsixties, rose at 4:00 a.m. to bake two hundred biscuits slathered with gravy for the National Guard. Military, firemen, and police came hungry from around the state. Volunteers such as Lorenda Gantz-Donham worked double-shift hours to feed them.

"We may be stinky and we may be bankrupt," said Lorenda, who had never before cooked for an army, "but we will be full."

On an urban farm in Tuscaloosa, where fourth graders once studied rows of turnips, the crops were poisoned with fiberglass. Tuscaloosa's Forest Lake was stripped of many of its oaks. But the founders of the Druid City Garden Project looked at the mess and saw another teachable moment. Andy Grace, a film professor, and his wife, Rashmi, tore out the ruined crops and planted sunflowers, zinnias, and marigolds, something pretty to look at as the neighborhood was rebuilt.

They reached out to local farmers for vegetables they could not grow themselves and turned them into collards and corn bread, roasted potatoes, homemade lasagna bursting with summer squash. A break from the shelters' emergency rations, often spooned from a can, these meals would be their next lesson: food heals.

They called their project the Soul Food Brigade. In the kitchen of an Episcopal chapel, the couple formed a unique supper club, a group of friends who had already shared a meal many evenings before, chopping hip-to-hip, weeping over cut onions, preparing a communal meal. Now they cooked for people who didn't have kitchens, for people who had driven hundreds of miles to ask a stranger "How can I help you?" They cooked meals that they would proudly serve company, prepared things that feed more than hunger. "This is the kind of food that we make when we're together," Andy said. "We wouldn't serve anything less."

■ ■ ■

People gave what they could. Nothing was too big or too small. Hair bows for Hackleburg. Free haircuts in Pleasant Grove. Portrait sessions for families whose memories were stolen by the wind. A thirteen-year-old girl from Arkansas found a temporary home for a family. Five friends in Mississippi filled a truck. Someone bought a brand-new house for a person he would never meet. A man who had lost everything to his own life's storms—divorce, a lost job, a wreck that left him in a wheelchair—gave blood. It was all he had left to give.

It was not only southerners who gave with great heart and imagination. The Yankees gave five hundred thousand dollars. A Los Angeles–based group called Calabama held a bikini car wash to raise funds for Tuscaloosa. Las Vegas gave cash. Texas sent gas cards. One New York lady dispatched a tractor-trailer full of tarps, just in time for the first Alabama rain. Japan sent eight thousand blankets to Alabama, a thank-you gift for all the help Americans had sent in the wake of the March tsunami.

A man in the little medieval town of Holt, England, saw a photograph of Holt, Alabama, where entire neighborhoods of modest homes had been mowed into the ground. Inspired by that image, Alan Heath rallied his church choir to hold a benefit concert for their sister town four thousand miles away. They sang gospel songs and great southern spirituals and auctioned off a quilt. They called the concert Heart to Heart; Holt to Holt, and they raised two thousand dollars.

The tiny town of Phil Campbell, Alabama, had been nearly wiped out by the EF5 that killed twenty-seven, destroyed three hundred homes, and demolished the high school. It was the eponymous destination of the Phil Campbell convention, a gathering of Phil Campbells (and at least one Phyllis) from around the world. In the wake of the storm, twenty Phil Campbells convened from as far away as England and Australia to rebuild their namesake town.

People still wrote checks to the Red Cross, still carried boxes of clothes to the Salvation Army. But help also flowed from house to house. Responding to tweets and retweets for help, strangers drove across town with a box of formula and hugged the mother with the hungry child. Synapse by synapse, whole communities knitted themselves together into a symbiotic phenomenon that transcended, or maybe even ripped away, the invisible walls that had once divided.

As complex as the system was, the needs were plain and simple. Hackleburg posted a need for juice boxes and children's underwear of every size. Fultondale needed chain saws and cardboard boxes dropped off at the command center—the library. Ohatchee needed manual labor. TES, Danielle's workplace, requested baby supplies. One woman from Etowah County had a message posted on James Spann's Facebook page, asking for help in fixing her house. Forty people came to her doorstep. Spann's Facebook page became such a valuable hub that the Red Cross began monitoring it.

The tragedy drove a die-hard alumnus of Auburn University, who answers her phone "War Eagle! This is Holly" to send truck after truck to rivals who yell "Roll Tide!" That said everything about the power of a crisis to unite. Holly Hart hated the University of Alabama Crimson Tide with the heat of a thousand suns.

"I'll tell you straight," she told everyone, whether they asked or not. "I cheer for Auburn and whoever is playing Alabama."

Yet here she was, one of a team of eleven staunch Auburn fans who gave everything to help the Tide's hometown. They could not explain it. They only knew one thing: in times of trouble, people help people. No matter what.

Toomer's for Tuscaloosa began as a Facebook group where victims and volunteers could connect online. The name was a twist on Tide for Toomer's, a group that had formed when a wayward Tide fan poured herbicide on the roots of the hallowed oaks that towered over Toomer's Corner in Auburn. It was sacred ground to Auburn fans, who honored the longstanding tradition of toilet-papering the trees. Fans of the Tide, acknowledging their brother's breach of the rules of warfare, had banded together and raised fifty thousand dollars for an effort to save the trees. They had called it Tide for Toomer's.

All but two of the eleven Auburn alumni behind Toomer's for Tuscaloosa had never met in person. But that did not seem to matter, and they came together behind the cause. Within two days, the Facebook group grew to more than twenty thousand people and would ultimately top eighty thousand. They would send help to more towns than they bothered to count—even to their own sworn enemies.

Equipped with a smartphone and uncommon sense, Holly Hart, an interior designer and mother of three, played dispatcher controller for waves of trucks sent by church groups, towns, and folks who have learned not to wait for help. She used a Facebook group as her command center where avatars moved semi-trucks and status updates brought real people face-to-face.

"This is social media, but how it is being used is more like the old-fashioned church phone tree," said James Chris Fields, a member of the Toomer's crew. And that is how a mother with grown kids, who had never been trained in emergency response, managed donations and cries for help from eighty-six thousand people.

"Anybody can make a difference in the lives of others if they're just willing to show up," said Holly. "None of us has any training in this. If each person gets out and helps one other person, it doesn't take long for this to be taken care of."

▪ ▪ ▪

The memory quilt that had flown seventy-five miles in the storm finally found its way back to the place where it took flight. Leah Meyer had tried to clean it but decided the rips and stains were another chapter in its beautiful story. One sunny day a few weeks after the storm, she unfolded it on a flat, dry place where a house once stood in the rural town of Phil Campbell.

Cradling her newborn son, Carrie Lynn Morgan, a mother of two, reached out to accept one of the last mementos that remained of her childhood. She had lost her house, and all the memories in it, to a fire some years ago. The quilt survived at her mother's house. She left it there, where she thought it would be safer. When April's tornado took that house—thank goodness no one was home—it left nothing behind but sky.

Leah did not know that story when she posted a picture of the quilt on a Facebook lost-and-found page. Carrie Lynn did not see that picture. She had no power, and her phone was dead. The news found her, though, through the old-fashioned grapevine, a little luck, and a friend who spotted a familiar smile before the post rolled off the screen.

"This quilt is my life, my journey through everything," she told Leah. "I see my baby pictures and realize how much my kids look like me."

Leah smiled.

"I'm glad we found you."

CHAPTER 33

BUT NOT DESTROYED

MONDAY, MAY 2, 2011—PRICEVILLE, ALABAMA

Chanel Chapman, the good friend of Danielle's who also worked the front desk at the Wingate, had driven up for the funeral from Tuscaloosa. She was still trying to grasp the existence of a world without her friend. Chanel's toddlers called her Auntie Danielle and did not care that her skin did not look like theirs, and the young mother had considered moving with Danielle to Florida, finding a place near the beach where her kids could play in the gentle surf with Danielle's little cousins.

Why would someone who cared so deeply for others be stolen from a world that needed her? Chanel remembered the day they had checked in a guest who seemed sad, so sad. Danielle had tried to cheer him up. The next day, housekeeping found his body in the bed. He had died in his sleep. Danielle sat in the office and cried until her worried boss sent her home early. It struck Chanel that it took a special person to feel that kind of compassion for a stranger. "No matter what anyone does in their life," Danielle had said, "nobody deserves to die alone."

■ ■ ■

Michelle had picked out her sister's outfit one final time. A lavender blouse had seemed to leap into her hands at Goody's. It felt like a sign, so she bought it. Never again would she be able to shop there without thinking of that moment. On her feet she placed the happy shoes that had walked across the stage.

Danielle's going to kill me, she thought, laughing briefly through the tears. *Her feet are going to hurt forever!*

Before they closed the casket, Michelle cut a lock of Danielle's hair to take to the beach and release in the waters that brought her sister peace. She placed in her casket a few favorite things: the radio she used for listening to UA football games and her purple stuffed dragon. Around her neck Danielle would wear her Joan of Arc medal to the grave.

The funeral was held at Annunciation of the Lord, the family's Catholic church, on a Monday at 3:00 p.m. Sunlight backlit the stained-glass window filled with angels whispering to Mary. A priest spoke of heaven as he sprinkled holy water on a sky-blue casket with a Celtic design that Danielle would have liked.

Terri saw Danielle's life spooling backward through the years, like an old home movie on rewind. She saw the woman about to graduate, the teenager who agreed to a blind date to junior prom with a cancer patient she had never met. The little girl who befriended a child in a wheelchair who could not go onto the playground. The baby with the wisest eyes.

As they played the next-to-last song of the funeral, Terri had a vision of Michelle's future. This home movie ran fast-forward. She saw her as a baby in Danielle's arms, as a sweet-faced toddler hiding behind her sister. She watched Michelle grow up, graduate, and get engaged. The vision ended with an image so bright and clear it seemed as real as a memory.

It was Michelle, five years from now, dressed in a white skirt. Beside her, Clay wore khakis and his MSU polo. Terri and Ed were dressed in wedding clothes. They encircled a baptismal fountain, smiling. In Terri's arms, wiggling in Michelle's tiny white christening gown, was a newborn baby girl.

That afternoon, they stood on the edge of a grave. It was a beautiful spring day, and just beyond the cemetery was an open field exploding with purple wildflowers. It was the ground where Ed's family was laid to rest, so she would not be alone. Her parents bought the plots on either side of her, so she would never lie next to a stranger. The family bowed in prayer.

Terri had chosen a special headstone with great care to detail. The shape of it mirrored the pointed arches of the stained-glass windows of their church. The stone was carved with the words Danielle had written on the whiteboard they found in the rubble:

> *We are hard-pressed on every side, but not crushed,*
> *perplexed, but not in despair;*
> *persecuted, but not abandoned;*
> *struck down but not destroyed.*
>
> —2 Corinthians 4:8

Michelle looked beyond the grave to the lavender field and felt her sister's presence. She picked a small bouquet and laid it on the casket. Her baby cousins did the same. They did not understand this moment, not yet, but they knew it was her favorite color. A little one turned to her mother and worried, "Dan-Dan can't breathe in that box!" Her mother hugged her and cried.

After the casket was lowered into the ground, Ed and Terri each took a shovel to the dirt and let it rain down on their daughter. Michelle, who had kicked off her heels in the field, walked barefoot to the edge of the grave. She dipped her small hand into the soil and sprinkled it gracefully upon her sister.

Before they left, a light breeze stirred the flowers in the field. It felt as if it was Danielle, whispering good-bye.

■ ■ ■

One hundred and seventy miles away, Loryn went down the aisle of her church one last time. As her mother wished, she was in a white dress.

A lady from church had taken the dress and scrubbed the red clay away, and the white cotton gleamed from the open casket. Ashley tucked into her casket a miniature crown and a sign that she hung on her doorknob: SWEET DREAMS. Loryn's grandfather, Ashley's father, had written her a letter, and they placed that with her, too.

One month and eight days after her twenty-first birthday—her grandfather and great-grandmother's birthday, too—Loryn Alexandria Brown was laid to rest in the small cemetery by her church. The grave sat in a peaceful spot in the shade of a stand of pines. There was no sound in the world quite as lonely as the sigh of the wind in those pines.

The headstone was black marble engraved with a photo that they had taken that Easter Sunday. Loryn stands in a white dress, hands on her hips, one red boot cocked out to the side. Her hair blows back off one shoulder, and she smiles. On the back of the stone is her senior quote:

> *Live life to the fullest, it's not the years*
> *in your life, it's the life in your years!*

CHAPTER 34

THE WEDDING

9:00 A.M., TUESDAY, MAY 3, 2011—BEVERLY HEIGHTS, TUSCALOOSA

By the time Dianne Rumanek arrived at the house, Loryn's grandfather was driving his bucket truck. True to his word, he was going to take the house down. He did not want strangers going through his granddaughter's things. This was one thing he could do in a helpless situation, one thing that made him feel less powerless.

"Loryn thought Pop-Pop could fix anything," he told Dianne. "I couldn't fix this. But I could be sure it's handled right."

The day was cold and drizzly. With its mechanical palsy, the backhoe lifted each wall carefully, one by one. As they rose, the families scurried under them, scavenging quickly for whatever they could find. One wall was still covered with Loryn's photos and notes, taped to the pink paint with clear Scotch tape.

The insurance adjuster was also there, scribbling on a clipboard.

"You want to go up?" Mr. Brown said.

The two men went up in the bucket and looked down upon the house. From up high, they could see the damage path and could tell that this was the most badly hit house in the neighborhood. It was the trees.

Mr. Brown had been trimming trees for fifty-five years, and he remembered the day, some years ago, when a previous owner had called him out to 31 Beverly Heights. Brown had counted twenty big red oaks and sweet gums, each three or four feet thick. "The trees are too big and too heavy," he had told the man, advising they cut them down. "Good storm comes along, and they're gonna go."

Now, overlooking the lot from the bucket truck, he counted fourteen trees on the house. The biggest, a red oak that looked nearly a hundred years old, had sliced it through the middle. The agent wiped tears from his eyes. He had never seen anything like this.

Dianne asked the agent whether he could pay Loryn's grandfather for bringing down the house. It was what he wanted. He should be the one. The agent checked her policy and told Mr. Brown what it could pay.

"Is that enough?" he asked.

Mr. Brown nodded slowly.

"That's about what I was thinkin'."

Danielle's family could not be here today. When Dianne called them to tell them they were taking down the house, Terri flatly described the week ahead.

"Tomorrow we have Will's funeral. Then we have Michelle's rehearsal on Thursday night, and the wedding on Friday."

"Seriously?" Dianne said.

"Dianne, the very last thing Danielle would want is for us to cancel this wedding," Terri said.

"You're stronger than me," Dianne said. "I don't think I could do that."

"We just need something to be happy."

■ ■ ■

FRIDAY, MAY 6, 2011—CULLMAN, ALABAMA

On the morning of the wedding in Cullman, the mother of the groom sat on the floor of her closet and wept quietly. Patti Whatley's house was thrumming with groomsmen and guests, and she could not let them hear her cry even though they had buried the maid of honor five days ago.

This is not how it's supposed to be.

She had overheard whispers in the grocery store: "They didn't postpone. It's going to be a sad wedding." Patti wanted to ask these ladies just how long they thought it would be until losing Danielle was no longer sad. One year? Two years? Five years? Ten? No amount of time would change the fact that Danielle was gone. That would never stop being sad.

"Are you going to reschedule?" well-meaning friends and family had asked in the nine days between the storm and the wedding.

"Not that I know of," said Michelle, alarmed and taken off guard the first time she heard the question. It had not even occurred to her.

She ran to her parents in tears. Should they postpone the wedding for a year? Terri and Ed felt strongly that Danielle would have wanted Michelle and Clay to move forward, to be happy. The whole family needed to come together in this moment of joy. No matter how long they waited, Danielle's absence would be present. Clay and his family agreed.

▪ ▪ ▪

Sacred Heart Church stood a few blocks from Cullman's torn downtown, its twin spires towering skyward, topped with gold crosses that caught the sun. On one of the state's biggest pipe organs, Pachelbel's Canon soared over wooden pews and an altar as intricate as lace. The bridesmaids glided down the aisle in long satin gowns the color of wet sand. One by one they lined up by the altar, holding small red bouquets. In the spot where the maid of honor would have stood, a white pedestal presented Danielle's bouquet—white hydrangeas with sprigs of eucalyptus, wrapped in a shimmering ribbon.

The small moments of comedy that punctuate every wedding lightened the gravity. The ring bearer sprinted down the aisle and nearly stepped on a bridesmaid's hem. Two flower girls tottered behind him, the tiny one crawling up the altar in her dress.

And then the music soared and the people rose and turned to the back of the sanctuary, waiting for the bride to emerge through the two great wooden doors. Behind them, Michelle was fighting the hiccups, which she got whenever she was nervous.

"Michelle, breathe," her father whispered. "Breathe."

The doors opened to a new chapter of her life. Clay stood at the altar, looking so handsome in a black tuxedo with a white vest and bow tie. In him, Michelle saw her harbor and her anchor, the man and the future meteorologist who would weather life's storms by her side. The aisle stretched before her, another small walk and another great journey.

At the altar, the priest said, "Love is both in this life and in the next life. Maybe Danielle will be with them during the darkest times, when they seem to be out of gas with each other. We won't be able to see her, but her presence will be there. She will be part of the gigantic unity of love that is God."

During the prayer, Clay took Michelle's right hand. In her left hand, she swore she could feel Danielle's. They always did that in church, and at the end of the prayer, they would try to crush each other's fingers. Danielle always won. Now Michelle thought she felt her sister's squeeze, and she almost laughed out loud.

They lit the unity candle and exchanged vows and rings. The priest wrapped their joined hands in his vestment. After they took their first Mass, the priest presented them to the church. The congregation leapt to its feet.

CHAPTER 35

HEALING

SATURDAY, APRIL 30, 2011—BIRMINGHAM, ALABAMA

On the weekend after the storm, James Spann put down his smartphone and closed his laptop. He pulled on a T-shirt and a baseball cap, loaded a chain saw and a few cases of water in the back of his SUV. His wife and son climbed in to join him for a day they all desperately needed, a day when they could help someone. Part of a caravan of baseball dads in pickup trucks, they drove out of the city and into the rural countryside northwest of Birmingham.

The storm had left eleven hundred miles of tornado tracks that stretched like scars across the South, through cities, forests, and no-stoplight towns. The storms were indiscriminate in their carnage, killing rich and poor, black and white, old men and infants. There was probably not a single person in Alabama who did not know someone touched by this.

Tornadoes are the Russian roulette of storms. In hurricanes, floods, earthquakes, and some other disasters, the damage is widespread. But tornado damage is acute and erratic, leaving one home destroyed next door to one barely touched. Because of this, people ask themselves, perhaps more than in any other disaster:

Why them? Why not me?

The only answer to this question is going out to help.

The Spanns drove to Walker County, the same rural county that had been hit in the April 3, 1974, Super Outbreak, where James Spann spent a pivotal night inside the hospital. They were driving to Cordova, where everyone knew everyone, and strangers could be spotted a half mile away and were often eyed with suspicion. A former mill town that dried up when the mills closed, Cordova before the storm was already fighting for all it had. The city could not afford a paid fire department, but its volunteers were as devoted and passionate as anyone who had ever held a hose.

Cordova had rolled snake-eyes; it was the one town in Alabama to be hit by two major tornadoes on April 27. In the morning, the EF3 had wrecked the downtown. Twelve hours later, almost to the minute, the EF4 struck the mostly empty downtown. Five people died in Cordova that day. Had the first one not hit when it did, and where, that number could have been much higher.

Some of the rescuers were also the victims. Brett Dawkins, the young lieutenant who rescued his aunt and jacked a house off his dead cousin, had come home after two or three days of recovery work downtown to find his house destroyed. He was so tired that he made himself a little pallet of clothes where his bed used to be, curled up, and fell asleep. Now he and his mother were living in the abandoned pharmacy building that had turned into the temporary headquarters of Fire & Rescue, whose station had also been lost. They put cots between the pharmacy shelves and hung a sheet for privacy. They showered at the homes of friends. Life would be this way for months.

Cordova's churches ran the recovery efforts and people from all walks came together. But it was not without its problems. Tragedy brings out the best in people, and also, sometimes, the worst. The mayor was criticized by the national news for enacting a ban on FEMA trailers downtown, though part of that, at least, had to do with the fact that they simply would not fit on those skinny lots. The *New York Times* published a story about a black teenage boy who woke up in the hospital saying that he, his mother, and his two white friends had sought shelter at a church and were turned away. When the second tornado had struck their house, his mother and two friends were killed. Anonymous donors had raised enough money to buy him a ticket to Hawaii to live with his brother. This raised many questions in and outside the little town. Some believed it a genuine effort to help a kid who lost everything, including his mother. Others speculated that certain people wanted to get the boy out of town before he could talk anymore. Few residents would go on the record to answer. Officials looked into it, but it was never resolved.

The tiny downtown of two-story brick storefronts was damaged beyond repair and condemned. The whole history of the town seemed tied up in those buildings, which would be reduced to a flat place in the heart of town, as if they had never existed. But the town could not afford to demolish them for three years, so the vacant buildings stood, a ghost town within a depressed town, an unavoidable reminder that haunted residents and children peering through the windows of school buses every single day.

On the outskirts of Cordova, Spann and the baseball-dad convoy pulled into the first driveway that looked hopeless. There, a double-wide trailer was eviscerated, insulation spilling out like guts. Nine children between twelve months and fourteen years old rambled about in the dust. Their parents, Tom and Heather Adams, had herded the kids into an underground storm shelter and ridden the EF4 out in safety, only to emerge into the daylight with the blinding disbelief that their home had been torn to shreds.

The Adams family—all eleven of them—were living in a tiny silver Airstream trailer parked in front of the uninhabitable double-wide. Heather had a one-year-old baby on her hip and a two-year-old at her knee, but she smiled at the men who pulled into her driveway. She had no idea why they were here.

James gravitated to twelve-year-old Patrick, a boy who dreamed of playing drums in a band. He was of the age James affectionately referred to as "knucklehead," and he introduced the boy to his own thirteen-year-old son, Ryan.

Patrick's ten-year-old sister, Adrianna, smiled and squinted up at James.

"Are you gonna forget about me in an hour?"

"No," James said.

"A year?"

"No."

"Two years from now?"

"No!"

"Knock-knock!"

"Who's there?"

"You said you wouldn't forget me!"

James laughed. How could he forget?

Spann and the baseball dads adopted the Adams family. Over the following months, they would make trip after trip to deliver food, clothing, cleaning supplies, toys. They got in touch with Habitat for Humanity and started building a home. A big one. It looked a bit like a stable, but that's not a bad thing for a couple with nine kids. They tried to get them on *Extreme Makeover: Home Edition*, but it didn't work with the TV show's schedule. They did, however, get the family moved into their brand-new home by December. Just in time to play Santa.

▪ ▪ ▪

After twenty-four nonstop hours on the weather desk, Jason Simpson had fallen with relief into the arms of his pregnant wife. Lacey and the dogs had ridden out the storm in a neighbor's basement, where a tornado had barely missed them. Simpson's family in Holly Pond finally got through to tell him that the family farm had been hit. The barn was gone and the land would never look the same. But none of that mattered, because despite the many close calls, none of his family had been hurt or killed.

The next morning, he woke up to the dreadful news: a death toll of one hundred and rising. He broke down. His wife, like Spann's, had never seen her husband weep like this and it worried her deeply. But Simpson did not want to talk about it. Not yet.

"I just want to go to work," he said.

The station sent him to Cullman with a camera crew to report on the mess downtown. On the drive, he saw power trucks coming in from other states, and his chest surged with relief and gratitude. They were not alone. Others were already there to help. In Cullman, he surveyed the roofless courthouse and the blasted buildings downtown, amazed that no one had died. Cullman had been warned with sixteen minutes of lead time, and people had gotten to safety.

The Sunday after the storm, Jason's and Spann's Facebook pages turned into living message boards for tornado relief. Jason noticed there was little traffic for many rural small towns, so he and his wife loaded their pickup with food and supplies. They did not know where to go at first, but decided just to drive until they ran across a place that needed help. They would not have to drive far.

They found Eoline Baptist Church, the only structure still standing in the little community of Eoline. People were clustered there under a tent, doling out food and stories. Some of them had lost every object they owned. But they were in good spirits, because they knew they could have lost much more. Their biggest need at the moment was paper plates to hold all the food. Jason smiled when he met the pastor overseeing this flock, because it was a pastor from another church in another town, giving Eoline's preacher a break to rest. Jason Simpson's healing began on the steps of that church.

The tornado that hit Eoline had been the same one aimed at his house and his pregnant wife. It was not the biggest funnel of the day, but its impact was profound. Even a small tornado can level a house. Whenever anyone asked him, as they would for years, "Will this storm be like April 27?" he would answer:

"If a tornado wipes out your house, that's your April 27. That's your day in hell."

▪ ▪ ▪

Brian Peters was crushed when he learned "his" tornado had killed four people in Cordova. The excitement he had felt quickly curdled into sadness and remorse. But the experience renewed the passion he poured into teaching storm-spotter classes, which left crop after crop of spotters reeling with awe at the majestic danger of the sky.

A few months after the storm, he was attending a weather conference when a young lady approached him with an unexpected question.

"Can I give you a hug?" she said.

He looked at her, puzzled. She could have been thirteen or sixteen, it was hard to tell. A group of smiling family members stood behind her.

"Um, okay," he said nervously. "Why?"

"You saved my life," she said.

"I what?"

"You saved my family's life."

In his forty-five years of meteorology, no one had ever told him that. Suddenly the noise of the conference vanished. It felt as if they were the only two people in the world. He let her hug him, and then he stepped back, wide-eyed.

"Okay, now you've got to explain what you mean by that!"

She and her family had lived in a mobile home near Cordova. When they heard his voice on the radio, they ran into their underground shelter. They crawled out to find their double-wide trailer twisted beyond recognition. She showed him a photograph he would never forget.

Retelling the story would choke him up for years.

CHAPTER 36

ONE STEP AT A TIME

SEPTEMBER 30, 2011—BIRMINGHAM, ALABAMA

Chelsea Thrash leaned on a pink cane as she limped across the stage before the sea of expectant faces. She had to walk slowly now, but every step she took was a tiny victory lap, because the doctors had initially told her she would never walk again. Now entering the fall of her junior year at the University of Alabama, she was a highlight speaker of the Trauma Symposium, a gathering of trauma nurses, doctors, surgeons, psychiatrists, paramedics, and emergency responders. She was there to tell her story of waking up on April 27 in the courtyard of the Charleston Square apartments in Tuscaloosa, unable to move her legs.

"My sorority's motto is 'Founded upon a rock,'" she joked. "And I was found upon a rock."

Chelsea had been thrown about 150 feet when the tornado blasted Charleston Square and landed like a rag doll upon a rock at the base of a tree that was now a stump.

Chelsea was taken to Tuscaloosa's Druid City Hospital and assigned the code name "November November." The doctors there assessed the gravity of her spinal injury—her L1 vertebra had been crushed like a soda can—and called for an ambulance to transport her to the hospital at the University of Alabama, Birmingham. As they examined her in this emergency room, flooded with people injured by the same tornado, the man on the gurney next to her flatlined.

"Mom, what if I don't make it?" Chelsea had asked her mother, Kelle Thrash, as they wheeled her into surgery. Her mother, who also happened to be a trauma nurse with thirty years' experience, looked into her daughter's frightened face, still caked with mud, framed by a mosaic of broken bathroom tiles tangled in her hair.

"You're going to make it," Kelle told her daughter.

The surgeons cut off the tip of Chelsea's rib and used it to rebuild the crushed vertebra. They treated a punctured diaphragm and picked shrapnel out of her flesh. They stabilized her spine. The operation took thirteen hours.

Chelsea regained consciousness hours later in the Intensive Care Unit with a tube threaded down her throat and a ventilator breathing for her. High doses of antibiotics were burning through her veins, combating the fourteen different types of bacteria detected in her system. A chunk of flesh around her ankle was missing, and a skin graft was taken from her leg to patch it. She was immobilized in a chest brace. She still could not move her legs. Lying there, she wondered whether she would spend the rest of her life in a wheelchair. Could she finish school? Would she ever walk again?

She was not able to sit up until days later, in the step-down unit, where she would transition into rehab. It took several people working together to haul her up into a seated position in bed. Her feet touched the ground for the first time since the storm, and she would never forget it. Her left foot felt nothing. But her right foot tingled.

That was the moment she inked the goal into her mind, the promise to herself that would drive her through many excruciating months of daily rehab and physical therapy: *I'm going back to school. In a wheelchair, on crutches, with a walker—whatever. No matter what it takes, I'm going back to school this fall.*

The first time she stood, with the help of a team of therapists and a machine that lifted her to her feet, the effort of standing for five long seconds left her drenched in sweat. Then she would stand for ten seconds, work up to fifteen. Learning to walk all over again was the hardest thing she had ever done. But the tingling in her right leg had grown into movement, and her left leg was waking up, too. She revised her goal: *I'm going to walk into class on August 20.*

Her mother filmed her first step, an exhilarating moment of triumph over suffering that was like scoring an Iron Bowl–winning touchdown. Chelsea muttered unladylike things through clenched teeth, but she worked with the fire of an athlete training for the Olympics. Her therapists were like coaches, pushing her through two-a-days to the limits of what they knew she could endure. They saw she was tough, and determined, and rarely inclined to the emotional trap of self-pity. On the days when they saw her struggling deep in the pain cave, they bribed her with whispered promises.

"Chelsea, if you can make it to the end of the hall, I'll bring you a Starbucks from the cafeteria."

On the bad days, her leg would buckle and she would fall to the floor, embarrassed, annoyed, and sometimes crying tears of angry frustration. Her therapist would give her a moment and say without pity:

"August 20. Here's a tissue. I'll come back in a minute and we'll do this again."

Between PT sessions, Chelsea watched movies or entertained the friends who came to visit her in the hospital. Her boyfriend had a two-hour daily commute to his internship in Montgomery, but he came to see her every day. Her little brothers and sisters brought her Coke slushees and Disney movies, which took her away from the TV news, a minefield of storm-related images so upsetting that she asked to have the TV disconnected. In the void, her days ran together, the weeks marked by the discharge of fellow storm patients she had come to know through rehab. One day, she was the last one left.

Chelsea got to go home in June, and her parents re-created her upstairs bedroom in a room on the bottom floor. Stairs were still Mount Everest. Her parents drove her to outpatient rehab every day, and she began filling out applications for financial aid, because the fall semester was now in sight. She bought herself a cute pink cane.

On the first day of class, a camera crew followed Chelsea as she limped on her cane into the lecture hall, and students craned their necks to see what all the fuss was about. Chelsea smiled and took things as she always had: one step at a time.

■ ■ ■

On hearing Chelsea's story, the doctors and nurses in the audience rose to their feet for a standing ovation. In the back of the room, James Spann listened and clapped. They had asked him to speak, too, but he had politely declined. It was still too fresh, too raw.

As Chelsea turned to leave the stage, the emcee announced that they had a little surprise for her. She turned around to face Adam Watley, the paramedic who rescued her on April 27. She hugged his neck and burst into tears.

Watley had not known, until someone called to invite him here, that Chelsea Thrash had survived. He had thought that of all the critical patients they rescued that day, none of them had made it. Those three babies he would never forget. When he heard that the girl with the broken back lived, and had even learned to walk again, it meant more than any award. Paramedics are in the business of saving lives, but they often never hear about the fates of the people they save, much less get to meet them. Now, face-to-face with his healed patient, who beat the odds by standing here, he felt the unfamiliar wetness of salty water streaming down his face.

CHAPTER 37

THE ANNIVERSARY

APRIL 27, 2012—CORDOVA, ALABAMA

The members of Cordova Fire & Rescue rose before dawn and gathered in their empty downtown. It still looked much as it had a year ago. Buildings crumbled at the edges. Storefront windows, blown out, had been boarded up. A chain-link fence surrounded the downtown eyesore to keep kids from poking around inside condemned buildings and getting themselves hurt. The trees that had survived were shorn of their branches and looked like telephone poles wearing kudzu sweaters. Places where beautiful homes once stood now had double-wide mobile homes parked upon the foundations of what used to be.

Brett Dawkins, now twenty-two and assistant fire chief, unfurled a giant piece of cloth, attached it to the ladder truck, and raised it as high as it would go. By first light, when Cordova's early birds began stirring, the first thing they saw when they came downtown was a giant American flag rippling in the morning air.

The fire department had lost five trucks to the storm. They had three now and parked them in the high school gymnasium, which they converted into the fire station. They would move later to the former Veterans of Foreign War building.

It was the one-year anniversary of the superstorm, and the town had not been forgotten. Bo Jackson—the Auburn football hero, the Heisman Trophy winner, the first athlete to go pro in both football and baseball, star of the "Bo Knows" Nike commercials—was coming to Cordova. Recently pronounced "the Greatest Athlete of All Time" by ESPN, Bo hailed from Bessemer, a poor black suburb of Birmingham. And when he saw the state of his state on TV, he wept. He lived in Chicago now with his wife and grown kids, but he still thought of Alabama as home and he wanted to help the state that raised him, that made him who he is.

So he came up with a somewhat crazy plan: ride a bike three hundred miles across tornado-torn Alabama to raise money and awareness. He would lead a philanthropic peloton across the state like some pied piper in skintight Lycra, drawing attention to places forgotten when the media circus moved on. He christened the endeavor Bo Bikes Bama, and decided the route—fifty miles a day for six straight days—should start in the northeast corner of the state and snake through the areas damaged by the storm. Magnanimously, he chose to end it with a party in Tuscaloosa, the home of the Crimson Tide, the bitterest rival of his own alma mater, the Auburn Tigers.

In Alabama, college football is a few prayers shy of religion, and a family containing fans of both the Tigers and the Tide is a house divided. In Alabama, "Roll Tide!" and "War Eagle" can mean anything from "Congratulations on the birth of your first child" to "A curse upon your children's children!" In Alabama, loving thy enemy as thyself is one thing, but loving the other side of the Iron Bowl is the business of Mother Teresa.

Today's ride started with a pep rally at Cordova Middle School, where Bo, who overcame a stutter as an adult, gave a touching pep talk to a sea of elementary school kids waving hand-drawn signs that read GO BO GO!

It was day five, and Bo was 200 miles into his ride. Having pedaled up hills that don't look all that steep from a car, he was tired and sore and suffering cramps that, by his own admission, "made me scream like a little girl."

He was not alone in the pain cave. He had recruited a number of celebrity athlete friends to join him: Ken Griffey Jr., Picabo Street, Al Joyner, and Scottie Pippen. None was an avid cyclist, but all made up for their lack of training with their ability to dig deep.

In rural Alabama, folks waved from their porches and from the side of the country road. And for once, the schism between War Eagle and Roll Tide disappeared, and they were all on the same team. Bo nearly fell off his bike when one fan hollered from a pickup truck, "Roll, Bo, Roll!"

Along the way, Bo stopped to talk with survivors, including children orphaned by the storm. Bryce Ferguson, who was ten, lost his parents and sister and sustained permanent brain damage from a blunt force hit to the head. He was now being raised by his grandmother. Ari Hallmark, six years old at the time of the storm, lost both parents, two grandparents, and a seventeen-month-old baby cousin in Ruth, Alabama. To help her cope with the loss of her family, a therapist encouraged Ari to write a book about her story, and at seven years old, Ari published *To Heaven after the Storm*, describing the moment that she looked up into the yawning mouth of the tornado and saw not death but a staircase leading up into the sky. She told of a tall, blonde woman who led her up those stairs, where, behind two doors with diamond handles, she saw her family one last time.

Bo Jackson could not recount Ari's story without tears streaming down his face. "I was so amazed at how resilient people can be after a tragedy," he said after meeting them. "To be six or seven years old and have it all taken away, that's enough to sink anybody. I explained to them that God has a plan for them; he has a plan for everybody. And when God calls you, no matter what, you've gotta go. I said, 'Whenever you want to talk to me, you call me. There are people who know how to get you in touch.' "

At the end of the ride, through donations from individuals and corporations, through auctions and entry fees and five-dollar text donations, Jackson raised six hundred thousand dollars in that first year for the Alabama Governor's Relief Fund, which pays for tornado relief and the construction of new community shelters. He promised to come back every year.

CHAPTER 38

REMEMBERING

APRIL 27, 2012—TUSCALOOSA, ALABAMA

Four families and their friends gathered around a new house at 31 Beverly Heights. Refreshments were served on the old front door, which rested across two sawhorses. It was the first time since the posthumous graduation ceremony that the families had been together. Newly planted trees were sending their roots into the soil.

Loryn Brown's family had picked a magnolia tree. Will's planted a dogwood. Danielle's chose a weeping cherry. Kelli had engraved their names on stone markers that the families could visit when they wished.

The house had been rebuilt in the fall with a new floor plan, in a different shape. Dianne Rumanek told the builders how it had fallen, and that they were building on sacred ground. On December 7, Danielle's birthday, Kelli placed a bouquet of purple zinnias in the new mailbox and tied on a balloon that said HAPPY BIRTHDAY.

Sean Rivers, a musician and a good friend of Loryn's, strummed a guitar and sang a song he wrote for her, "Mind on Tuscaloosa." Ed unscrewed a plastic bottle of water, took a sip, let Terri drink, then poured the rest on Danielle's tree. It would become their tradition. Loryn's Maw Maw and Will's Paw Paw met and traded memories. Their mothers spoke about how perfect a couple they would have made.

Kelli had prepared a short speech about her friends. But when she stood in front of the group, she opened her mouth and nothing came out. She stepped back and let the others speak.

■ ■ ■

Since the storm, Kelli had suffered from anxiety and panic attacks so debilitating that they threatened her ability to live a normal life. Any mention of tornadoes, in news or conversation, would trigger a memory and send her running out of the room to cry and to call her mother or Eric.

Her turnaround began in the parking lot of Bruno's grocery store. She had run out of class after someone uttered the word, "tornado," feeling a suffocating anxiety. She got in her car and started to drive home, but had to pull over and cry. And there, in the parking lot of Bruno's, she had an epiphany:

Nobody's dying today. There's no tornado coming.

She grasped for the first time that the threat was inside her, not in the sky. Her thoughts were creating the danger.

She began seeing a counselor and learned how to talk herself through the panic, how to catch herself before she spun out of control. It did not stop her mind from racing, and even though she could logically observe herself spiraling into a meltdown, it did not stop the emotions. But at least now she could calm herself down.

What she had learned she paid forward to her patients every day in her new job. She had gained a new level of empathy, and although she still struggled with irrational fears of losing someone close to her, she had learned to manage those feelings. After finishing her master's in social work she was hired by a psychiatric hospital to work with people in crisis. She still panicked every time the weather turned, but now she had a weather app on her phone, and an emergency plan with friends and family.

She and Eric had gotten married two months after the storm, realizing that tomorrow may never come. Eric had had an epiphany while holding Kelli beside the fallen house. When he saw that playing card facedown in the dirt and flipped it over to reveal the queen of hearts, that was the moment he realized he was ready to spend his life with this girl in his arms. He had felt that the universe was giving him its blessing. Not long after, he proposed with a ring of stones set in the shape of a flower—perfect for his modern hippie. On a sweltering day in July, they got married, barefoot, beside Lake Nicol. They got a small house and a big, happy dog. On the wall of the dining room they hung the old front door of 31 Beverly Heights, a door to the past, a daily reminder to live mindfully today, because tomorrow may never come.

▪ ▪ ▪

Will's mother still cried every day at 1:15 p.m., because that was the time when Will should be calling. His father cried, too. He had towed Will's truck back home and let it sit out in the field. Will never knew that Darrell had been fixing him up a dualie like his as a graduation gift. He didn't have the heart to do much with either truck now.

They buried Will near his Nana. The family Jack Russell Terrier, Bubbles, fell into a depression. She ran straight to his grave and lay down beside it the first time she ever saw it. They had kept his room more or less as he left it. Jean could not bring herself to clean it up, though she did pick a few of his clothes off the floor. She used his laptop until the screen went out, and his sister wore his clothes.

The family would never stop wondering why things happen the way they do. Why someone who had so much to give the world would have died before having the chance. His sister pictured him with Nana.

Taylor had gone to visit each of the families. She spent a night on the farm with Loryn's sisters and brother. She and Michelle became close, leaning on each other as orphaned siblings who had to find their way through the new and unfamiliar life of an only child. Taylor spent the night before the memorial with Kelli and Eric and got to know them as well. She was still hotheaded, and her grief usually manifested as anger. But she had found in the tragedy a new direction for her life.

After the tornado, she enrolled in nursing school, with an interest in emergency medicine.

Will's cousin had started a memorial scholarship fund in Will's name. It was just what Jean and Darrell needed to begin their healing process. It was a way to channel their energy and emotions toward something that could make a difference. Nothing would ever take away the void and the pain, but the one thing that made them feel better was helping others. They organized an annual memorial car show, where avid restorers of antique cars paid ten dollars to park on the baseball field and look under one another's hoods. They auctioned off engine blocks and donated parts, and sold raffle tickets for door prizes. That first year, they raised ten thousand dollars. They had a town-wide yard sale, which raised a few thousand more. They raised enough to grant two college scholarships each year, to a male and a female athlete from Priceville. This year, the male recipient's name was Chance, and he wore the number 11.

Will's football number was 11, as was his daddy's. Chance Ellsworth chose the number because Will had been a mentor to him. After Chance, the Priceville football coach promised to retire that number as long as he was coach. Will had also played under number 7, because he admired University of Alabama quarterback Jay Barker. That year, when the cows began to calve, Darrell came back to the house one morning looking especially pale and red-eyed.

"I got two cows that just calved," he told Jean.

"Okay."

"The first cow was number seven."

"Okay."

You know what the next one was?"

"Number eleven."

It felt like Will was sending them a message:

It's gonna be okay.

■ ■ ■

Loryn's mother visited her grave every week and made sure she never lacked decorations. On game days she ordered a red and white spray of carnations shaped into a big Alabama *A*. When Beyoncé had a baby girl, they bought an IT'S A GIRL! wreath and placed it on Loryn's grave. On Halloween, the girls painted polka dot pumpkins. On Christmas, Ashley put up lights and a tree.

She had found little things as she sorted through the objects they had gathered from the house. There was a sketch pad that was mildewed from its time in the rain. It was blank, but she could not bring herself to throw it out. She flipped through one last time and found a page that she had missed. It was one of the only pages free of mud or mold, and on it Loryn had drawn an angel, with curly hair, standing on a cloud. In a copy of *Chicken Soup for the Soul*, a twig and a white azalea had blown into the pages. She opened it up to the page they marked, and it contained a poem called "Angels Among Us."

She felt that she would never be the same mother that she was when Loryn was alive, but she treasures every moment with her living kids. The smiles seem brighter. The hugs seem tighter. And she believes that the three simple words "I love you" can never be overused.

The kids are magnificently resilient, and they still cry and miss Sissy, but they're okay, too. Anna, though, went through a very hard time and began to withdraw. Born in a family of ardent huggers, she lost her will to hug. Before, she would climb into Loryn's arms and attach herself to her sister all weekend like a monkey. Loryn would always make her mother give two-arm hugs, not the one-arm side hugs that did not count. "Mama, put down that laundry basket and give me a two-arm hug!" she would say. Ashley had to teach Anna how to hug again. She made her give a two-arm hug every single night for thirty-one days. Even if she was staying over at a friend's house, she had to hug her friend's mom with two arms before going to sleep that night.

Whenever the weather turned, the kids would all pull on helmets and huddle in the hallway, remembering. Anna worried the hardest.

When a rash of tornadoes pummeled the South on Christmas Day in 2012, Anna was inconsolable.

"It's going to be okay," Ashley told her kids. That's what a mother says.

"Mama, it's not going to be okay," Anna said. "It wasn't okay when Sissy didn't come home."

Christmas was the hardest time of year, especially for Ashley. How does a mom learn to shop for one less kid? She didn't have the heart anymore to decorate like she used to, or put up a tree in every room. Everything meant to bring her cheer only made her think of Loryn.

One day that first December, Ashley came down with an awful flu and crawled into bed with Loryn's quilt, which she had never slept with before. When she woke up in the middle of the night, she saw a white mist floating across the room. Not much of a drinker, she thought at first it was the NyQuil talking. She reasoned it was moonlight bouncing off the pond and streaming through the blinds. But when she closed them, it was still there. She thought it was steam rising from the iron. The iron was cold.

"What is that?" she heard herself say aloud. It started to move to the door. "Wait, don't go."

It moved to the corner of the bed, the corner where Loryn used to sit. She just lay there, looking at it, unafraid. Then she took out her camera, snapped a photo, and fell back asleep. Days later, the memory of it came back like a dream. She told her husband about it, and he looked at her as if she was crazy. *Was it a dream?* Then she remembered the picture on her phone.

There it was, just as she remembered it. A white, shapeless mist hovering over her bed. To this day she cannot explain it. She does not believe in ghosts, because she knows her daughter is in heaven. Whatever it was, she felt that it was given to her to get her through the heartache of that first Christmas.

Loryn's family started a memorial scholarship fund, too. Shannon's fame as a coach and a UA football player helped them raise enough money to reach endowment. Then they started another one and endowed that, too. Ashley reads all the applications and chooses the recipients. The first one reminded her of Loryn.

■ ■ ■

One Friday night in autumn, two north Alabama high school football teams lined up to play for a memory. Each team was led by a coach who had lost a daughter to a storm: Shannon Brown, the coach of Ardmore High, reeling from the loss of Loryn, and Dirk Strunk, coach of Priceville High School.

Four years had passed since Strunk's own sixteen-year-old beauty, Katie, was killed when a twister struck Enterprise High on March 1, 2007. Katie had been hunkered in the hallway with friends, near the classroom where her mother, Kathy, was teaching. Eight students died that day.

Weeks after that storm, Ashley drove Loryn and some friends to the beach for spring break on March 17, 2007, Loryn's seventeenth birthday. They often passed through Enterprise, and that day they made a detour by the school. The girls were struck by what they saw.

"Those kids were our age," said Loryn's friend.

The girls let that sink in.

"You know," said Loryn, "none of us know we will make it through today."

After April 27, 2011, Kathy wrote a letter to Loryn's mom, sharing the sorrow that other mothers could only try to imagine. Ashley Mims took some comfort in knowing that she did not mourn alone. Coach Strunk had reached out to Shannon Brown and Darrell Stevens, telling them the same.

"We're in a club nobody wants to be in."

The Ardmore players wore on their helmets a special gold sticker with Loryn Brown's initials. Odd-numbered Priceville players wore Will's, while the evens honored Danielle.

Three families sat hip to hip in the stands, seesawing between pride and sorrow, leaning on one another through every play. Ashley Mims had spent the night at Will's house, where she stood in Will's room and got to know the boy who had held her daughter's hand until death pried them apart.

Jean and Darrell Stevens blinked away tears in the stadium lights as they watched Chance Ellsworth retire the number 11 in the last home game of Priceville's season.

▪ ▪ ▪

On January 9, 2012, Tuscaloosa's biggest healing moment came when the University of Alabama Crimson Tide swept over LSU to win their fourteenth national championship. Watching the march to victory on TV, Shannon Brown paused from the gripping game to send a quick message from his phone. It popped up on Loryn's Facebook Page, where friends continued to send her greetings.

10:00 p.m.	Shannon Brown	Hey honey, we are gonna win this one for you!
12:51 a.m.	Brandon White	ROLL TIDE sweet girl. When Trent took that ball into the end zone all I could think about was how excited you would be.
1:02 a.m.	Sean Rivers	Loryn, this one is for you, baby! I know you're celebrating with my dad and grandparents in heaven. We miss you! Roll Tide!

The next day, after the victory celebration, Alabama long-snapper Carson Tinker left the New Orleans Super Dome with his team to fly back to Tuscaloosa. It would have been Ashley's twenty-third birthday. In Tuscaloosa, three homemade crosses were planted in a quiet field across the street from where the girl he loved was ripped from his arms by the wind. The crosses marked the spot where Ashley Harrison was found lying near their dogs, who also died. Friends had decorated her memorial with lay crimson-and-white shakers and other tokens from the game and left golf balls for her dogs. In his wallet Carson carried a note she'd written that said, "Just remember I love you. ♥Ash." The signature from that note was stamped on the pink memorial bracelets sold to raise money for her scholarship, along with the phrase she often said to her family:

I love you as big as the sky!

■ ■ ■

Michelle still had good days and bad days. On the bad ones, she knew she could go home to cry on Clay's shoulder. He did not even need to say anything.

She did not want sympathy. She hated the looks she got from people who gave her sad smiles of pity. She hated just as much the judgment she felt when she did not show her grief. She experienced the whole spectrum of emotions every day, from sadness to anger to injustice to peace. She felt selfish for wanting her sister back on earth when she believed that she was in a place free of pain or sorrow. She told herself that nobody wanted to hear about her pain, but she did not want to be here if Danielle was not.

She did not want to hurt Clay when she told him that. She just wanted to be with her sister. Danielle's hugs could fix any hurt. Her laugh brightened any day. Without her, the world just did not hold the same beauty as it did before.

She wished that she could dial Danielle's number and hear her voice. Or send her a text about nothing. She even missed the things she hated the most, how anytime she vented, Danielle would force her to see the situation from another point of view. Danielle saw the good in everyone. It was something Michelle struggled to emulate.

Recently, she overheard her dad and uncle joking about something in the car. It struck her then, the realization that she would never again have that. The thought of facing sixty sisterless years terrified her. She still wept a lot, but counseling sessions with her priest had taught her how to control her crying spells. And she had a dream that would help her face a world without Danielle.

In the dream, she is standing in billowing clouds. In front of her towers a golden gate. It slowly opens. On the other side, she sees Danielle, smiling, so pretty in her favorite little black dress. The sisters run to each other and embrace. The dream hug feels so strong, so real. Michelle can smell her sister's hair.

Then Michelle feels herself being pulled away. Danielle is still smiling, but now it is a sad smile. She uses no words, but her kind brown eyes say everything.

It is not your time. But I will see you again.

Michelle is now outside the gate, looking in at her smiling sister.

And then she wakes up.

CHAPTER 39

THE MASTER

JANUARY 28, 2013—BIRMINGHAM, ALABAMA

Johnny Parker stood in a crisp black suit before the green screen at ABC 33/40, beaming into the studio lights. On the TV monitor, a radar splashed behind him. He posed for pictures, gesturing in front of the weather map he could not see, and shaking hands with James Spann as they stood behind the weather desk. Spann had invited him to the filming of WeatherBrains, the online video talk show that he hosted every week. Guests typically joined the show remotely, using Google Connect and a webcam. But Johnny had driven two and a half hours with his family to be on the show in person.

Johnny had filled out, and with a beard and glasses, looked more than the year and a half older than he did when the superstorm hit, but he still had a scramble of dishwater curls and a boyish, effervescent smile. He sat down at the news desk with Spann and Bill Murray, a meteorologist who regularly appeared on the show. Murray had taken an interest in the aspiring weatherman and made efforts to support him. Johnny's mother, Patti, sat by his side, gently filling in the gaps in the moments when words would not come.

As the cameras rolled, Johnny told his story. Even though he still struggled to speak, he was comfortable in his element, confident among his people. Together they described the experience few meteorologists in the world would ever live to tell about: surviving an EF5.

The house where the Parkers had lived for twenty years had taken a direct hit. But the interior walls had stood up to the two-hundred-mile-per-hour winds that spiraled within the funnel. They had survived, amazingly, without so much as a bruise. But the front and the back of their home had been shorn off, and the hallway had become a wind tunnel that sprayed debris through the house like buckshot. The windowless bathroom at the core of the house was the island of safety, and their last-second escape from the hall had saved their lives. They had preserved the strip of drywall stamped with childhood handprints, but the rest of the house was torn down.

Johnny described his defining moment of meteorological instinct. Just before school was dismissed a little early on April 27, a teacher had asked him what he thought the weather would do. The words stumbled out of his mouth before he even realized they were coming.

"I told him, 'Even if our town does not get hit by one today, in the near future, we will be hit,'" Johnny said. "After I told him that, that's when I realized what would happen."

Smithville High was still using portable trailers as classrooms—with underground shelters nearby—when Johnny graduated the following May. He had his class ring engraved with waves and a tornado. Now he was a college student, enrolled in online meteorology courses at Itawamba Community College near home. He would later transfer to Spann's alma mater, Mississippi State.

A few months after the tornado, Jason Simpson conspired with a colleague from Mississippi to get Johnny and his family to Birmingham to introduce him to a special guest. Johnny did not know at first who it was, only that he was making the two-hour drive from Atlanta specifically to meet him. When a familiar face from the Weather Channel walked in the door, Johnny felt ten feet tall.

"Jim Cantore," Johnny announced proudly on WeatherBrains, "gave me his own Weather Channel jacket."

That blue rain shell, embroidered with Cantore's name, had weathered at least one whole season of storms, and Johnny wore it rain or shine. Cantore had a special appreciation for Johnny's intelligence and determination to overcome impediments. His own two children were born with Fragile X Syndrome, a chromosomal abnormality that placed them on the autism spectrum. Cantore signed up for Johnny's forecasts, and the two became friends who e-mailed each other whenever the weather got interesting.

Patti Parker recounted the day after the storm, Johnny's seventeenth birthday. She had dug through the house to salvage his gift: a NOAA T-shirt. He loved it. The family shared a cake and a brief birthday celebration, a nice respite from what would grow into long months of cleanup and recovery.

They lived in a temporary house for much of that time, as Patti worked around the clock for United Way, overseeing storm relief. They wore donated clothes and ate donated food and occasionally their restaurant tab was picked up anonymously. Once, while she was standing in the checkout line at Walmart, Patti unloaded at least one hundred dollars' worth of groceries from her cart. When she reached into her purse for her wallet, the checkout lady smiled and said the stranger in line ahead of her had quietly offered to pay.

The tornado devastated the heart of Smithville, but not its soul. It gutted four churches and more than 150 homes. It ravaged Town Hall, the post office, the police station, and almost every business, including Mel's Diner and the Piggy Wiggly. It killed sixteen people. Some of the dead were found naked in fields, stripped of their clothes by the winds.

The people who got through it best were able to look at the mess and see meaning.

Johnny's pastor had carefully salvaged the fragile stained-glass window of Christ from the ruins of Smithville Baptist. That it would survive, with just two small cracks, may or may not have been a sign. But to the people who had seen their town scoured by the sky, it was not a matter to question. All they wanted was someone to make sense of it. Pastor Wes White, a man who described himself as a better hugger than a prophet, did the best he could. Sixteen neighbors and friends were gone forever. He held five funerals in four days. "We do not grieve as those who have no hope," he preached through the days of mourning. "For the believer, there is no period at the end of our life, only a comma."

Even in rubble, even in pieces, the church was there for people to lean on. On the Sunday after the storm, his congregation built a giant scrap-wood cross, stuck it into the soil in front of the ruins, and held church in the parking lot. "Our beautiful church building is no longer here, but our church has never been more lovely," the pastor told them that day. "I believe our God is going to take our devastation and turn it into something beautiful."

Pastor Wes now presided over a church that had grown not only in size but in members, despite the town's population decline. Smithville Baptist was rebuilt bigger and better, with a modern sanctuary, a cozy nursery, and a new youth wing for teens. The stained-glass window watched over the pews and the altar, a sign of what stands in a storm.

The storm blew some people to a place from which they will never quite return. But others were blown to a better place. The Parkers lost their home, but the tornado scoured a clean slate for the dream house Patti had been sketching in her mind for years. Now those rooms were a daily reality.

Just as the Super Outbreak of 1974 had forged James Spann, the Smithville EF5 was the catalyst that transformed Johnny's weather hobby into a viable career. He still rose before first light to write his forecasts, and now he used complex meteorological software and other tools of the pros. His parents helped him create a private weather company, Parker Weather Service, and he had chosen a unique title for his business cards, inspired by his love of Jedi: Master Meteorologist. He had typed so many forecasts he wore the letters off his keyboard. He now had more than a thousand subscribers, including Jim Cantore and James Spann.

On the show, Spann acknowledged the impossibility of understanding all this family had endured. Of the thousands of tornadoes he had forecast, he had never stared into the teeth of one.

"I have been doing this for thirty-four years, and I have never been in a tornado," Spann said. "I don't know what you feel like, but I'm sorry you had to go through that. That pain never goes away. It fades away, but it never goes away."

Spann looked at Johnny and saw a boy who reminded him of his eighteen-year-old self. He also saw the future. Spann was not ready to retire just yet; he wanted to fix the warning system and develop a new weather model to pass on to the next generation. Johnny was coming of age in just the right era, with tools that helped him transcend limitations to do just what he loved.

"God spared your family for a reason," James told Johnny. "You're taking something bad and turning it into something good."

■ ■ ■

Somewhere in the world, right now, the atmosphere is stirring. Great invisible paisleys are swirling in a perpetual dance of infinite complexity. Winds are coursing above the land in waves and streams and eddies, heating and cooling and flowing, yielding to pressure in the immutable ways that water surrenders to gravity.

Somewhere, thunderstorms are purpling the sky, gathering and spreading with whistling speed and bruising rain. Below them waits a road, a town, a church. And somewhere, a future meteorologist, scanning the coiling sky.

Nature holds mysteries and power we barely fathom. It can, and will, inflict unimaginable suffering. But the same forces that destroy the walls that protect us also bring down the walls that divide us. And when everything else is stripped away, what stands is a truth as old as time: The things that tear our world apart reveal what holds us together.

EPILOGUE

April 2011 became the most active tornado month on record, with 757 tornadoes confirmed throughout the United States. Two hundred of them occurred on April 27, the most ever recorded in a single day. It is tricky to compare outbreaks, which have some similarities but inevitable differences, but many experts consider the April 25–27 outbreak the worst on modern record, narrowly exceeding the April 3, 1974, Super Outbreak. "In the period from 1960-2011, there have been about 100 tornado outbreaks that would qualify as 'major' events and these two (April 3, 1974 and April 27, 2011) are, by far, the highest rated," wrote Chuck Doswell, the respected research meteorologist who studies tornadoes. "The 2011 outbreak is the highest ranked outbreak (by a very tiny margin over April 3, 1974) since 1960."

But the atmosphere was still restless. On Sunday, May 22, 2011, the small town of Joplin, Missouri, was obliterated by an EF5. The deadliest single tornado since record keeping began in the 1950s, it killed 158 people and injured more than a thousand.

In both storms, the warnings were excellent. But many people did nothing. Why? Social scientists found that many people had grown complacent and did not immediately take shelter after hearing a warning. Many first sought confirmation from another source—the news, a phone call, a look outside—actions that cost precious minutes and sometimes lives. Some people got the warnings and did nothing at all.

The false alarm rate (FAR)—the percentage of occasions when a warning is sounded and no tornado occurs—contributed to complacency. In one survey of Joplin residents, some people said they are "bombarded with [sirens] so often that we don't pay attention."

These tragedies were catalysts to improving the warning system. To enhance public understanding, meteorologists added qualifying statements that better express uncertainty. They adopted stronger wording—phrases such as "catastrophic damage" and "well-built houses swept clear from their foundations"—to differentiate strong and violent tornadoes. Many National Weather Service offices have implemented dual-polarization (dual-pol) radar, which can better distinguish debris from precipitation. By helping meteorologists identify tornadoes with higher accuracy, dual-pol is expected to reduce false alarm rates considerably.

The Birmingham office of the National Weather Service scrutinized its warning process in an effort to reduce its False Alarm Rate, which at the time of the April 27, 2011, outbreak was around 80 percent*—the same as the national average. Three years later, it was around 40 percent, according to Kevin Laws, chief scientist at the Birmingham NWS office.

Tornadoes are rare. Only a small fraction of thunderstorms produce them, and EF4 and EF5 tornadoes are exceptionally rare, accounting for less than 1 percent of all twisters. Only one EF5 is recorded in the United States in a typical year. In 2011 there were six. Four struck on April 27. Statistically, an event of this magnitude occurs only once or twice a generation. But it can, and will, happen again. And the next one might be bigger.

* This number is an average FAR from October 2007 to March 2011; scientists considered April 2011 an "anomalously active month" and did not include it here.

ACKNOWLEDGMENTS

This book came to be through a perfect storm of all the right people in my life.

My agent, Jim Hornfischer, coached, cheered, and prodded me to new heights with his singular blend of literary instinct, incisive edits, and uncoated honesty. For me, this was the perfect recipe. Senior editor Leslie Meredith championed this story and gently guided me through the terrifying first draft with wisdom and tact, then refined each sentence with laserlike precision. Associate editor Donna Loffredo weighed in during critical moments and helped us keep momentum.

I have been blessed with a first-class team of "editorial rabbis" who have mentored me throughout my career, and every single one of them is a lifeline I call on frequently. Ed Mullins, Don Noble, Kristi Ellis, and Bailey Thomson informed my undergrad and graduate years in J-school at the University of Alabama. Russ Mitchell groomed me as a cub reporter and advised every career change since. Mike Wilson has been my trusted friend and Jedi Master for more than a decade, and always, always makes time for my questions with thoughtful, prescient answers. *Helped me . . . he has.* Tanner Latham, who knows me better than I know myself, has never stopped believing in me and in the transcendent power of storytelling. George Getschow and the Mayborn tribe—especially the Archer City Class of 2014—made me realize, on the beer-soaked tailgate of a pickup truck lit by shooting stars, that I had finally found "my people." Noah Bunn led me to Mayborn. Bob Shacochis asked the hard questions that made me think harder and aim higher. Julie Chapman and Eric Calonius laughed with me through my publishing faux pas. Book whisperer Joel Achenbach talked me through the art of beginnings and endings, and taught me that humor and science are not mutually exclusive. My friend and UA colleague Dianne Bragg helped me see my blind spots, and saved me from myself. Rick Bragg—friend, confidant, and tone-poem coach—endured three years of my editing, wrote a beautiful foreword, and guided me through the wonderful world of book publishing. Thank you for weathering the oscillations between Grasshopper and Crankypants.

I am indebted to the families who lost somebody, who recounted the intimate details of the most painful days of their lives so that I could capture a mere iota of what that person brought to their world.

Terri and Ed Downs equipped me with an arsenal of documents, text records, memorabilia, and memories, and made me feel like a member of their family. Michelle Whatley endured floods of tears to revisit the emotions that have taken her years to overcome, and her husband, Clay Whatley, supported both of us through that process. They all helped me get to know Danielle so well that she visited me in a vivid dream. I believe that her story will continue her legacy of helping others.

Will Stevens's family, especially Jean, Darrell, and Taylor, invited me into their home and shared a lifetime of stories about their charming boy. I often think of Will when I look at my athletic, brown-eyed son, and I hug him extra hard. Loryn Brown's mother, Ashley Mims, shared videos, photographs, and stories that brought Loryn to life in my mind and, I hope, on these pages. Little bits of her unforgettable personality are now embedded in my psyche. Loryn inspired me to embrace bling.

The book contains too many supporting characters to name, but I am grateful to all who shared their stories, including some who did not make it into the final draft, yet still informed my understanding of a massively complex event. Special thanks goes to Tuscaloosa Fire & Rescue Deputy Chief Chris Williamson, who identified and introduced me to all the right sources, and who trusted me with invaluable maps, tapes, and resources. Tuscaloosa Mayor Walt Maddox did an unforgettable job in guiding the city through its crisis and shared personal revelations instead of canned quotes in our interview. Fire & Rescue Station 7 and Station 2 contributed greatly to the details and on-the-ground narrative.

I've attempted to describe the science in a way that is accessible to nonscientists, an effort that would have been laughable without the help of a crew of meteorologists who fielded my incessant interrogation for more than a year. At the National Weather Service, Jim Stefkovich and Kevin Laws were instrumental to my weather education, as was the retired NWS meteorologist Brian Peters, who showed me tools and resources that helped my understanding and reporting. Special thanks to James Spann for trusting me to tell his story, Chuck Doswell for vetting my metaphors and winnowing out my "seriously flawed concepts," Greg Carbin for his reports and big-picture perspective, and Tim Coleman for sharing unpublished videos that helped me re-create the chase scene and dialogue.

For the seeds of this story, I am utterly grateful to *Southern Living*, especially former editor Lindsay Bierman, who envisioned a heavily reported tornado feature that would fit in the pages of a lifestyle magazine. He selected me to lead a team of reporters and writers who canvassed disaster zones in six states, devoted the pages we needed to tell the story, and trusted me to write my heart out. Erin Shaw Street, Robbie Caponetto, Jason Wallis, Art Meripol, David Hanson, Stephanie Granada, and Cory Bordonaro all contributed poignant facts, words, and images. Rick Bragg wrote the heart-wrenching first essay of that feature and guided me through my writing of the rest, at times sitting beside me at the keyboard, putting music in the words. The resulting story, "What Stands in a Storm," won three professional awards and generated hundreds of e-mails and comments from readers who made me believe that this story should be a book. *Southern Living* publisher Greg Schumann encouraged me to seize the opportunity, and managing editor Candace Higgenbotham graciously granted me rights to use some of the material from the magazine story. I'm grateful to the whole staff for supporting the book and keeping me on the masthead when I decided I had to leave my post in order to make it happen.

Gracious hosts gave me a place to wrestle with words on writing retreats in wonderful, nurturing places. Dede Clements, a patron of many artists and writers, let me haunt her lovely historic Edgeworth Inn in Monteagle, Tennessee. Dan and Lisa Brooks lent me their magnificent cabin in Blue Ridge, Georgia, during the "blizzard" of 2014.

It took a great leap of faith—quitting a good job with no book contract in hand—to tell a story that needed to be told. For that I thank my family for their unflagging support. My husband, Eddie Freyer, has been urging me for more than a decade to chase my dream of writing books, and was ready before I was to make the freelance leap. He has been a solid partner in everything from canyoneering to parenting, and even became a damn fine writer along the way. My mother, Joyce Cross, helped transcribe hours of interviews and fed me through all-night writing sessions at her house. She will always be my biggest fan. My late father, Ken Cross, was the first editor to make me cry (third grade) and once told me, "To be a writer, you need a callus on your psyche an inch thick." His best advice—"Tough luck, cream puff" and "Suck it up!"—rings in my ears whenever the going gets tough. My branches of awesome in-laws—the Freyers, the Nagels, and the Ashes—sent great love and words of support from afar, and never rolled their eyes at hearing, for the umpteenth time, about tornadoes.

My son, Austin, understood and forgave me for the snuggles and bedtime stories lost to my weeklong writing retreats. When he was five, he threw a penny in a fountain. I told him he should not speak his wish aloud, or else it may not come true. He informed me it already had.

"What is it?" I asked.

He looked at me with ancient eyes.

"For you to be a writer."

IN MEMORIAM

This book is dedicated to the Alabamians who lost their lives and to the people who face a world without them.

(1) BIBB COUNTY

Ricky Paul Smith, 55

(9) CALHOUN COUNTY

Ruby Douthitt, 61

Michael Forrest, 54

Tina Forrest, 50

Francis Arvella Jones, 72

Linda Sue Lipscomb, 63

William Thomas Lipscomb, 67

Vernon Spencer Motes, 33

James Romaine, 65

Angel Stillwell, 13

(2) CULLMAN COUNTY

Lloyd Winford Harris, 68

Keenan Jonathan Sullivan, 20

(35) DEKALB COUNTY

Chelsie Black, 20

Charlotte Bludsworth, 36

Belinda Boatner, 67

Eddie Joe Bobbitt, 71

Gene Bullock, 65

Marcella Wells Bullock, 64

Jewell Elizabeth Tinker Ewing, 73

Emma Ferguson, 6

Jeremy Ferguson, 34

Tawnya Ferguson, 32

Carol Lisa Fox, 50

Hannah Goins, 3

Kenneth "Buddy" Graham, 56

Linda Graham, 62

Violet Hairston, 90

Harold Harcrow, 74

Patricia Harcrow, 75

Jody Huizenga, 28

Lethel Izell, 86

Jimmy Michael Kilgore, 48

Courtney McGaha, 15

Martha Michaels, 72

William "Buddy" Michaels, 70

Eula Lee Miller, 80

Ida Ott, 87

Timothy Ott, 53

Esther Rosson, 81

Peggy L. Wanda Sparks, 55

Terry "Tub" Tinker, 50

Daniel Vermillion, 42

Jilda Jo Vermillion, 44

Judith White, 63

Wayne White, 68

Hubert Wooten, 70

Juanita Wooten, 70

(6) ELMORE COUNTY

Candice Hope Abernathy, 23

Kammie Abernathy, 5

Melissa Ann "Missy" Myers Gantt, 43

Alice Herren Lee, 74

Martha Ann Gray Myers, 67

Rebecca Herren Woodall, 70

(4) FAYETTE COUNTY

Jeffery Kemp, 60

Reba Kemp, 60

Leon Spruell, 76

Sylvia Spruell, 69

(25) FRANKLIN COUNTY

Donna Renee Berry, 52

Nila Black, 68

Zan Reese Black, 46

Jack Cox, 78

Charlene Denise Crochet, 41

Donnie Gentry, 63

Patricia Ann Gentry, 50

Donald Ray Heaps, 49

Lester William Hood, 81

James Robert Keller Jr., 53

Rickey Ethan Knox, 10

Amy LeClere, 33

Jay W. LeClere, 45

Dagmar Leyden, 56

Claudia I. Mojica, 38

Edgar Mojica, 9

Kelli Thorn Morgan, 24

Mike Morgan, 32

Edna Lucille Bradley Nix, 89

Martha Lou Pace, 64

Georgia Scribner, 83

Jack E. Tenhaeff, 67

Sonya Black Trapp, 47

Carroll Dean "C.D." Waller, 76

Gerri Waller, 64

(6) HALE COUNTY

Cora L. Brown, 68

Gerald C. "Jerry" Brown, 70

Jerry Lee Hodge, 61

Henry Lewis Jr., 26

Frankie Joe Lunsford, 55

Elizabeth C. White, 25

(8) JACKSON COUNTY

Kathy Gray Haney, 46

Ann Satterfield, 81

Herbert Satterfield, 90

Janie Shannon, 80

Shelby Jean Shannon, 58

Branen Warren, 13
Elease Whited, 75
John Whited, 77

(22) JEFFERSON COUNTY

Milton Edward Baker Sr., 68
Bessie Reynolds Brewster, 72
Iva Mae "Nana" Cantrell, 73
James Jerry Clements, 66
Cheryl Denise Cooper, 47
Canatha Hyde Earley, 71
Mae Belle Garner, 87
Janet Elaine Hall, 55
Garrett Lee Jones, 25
Jennifer Leonard Jones, 25
Reba Jones, 76
Haley Alexis Kreider, 8
Michael David Kreider, 10
Michelle Pearson Kreider, 30
Carrie Grier Lowe, 26
Ernest C. Mundi Jr., 53
Kenneth Ray Nation, 64
Deniece Kemp Presley, 57
Ramona Sanders-Walker, 47
Louella Bell Thompson, 81
Tracy Traweek, 39
Nancy Wilson, 56

(14) LAWRENCE COUNTY

Matthew Chase Adams, 21
Earl Lewis Crosby Sr., 63
Mike Daworld Dunn, 58
Aurelia Guzman, 12
Zora Lee Jones Hale, 80
Lyndon Lee "Doby" Mayes, 74
Mary C. Mayes, 76
J. W. Parker, 78
Donald "Duck" Ray, 73
Helen Smith, 84
Horace Grady Smith, 83
Allen Oneal Terry, 49
Herman Oneal Terry, 80
Edward "Ed" Vuknic, 66

(4) LIMESTONE COUNTY

Carol Jan McElyea, 47
Glen Riddle, 55
Janice Riddle, 54
Shannon Gail Sampson, 39

(9) MADISON COUNTY

Gregory John Braden, 58
Katelyn "Katie" Cornwell, 15
Harold "Butch" Fitzgerald, 65
Milinia Nicole Hammonds, 32
Ronnie McGaha, 42
Bobby Joe Moore, 61
Philomena Muotoe, 79
Fred Post, 72
Rachael Renee Tabor, 37

(24) MARION COUNTY

Rodney Gene Ables, 51
Bridget Barnwell Brisbois, 34
Michelle Brown, 43
Robbie "Peachie" Cox, 68

Tina Donais, 36
Chris Dunn, 32
Charles Tommy Garner, 75
Mae E. Garner, 79
Ed Hall, 53
Teresa Gay Hall, 50
Tammy Laveen Johnson, 53
Donna Lee "Leah" Jokela, 77
Kaarlo Jokela, 76
Linda Faye Knight, 57
Freddie Lollie, 81
Vickey Lollie, 55
John Lynch, 70
Cledis Inez McCarley, 69
Vicki Lynn McKee, 47
Faye O'Kelley, 70
Jacob Ralph Ray, 5
Virginia Revis, 53
Ken Vaughn, 24
Jeanette Cochran Wideman, 52

(5) MARSHALL COUNTY

Ann Hallmark, 54
Jayden Hallmark, 17 months
Jennifer Hallmark, 31
Phillip Hallmark, 56
Shane Hallmark, 37

(14) ST. CLAIR COUNTY

Oberia Layton Ashley, 86
Precious Necale Fegans-Hartley, 27
Leah Isbell, 7
Ronnie Isbell, 56
Tammy Isbell, 32
Bertha S. Kage, 91
Thomas Carl Lee, 64
Stella "Mae" Lovell, 97
Gayle McCrory, 56
Sandra Pledger, 68
Albert Sanders, 44
Angela Sanders, 44
Charlie Wolfe, 68
Nettie Wolfe, 68

(1) TALLAPOOSA COUNTY

Katherine Massa, 70

(52) TUSCALOOSA COUNTY

Minnie Acklin, 73
Ovella P. Andrews, 81
Jeffrey Artis, 51
Scott Atterton, 23
Jennifer V. Bayode, 35
Caiden Blair, 7 weeks
Michael Bowers, 3
Loryn Alexandria Brown, 21
Samuel Brasfield, 50
Mary Darlene Bryant, 43
Hugh Graham Davie, 55
Ta' Christianna Dixon, 11 months
Danielle Downs, 24
Arielle Edwards, 22
MaKayla Edwards, 4
Melgium Farley, 58
Thomas Hannah, 74
Cedria Harris, 9

Keshun Harris, 5
Ashley Harrison, 22
Robert Gene Hicks, 83
Shena Hutchins, 26
Carolyn Ann Jackson, 50
Jacqueline Jefferson, 45
Leota Jones, 97
Helen Kemp, 80
Thelma May Bennett Krallman, 89
Tennie Mozelle Lancaster, 95
Davis Lynn "Gordo" Latham, 57
Lee Andrew Lee, 88
Velma T. LeRoy, 64
Dorothy Lewis, 61
Thomas D. Lewis, 66
Yvonne Mayes, 61
Christian A. McNeil, 15 months
William Robert McPherson, 85
Zy'Queria McShan, 2
Melanie Nicole Mixon, 22
Perry Blake Peek, 24
Lola Pitts, 85
Terrilyn Plump, 37
Colvin Rice, 78
Kevin V. Rice Sr., 36
Annie Lois Humphries Sayer, 88
Judy Sherrill, 62
Morgan Marlene Sigler, 23
Marcus Smith, 21
William Chance Stevens, 22
Justin Le'Eric Thomas, 15
Patricia Hodo Turner, 55
Willie Lee "Trey" Turner III, 21
Helen Wurm, 98

(9) WALKER COUNTY

Kathleen Brown, 64
Jonathan Doss, 12
Justin Doss, 10
Harold Ray Jett Jr., 47
Pamela O. Jett, 43
Annette Singleton, 46
Wesley Starr, 46
Bryant Jackson Van Horn, 21
Lucille Waters, 88

MEMORIAL SCHOLARSHIPS

Danielle Downs Memorial Fund
Air Force Aid Society
241 18th Street S Suite 202
Arlington, VA 22202
Make checks payable to ASAF with "Danielle Downs Memorial" on the memo line or donate online at ASAF.org

Loryn "Lo" Brown Endowed Scholarship
National Alumni Association of the University of Alabama
Attn: Scholarship Department
P.O. Box 861928
Tuscaloosa, AL 35486
Make checks payable to "Alumni Fund" with the endowment name on the memo line.

Will Stevens Scholarship Foundation
P.O. Box 128
Somerville, AL 35670

INDEX

Note: Italic page numbers refer to illustrations.

D

ABOUT THE AUTHOR

Kim Cross is an editor at large for *Southern Living* and a freelance writer who has received awards from the Society of Professional Journalists, the Society of American Travel Writers, and the Media Industry Newsletter. Her writing has appeared in *Outside*, *Cooking Light*, *Bicycling*, *Runner's World*, the *Tampa Bay Times*, the *Birmingham News*, the *Anniston Star*, *USA Today*, the New Orleans *Times-Picayune*, and CNN.com. She teaches advanced reporting at the University of Alabama, where she received her undergraduate and master's degrees in journalism, and often speaks at the Mayborn Literary Nonfiction Conference in Grapevine, Texas. Cross is writing her next book with Amber Smith, a war memoir called *Danger Close*. She lives in Birmingham, Alabama, with her husband and son.

For photographs, videos, maps, and other information on the storm, please visit whatstandsinastorm.com. Follow Kim on Twitter and Instagram at @kimhcross and on kim-cross.com.